# INDIGENOUS ENCOUNTERS
# WITH NEOLIBERALISM

**Women and Indigenous Studies Series**

The series publishes works establishing a new understanding of Indigenous women's perspectives and experiences, by researchers in a range of fields. By bringing women's issues to the forefront, this series invites and encourages innovative scholarship that offers new insights on Indigenous questions past, present, and future. Books in this series will appeal to readers seeking stimulating explorations and in-depth analysis of the roles, relationships, and representations of Indigenous women in history, politics, culture, ways of knowing, health, and community well-being.

Other books in the series:

*Standing Up with Ga'axsta'las: Jane Constance Cook and the Politics of Memory, Church, and Custom,* by Leslie A. Robertson with the Kwagu'ł Gixsam Clan

*Being Again of One Mind: Oneida Women and the Struggle for Decolonization,* by Lina Sunseri

*Indigenous Women and Feminism: Politics, Activism, Culture,* edited by Cheryl Suzack, Shari M. Huhndorf, Jeanne Perreault, and Jean Barman

*Taking Medicine: Women's Healing Work and Colonial Contact in Southern Alberta, 1880-1930,* by Kristin Burnett

# INDIGENOUS ENCOUNTERS WITH NEOLIBERALISM

## Place, Women, and the Environment in Canada and Mexico

Isabel Altamirano-Jiménez

UBCPress · Vancouver · Toronto

21 20 19 18 17 16 15 14 13      5 4 3 2 1

Printed in Canada on FSC-certified ancient-forest-free paper (100% post-consumer recycled) that is processed chlorine- and acid-free.

**Library and Archives Canada Cataloguing in Publication**

Altamirano-Jiménez, Isabel
  Indigenous encounters with neoliberalism : place, women, and the environment in Canada and Mexico / Isabel Altamirano-Jiménez.

(Women and indigenous studies series, 1924-1410)
Includes bibliographical references and index.
Also issued in electronic format.
ISBN 978-0-7748-2508-5 (cloth); ISBN 978-0-7748-2509-2 (pbk.)

  1. Inuit – Nunavut – Case studies. 2. Niska Indians – Case studies. 3. Indians of Mexico – Mexico – Chiapas – Case studies. 4. Zapotec Indians – Mexico – Juchitán de Zaragoza – Case studies. 5. Inuit women – Nunavut – Case studies. 6. Niska women – Case studies. 7. Indian women – Mexico – Chiapas – Case studies. 8. Zapotec women – Mexico – Juchitán de Zaragoza – Case studies. 9. Neoliberalism – Canada. 10. Neoliberalism – Mexico. I. Title. II. Series: Women and indigenous studies series

E78.C2A398 2013               305.897'071               C2013-900501-3

Canadä

UBC Press gratefully acknowledges the financial support for our publishing program of the Government of Canada (through the Canada Book Fund), the Canada Council for the Arts, and the British Columbia Arts Council.

This book has been published with the help of a grant from the Canadian Federation for the Humanities and Social Sciences, through the Awards to Scholarly Publications Program, using funds provided by the Social Sciences and Humanities Research Council of Canada.

UBC Press
The University of British Columbia
2029 West Mall
Vancouver, BC V6T 1Z2
**www.ubcpress.ca**

*To Eren and Camilo*

# Contents

# Abbreviations

| | |
|---|---|
| CI | Conservation International |
| CIESAS | Centro de Investigaciones y Estudios Superiores en Antropología Social |
| COCEI | Coalición de Obreros, Campesinos y Estudiantes del Istmo |
| COCOPA | Comisión de Concordia y Pacificación |
| EZLN | Ejército Zapatista de Liberación Nacional |
| ICC | Inuit Circumpolar Conference |
| ILO | International Labour Organization |
| IMF | International Monetary Fund |
| IQ | Inuit Qaujimajatuqangit |
| ITC | Inuit Tapirisat of Canada |
| ITK | Inuit Tapiriit Kanatami |
| LCAC | Land Claims Agreements Coalition |
| MBC | Mesoamerican Biological Corridor |
| MLA | member of the Legislative Assembly |
| NAFTA | North American Free Trade Agreement |
| NDP | New Democratic Party |
| NGO | nongovernmental organization |

| | |
|---|---|
| NIC | Nunavut Implementation Commission |
| NLCA | Nunavut Land Claims Agreement |
| NTC | Nisga'a Tribal Council |
| NWT | Northwest Territories |
| PRD | Partido de la Revolución Democrática |
| PRI | Partido Revolucionario Institucional |
| PROCEDE | Programa de Certificación de Derechos Ejidales y Titulación de Solares |
| SEMARNAT | Secretaría de Medio Ambiente y Recursos Naturales |
| TFN | Tunngavik Federation of Nunavut |
| UN | United Nations |
| UNDRIP | United Nations Declaration on the Rights of Indigenous Peoples |
| UNESCO | United Nations Educational, Scientific and Cultural Organization |
| WCIP | World Council of Indigenous Peoples |

# Acknowledgments

Academic work is seldom an individual activity. Individuals and institutions supported this project at different stages and in different ways. I am grateful to the people who participated in my doctoral research, to my supervisors, as well as to my colleagues Val Napoleon and Robert Nichols for the productive discussions that have enhanced my thinking. I am grateful to the anonymous reviewers for their intellectual generosity and insightful comments. I am grateful for the generous support I received from the Canadian Circumpolar Institute at the University of Alberta, the Consejo Nacional de Ciencia y Tecnología (National Council for Science and Technology) in Mexico, and the Centro de Investigaciones y Estudios Superiores en Antropología Social (CIESAS) (Centre for Research and Advanced Studies in Social Anthropology) in San Cristóbal de las Casas, Chiapas, where I was hosted as a guest researcher. I thank Robert Lewis for his dedication in editing this manuscript and Ann Macklem for overseeing the production of this book. Last but not least, I thank Darcy Cullen for her support throughout the different stages of the editorial process. Quixhe latu.

A section of Chapter 3 was published in *Canadian Woman Studies* 26, 3-4 (2008): 128-34, and later reprinted in Monture and McGuire (2009).

# INDIGENOUS ENCOUNTERS WITH NEOLIBERALISM

# Introduction

—————— The Articulation of Indigeneity
and Neoliberal Governance

"Government Labels Environmentalists 'Terrorist Threat' in New Report." This was the headline on 10 February 2012 in the *Vancouver Observer*. The article said that the Government of Canada had presented its new counterterrorism strategy, which notes that low-level violence by domestic "issue-based" groups remains a reality in this country. In its list, next to white supremacy, we can find environmentalism (Stoymenoff 2012). Three months later, Allan Adam (2012), chief of the Athabasca Chipewyan First Nation, wrote in the *Edmonton Journal,* "From a First Nations perspective, it doesn't matter whether we stand on the coast of B.C. [British Columbia] or in the heart of the oilsands – our struggle is largely one and the same. We don't want our lands, our rights, or our people to be sidelined and destroyed by irresponsible development." Are Indigenous peoples eco-terrorists?

A year and half earlier, in December 2010, at the opening ceremony of the United Nations (UN) climate change talks in Cancún, Mexico, Simona Gómez, an Indigenous woman, addressed the audience before Mexican president Felipe Calderón. Gómez explained how she and other Indigenous female forest dwellers, who heavily depend on the forest for food and wood, have found a new way to protect the environment and, at the same time, reduce their workload. She said that with the help of the Mexican government, her community had begun to use more "fuel-efficient" stoves and kilns. Gómez was showcasing a new gender initiative launched at Cancún, which ensures that women are an integral part of the UN Collaborative

Programme on Reducing Emissions from Deforestation and Forest Degradation in Developing Countries.

What do these stories have in common? They highlight the complex relationship that exists between the market, colonialism, Indigenous peoples,
and gender. The first story speaks of how the expansion of global markets
requires more natural-resource extraction and how this demand continues
to dispossess peoples. If Indigenous peoples resist dispossession, they are
perceived as a "threat" to the "white, male control of natural resources"
(Strang 2009, 249). There are also some racialized gender issues in these
stories. Whereas natural resources are considered a white, male domain,
caring for the environment is Indigenous peoples' and women's responsibility. These stories are about who has the right to control resource extraction
and who bears the cost of protecting the environment. These stories are
about how nature and difference are produced and gender inequalities reinserted when place is neoliberalized. Thus knowledge of how indigeneity
is defined in relation to the environment is useful in understanding how
gender is produced and how socio-natures are neoliberalized in both the
global North and South. Socio-natures are a product of the relationships
established by human-nonhuman interactions. These relationships and
interactions are subsumed within the process of neoliberalization (Nast
2006; Bakker 2010).

Although the governance of nature is often considered an apolitical exercise, the management of resources is implicated in relations of power and
informed by hegemonic knowledge that authorizes who has the truth about
how nature should be managed (Peet and Watts 1996; Harcourt and Escobar
2002). Environmental and resource policies and interventions are embedded in power relations that reproduce inclusions and exclusions and particular understandings of gender and nature (Kabeer 2005; Leach 2007).

If policies and interventions have produced hegemonic understandings of
nature and Indigenous women, Indigenous peoples have responded in different ways. In their demands for recognition, territory, and self-determination,
Indigenous peoples have articulated meanings of indigeneity and cultural
difference that are intelligible to the state and other transnational actors and
institutions. In doing so, these peoples have reproduced the problematic
distinction between "authentic" or "intelligible" and "inauthentic" indigeneity, a distinction that perpetuates structural inequalities (Povinelli 2002;
Hale 2005). In challenging these inequalities, Indigenous peoples have also
attempted to expand the grid of intelligibility that neoliberalism has imposed
on indigeneity and have also articulated non-state-centred understandings

of identity. Thus determining the meanings of indigeneity in terms of resistance to and integration into the neoliberal project is important to understanding the complexity of Indigenous peoples' struggles and to questioning essentialized Indigenous identities.

This book builds on the work of critical geographers and anthropologists who have argued that identity and the environment constitute two axes of neoliberalism and that state practices shape the spatial and social reconfigurations of landscapes and communities (Brosius 1999; Chapin 2004; Castree 2005; Perreault and Martin 2005; Robbins 2006; Baldwin 2009; McAfee and Shapiro 2010). This book examines how indigeneity, gender, and the environment have been articulated under neoliberalism in Canada and Mexico. Specifically, this book asks: What kinds of social configurations result from the intersection of indigeneity, gender, neoliberalism, and the environment? How do neoliberal governance and environmentalism inform local agency and the global articulation of indigeneity? What effect does the global articulation of indigeneity have on Indigenous places? How are meanings negotiated in place? How does neoliberalism materialize in places with different colonial histories?

To address these questions, I put forward a set of interrelated arguments. First, Indigenous understandings of place are grounded in specific locations that are heterogeneous. Second, the articulation of indigeneity is a contingent product of global articulation and local agency; different articulations of indigeneity have different effects on different places. Third, the neoliberal spatial and economic reorganization of Indigenous peoples' places rests not only on the liberalization of the natural environment per se but also on schemes aimed at commodifying "saved" or "untouched" nature for the global market. Fourth, although neoliberalism is a hegemonic project, it has materialized differently in diverse places. A critical approach to neoliberalism starts by considering how its processes unfold in specific locations in which neocolonial power is exercised. Fifth, the articulation of indigeneity is both produced and productive. Through the articulation of specific understandings of nature and indigeneity, the inequalities between men and women are maintained and reinscribed in struggles over resources. Through alternative and place-based articulations of indigeneity, Indigenous peoples have challenged such inequalities.

*Indigenous Encounters with Neoliberalism* does not undertake a comprehensive comparison of Indigenous experiences in Canada and Mexico. Rather, the book shows how the articulated nature of indigeneity implies a sense of the political, consensus building, exclusions, alliances, and antagonisms on different scales. Indigenous peoples do not have a unique trajectory; their politics are motivated by specific aspirations and are shaped by different colonial entanglements.

### Indigeneity, Meanings, and Articulation

As a concept, indigeneity has been defined in "criterial" and "relational" ways (Merlan 2009). Criterial definitions identify conditions that enable a diversity of peoples from around the world to identify as Indigenous. These definitions rest on the understanding that Indigenous peoples were the first to occupy the land and on their shared experiences of colonization (Alfred and Corntassel 2005; Abele and Rhodon 2007; Turner and Simpson 2008). In complex ways, these criterial definitions are informed by racialized constructions connected to colonial and government recognition. However, all of these criteria are represented as part of a self-evident category. Relational definitions, on the other hand, emphasize relationships between Indigenous peoples and "Others." Indigeneity also refers to multiscalar politics involving the state, international organizations, networks, place, and academics, all of which shape the "collective social, political, cultural, and economic interests of Indigenous peoples" (Bennett 2005, 73). Indigeneity is a product of the articulatory practices of Indigenous peoples and different sites, and it constitutes a field where power, social practices, knowledge, governance, and hierarchies are produced, contested, negotiated, and altered in the process of producing the meanings of indigeneity. The concept of articulation is useful in characterizing the diversity of peoples making indigeneity claims and the multiscalar politics of indigeneity production.

Indigenous peoples construct their identities based on meanings and social practices situated in place. Under neoliberalism, these meanings are disarticulated to establish new cultural meanings that depoliticize Indigenous peoples' claims. Articulation theory is useful in understanding how cultural assemblages are produced to mediate economic formations. Thus articulation of meanings does not always involve radical contingency; rather, its possibilities are historically constrained by structural relations of domination (Clifford 2001, 472). Although Indigenous peoples are agents shaping the articulation of indigeneity, the sites involved create a complex field in which Indigenous peoples negotiate a balance between local needs and global wants.

I see the intersection of power and space as being useful in understanding the specific discursive, social, and material effects of neoliberalizing socio-natures on how indigeneity is defined, policies are framed, political possibilities are envisioned, and gender hierarchies are reproduced. In mapping the different scales on which political relations are configured, I hope to demonstrate that the interactions between the global, state, and local levels are neither natural nor inevitable. Such interactions result from people's agency and occur in specific contexts.

## Neoliberalism, Indigeneity, and the Environment

In recent decades, there has been a considerable expansion of the literature on neoliberalism. Debates have focused on either conceptual discussions or contrasting research agendas. There has also been a diversity of studies on neoliberalism in practice. Larner (2003) points out that this diversity of accounts suggests that there is no single or unitary neoliberalism. Rather, we can understand neoliberalism as a process that involves a multiplicity of – often contradictory – effects and practices. Neoliberalism is hegemonic but not total. Although neoliberalism is a contradictory and messy process that has materialized differently across diverse geo-political spaces, there are important commonalities that account for patterns (Castree 2009).

Neoliberalism has usually been treated exclusively as an economic project involving deregulation, privatization, individualization, and transformation of the state-citizen relationship. However, as a form of governance, neoliberalism involves practices, knowledge, and ways of inhabiting the world that emphasize the market, individual rationality, and the responsibility of entrepreneurial subjects (Hale 2005; Brodie 2010). The reorganization of society under neoliberalism occurs along the lines of decentralization of power, reduction of state intervention in the market, affirmation of basic human rights, re-regulation, and development of civil society and partnerships. The recognition of cultural difference and the "compensatory measure" of granting collective rights to "disadvantaged" social groups are integral to neoliberalism. These cultural rights, along with the socio-economic components, distinguish neoliberalism as a specific form of governance that shapes, delimits, and produces difference (Hale 2005, 12-13).

Through interconnections between the global discourse of rights, environmentalism, and the market, neoliberalism opens up a space for the recognition of Indigenous rights as well as for the institutionalization of management practices that have uneven implications for Indigenous places and for Indigenous peoples' senses of place (Swyngedouw 2009, 122-23). As a mode of governance, neoliberalism expands the scope of what is considered "nature" to include relationships between the human and nonhuman world, moving beyond nature as a resource to the concept of "socio-natures."

Swyngedouw (2009) and Bakker (2010) point out that the concept of socio-natures is useful in accounting for how human bodies, genetically modified organisms, feelings, and environmental services are transformed into commodities under neoliberalism. Thus moving beyond an anthropocentric understanding of nature is useful in addressing the full range of strategies and socio-natural entities being subsumed within processes of neoliberalization. Neoliberalization strategies vary depending on the target and include property rights, governance practices, and different types of socio-natures (Bakker 2010, 717). In some places it might be easier to pursue strategies that target socio-natures, and in some others a focus on property rights may be more lucrative.

Since territorial and resource conflicts are among the most pressing issues for Indigenous peoples, it is crucial that we consider how power and knowledge shape the processes through which rights are secured and gender is reinscribed. The legal protection of Indigenous lands has opened the door to new forms of economic autonomy, political participation, and the conceptualization of new forms of Indigenous land tenure (Stock 2005, 86). One of the serious consequences of linking rights with economic development is that nature and natural resources are almost exclusively depicted as economic potential, a depiction that does not always match Indigenous peoples' understandings of their place-based relationships with nature. Writing on the Maori experience in New Zealand, Bargh (2001, 252) argues that "re-colonisation is the embedding and re-embedding of Neoliberalism utilising multiple avenues including institutional, state, corporate and intellectual pressure."

**Producing Place, Producing Gender**

Although places exist as specific locations, people construct them according to their own subjectivity. Feminist geographers have produced an important literature that reflects on the spatiality of cultural practices, identity formation, and meaning production. They argue that because people's lives unfold in specific locations and because environments are socially constructed, we need to consider what meanings people attribute to the relationships they build with place (Benwell and Stokoe 2006). From this point of view, Indigenous peoples' sense of place stems not only from their specific roles, practices, and responsibilities but also from their established relationships with identifiable natural and cultural landscapes (McKinley 2007). Moreover, place is crucial to defining what it means to be "Indigenous" and a "woman" in specific locations.

Significantly, this approach highlights how the production of nature brings into existence categories of social difference, including gender. Feminist critical geography is also useful in understanding how place is imagined and reified. Spatial representations are important for political purposes because they anchor historic claims to land/territory and validate identities. Since places are loci of collective memory and political identities, Indigenous peoples' ability to mobilize identity into forces of solidarity depends largely upon the specificities that determine the construction and maintenance of their identities. Although interactions between the local and the global enable Indigenous peoples' politics, they also constrain Indigenous peoples' possibilities. I argue that struggles involving place are struggles over who controls how place is lived and imagined. How place is represented, what stories are heard, in what forums they are told, and for what purposes are political phenomena. Thus the issue of which stories are recovered and which ones are erased has consequences for different groups of people and for how place is imagined in terms of a collective, unified, Indigenous nation.

Global articulations of indigeneity have an effect on place, a fundamental component of Indigenous identifications. Place is simultaneously powerful and constrained by neoliberal governance. Place is heterogeneous; however, essentialized traits bring us face to face with contested local experiences and visions of "identity," "belonging," "exclusions," "rights," and "responsibilities." The adoption of global discourses of indigeneity at the local level, although politically empowering, raises a number of extremely political questions. Who defines "Indigenous" and what is "authentic" or "traditional"?

Feminist theory on gender and nationalism is relevant to understanding the discursive and material effects of reproducing place. As a discourse of power, the language of nationalism enables local Indigenous peoples to define themselves with the authoritative vocabulary of peoplehood. In this process, gender roles are constructed, traditional and historical models are evoked, and symbols, customs, and political and social practices are selected in asserting the right to a homeland and self-determination. Nationalist rhetoric uses culture, tradition, gender roles, and sexuality as border guards aimed at controlling and maintaining a fixed, homogeneous, stable identity. However, rather than expressing the "organic" and "timeless essence" of indigeneity, nationalism becomes a battleground over how culture and belonging are defined and how decolonization is envisioned. Therefore, the intersection of power and space involves both the discursive and the material, which are codified in how indigeneity is defined, policies are framed, resistance is constituted, and possibilities are envisioned.

## Why Canada and Mexico?

Conducting the research for this book has taken me on a journey as an Indigenous academic. I first became interested in comparing Canada and Mexico when, as an undergraduate student of social anthropology, I was invited to participate in a research project on the movement for Indigenous Hemispheric Resistance to the Fifth Centennial of the "Discovery of the New World" in 1992. As an Indigenous transnational undertaking, the Indigenous Hemispheric Resistance movement was an important effort to build alliances throughout the Americas.

A striking political difference was found along the English-Spanish divide, or between "rich" and "poor" countries. For instance, whereas some Indigenous representatives from Canada insisted on reclaiming "sovereignty" and "land title," Indigenous organizations from Mexico insisted on "human rights" and to some extent "dignity." Was this transnational difference a result of the global North-South divide? If not, what else was behind the difference between these claims and their distinct language? I argue that the contrast resulted from different forms of dispossession, exploitation, and othering as well as from spatially and economically distinctive colonial and neocolonial projects.

Settler and extractive colonialism pursued different strategies, modes of governance, and operation. As a specific type of colonialism, settler colonialism relied on a logic of racial disappearance and spatial seclusion (Wolfe 2006, 388). As a "structure" (Wolfe 2006), settler colonialism heavily relied on the acquisition of land. Mythical notions such as "vacant land," "empty land," and "wilderness" erased prior Indigenous connections to the land. In contrast, in Mexico, extractive colonialism implied that Indigenous peoples were recognized as *subjugated peoples* who had to render tribute and pay taxes to the colonial authority. Although the configuration of intimate colonial spaces disciplined bodies, the colonized also generated clandestine practices and strategies aimed at resisting, adapting, and remaking such spaces. A historically grounded comparative analysis reveals how reclaiming certain Indigenous rights and mobilizing certain concepts in the present stem not only from the opportunities opened by global articulations of indigeneity but also from different geographies of colonialism.

Before the North American Free Trade Agreement (NAFTA), the intellectual value of comparing Canada with Mexico appeared limited. Each nation shares a geographical space in North America, and each has evolved as a colonial society superimposed on Indigenous populations. Canada belongs to the so-called global North and Mexico to the global South, but both countries subscribe to NAFTA, bringing the North-South divide to a different scale. That neoliberalism is uneven and fragmented in different places suggests the existence of territorialized power hierarchies among and within countries. Thus the examination of specific locations enables a different reading of the complexities of Indigenous peoples' political actions and their engagement and disengagement with global discourses. At the same time, this examination reveals how neoliberal policies selectively and unevenly target Indigenous peoples in different places.

The four studies presented in this book – Nunavut, the Nisga'a, the Zapatista *caracoles* (administrative centres) in Chiapas, and the Zapotecs in Juchitán, Oaxaca – are a window onto the diversity of Indigenous peoples' responses to neoliberalism and different strategies of neoliberalization. Both the Nunavut and the Nisga'a self-government agreements resulted from land claims negotiations with the Canadian government. Through these agreements, the Canadian government made important promises in return for reconciling the Crown and Indigenous interests and for ensuring development in more than half of Canada's land mass and exploitation of the resources contained therein. The terms and fulfilment of these modern agreements offer some important insights into the questions of how indigeneity is defined, how rights are recognized in Canada, and how self-government is exercised. The Zapatista *caracoles,* on the other hand, constitute a de facto and non-state-driven autonomous political project. By selectively delinking from the global economy and the state, the Zapatistas have sought to control place, give themselves a law, and articulate a meaning of indigeneity that is inclusive and place-centred. Finally, in the study on the Zapotecs in Juchitán, I demonstrate how the Oaxaca Indigenous Law of 1998 differentiated between Indigenous communities according to their social organization, livelihoods, and environments. The two Mexican studies are relevant in terms of the importance Indigenous communities place on communally owned land and in terms of the strategies used to reorganize Indigenous economies in southern states. These studies offer important insights for understanding how neoliberalization processes unfold differently in specific locations in which nature is unevenly produced.

The cases presented here demonstrate different strategic responses to broader colonial and global economic processes affecting place. They exemplify how, in resisting or integrating into neoliberalism, different peoples draw on different sources of power, engage with different discourses, create alliances that are not always transnational, develop varied political and social practices, and mobilize different concepts. Indigenous peoples' engagement or disengagement with neoliberalism is shaped by their specific under-standings of who they are in the world. Thus these engagements and dis-engagements have not only discursive but also material consequences for Indigenous peoples' everyday practices.

## Looking Back

How did this book become what it is? It is difficult to specify the exact mo-ment when I decided upon the topic of this book. The choice was shaped, in part, by who I am as a Zapotec woman. As I started my doctoral research, I focused on the relationship between Indigenous nationalism, gender, and tradition. I became concerned that most theories of nationalism do not even consider Indigenous nationalism and that postcolonial critiques of national-ism and gender mostly reflect the experiences of women of colour. The few studies on gender and Indigenous self-determination foreground the voices of Indigenous female scholars. However, few theorize about Indigenous nationalism. The studies that address Indigenous women's experiences with self-determination processes are divided between those that openly support Indigenous feminisms and those that strongly criticize feminism. Aware of this distinction, I formulated the following questions for my doctoral dis-sertation: How is Indigenous nationalism different from other types of nationalism? What kinds of cleavages and disparities exist in our commun-ities? In what ways do Indigenous women relate to nationalism? How do Indigenous men and women envision decolonized spaces?

I was committed to including Indigenous people's perspectives, particu-larly women's voices. I asked for guidance about the proper cultural protocols for contacting different Indigenous communities. I sought research-ethics approval from the University of Alberta and the Nunavut Research Institute as well as permission from authorities. I was accepted as a student research-er at the Centro de Investigaciones y Estudios Superiores en Antropología Social (Centre for Research and Advanced Studies in Social Anthropology) in San Cristóbal de las Casas, Chiapas, where I had the opportunity to work, once again, with Araceli Burguete, a long-time Indigenous activist and, later, scholar.

There were some limitations on this research as well. In places like Chiapas, where a low-intensity war has developed, my research became "flexible." Instead of focusing on one location, my research became itinerant. I followed research participants around at meetings and gatherings and did volunteer work for an Indigenous women's co-operative operating in San Cristóbal de las Casas. In Oaxaca I also interviewed Zapotec leaders and activists mostly at meetings and forums. In Nunavut I concentrated mainly on Iqaluit, and in the Nass Valley of British Columbia I focused mainly on New Aiyansh. This research was conducted between January 2003 and September 2004. Eighty people agreed to participate, and I followed the "snowball" approach. In writing my dissertation, I did not draw from all of the interviews or regard the participants as representing the overall views of the different locations. Rather, I saw places as heterogeneous and the views of the participants as expressing this complexity. A constant theme in these conversations was economic development. However, my dissertation's contribution in this regard was limited.

As I worked on my doctoral research, I also did some research concerning the intersection of Indigenous rights and neoliberalism and concluded that Indigenous nationalism is closely connected to neoliberalism (Altamirano-Jiménez 2004, 2007). Although the convergence of these two lines of research was clear in the case of the Zapatista movement, I had some difficulties accounting for specific neoliberalization processes in the other locations. This was partly because only a few studies explicitly connect neoliberalism and Indigenous rights in Canada (Stewart-Harawira 2005; Bargh 2007; Feit 2010). The limited literature on this subject suggests that neoliberalization in countries like Canada and New Zealand has somehow provided progressive opportunities for Indigenous peoples. Nonetheless, a superficial review of the two bodies of literature suggests that neoliberalization has provided better opportunities and expansive rights for Indigenous peoples in the global North than in the global South, where these peoples seem to be resisting neoliberalism.

As I continued to conduct research on this topic, I realized that part of this superficial account of Indigenous experiences was that many studies fail to compare countries of the global North with those located in the global South in order to understand the diversity of expressions. More important, these studies fail to fully consider how different colonial modes of governance have shaped contemporary Indigenous experiences and reinserted gender inequalities. Anthropologists and critical geographers have contributed an important body of literature that explores the connection between neoliberalism and the environment. Scholars have detailed how notions of property rights and resources are crucial to how ecological systems are being reworked through colonialism, capitalist development, and neoliberalism in specific locations (Neumann 2004; Robbins 2004). From this perspective, taking this spatial element into account to explain neoliberalism's locally contingent forms remains important (Jessop 2002; Perreault and Martin 2005; Magnusson 2009).

This book draws on the foregoing body of literature, my doctoral dissertation, and research on neoliberalism and Indigenous peoples. This comparative research applies the insights of various approaches, including Indigenous feminism, feminist ecology, critical geography, political economy, articulation theory, and colonial studies. I combine these approaches because traditional political science, although useful, is insufficient to account for how neoliberalism as a mode of governance unevenly produces subjects, places, spaces, and nature. I think these approaches help us to provide a more nuanced analysis of the diversity of Indigenous peoples' responses to neoliberalism in both "poor" and "rich" countries. Furthermore, these approaches are important to revealing the variety of political-economic, cultural, environmental, and symbolic processes through which gender is produced. By exploring Indigenous peoples' relations both *to* and *in* place within different locations, this study attempts to uncover the contingencies, fixities, and complexities of materializing neoliberalism and the fluidity of indigeneity.

Chapter 1 focuses on the theoretical and historical approaches that are used to map the different scales on which indigeneity is produced. By looking at the effects that sites of articulation of indigeneity have on the negotiation between specific places and the global, this chapter shows how colonial formations shape patterns of relationships between Indigenous peoples and the state, gender relationships, and political actions. Chapter 2 explores how neoliberal understandings of the self, difference, and the market are grounded in colonial legacies and how neoliberalism shapes state practices and articulations of indigeneity. By analyzing the intersection of Indigenous identity, rights, the environment, and neoliberalism, this chapter shows how indigeneity articulations shape Indigenous political (im)possibilities and gender inequalities.

Chapters 3, 4, 5, and 6 explore how indigeneity is articulated in different places and how articulations mediate economic processes that continue to reproduce racial and gender inequalities. Chapter 3 shows how contested visions of Arctic sovereignty complicate the Inuit's struggle to expand the grid that neoliberalism has imposed on indigeneity and to control their homeland. Chapter 4, on the Nisga'a of the Nass Valley, explores how private property highlights the contradictory character of indigeneity articulation as it intersects with neoliberalism. As a form of governance, neoliberalism disarticulates established meanings and establishes new ones. Under neoliberalism, the recognition of indigeneity is shaped by imperatives that fail to maintain difference.

Chapter 5, on the Zapatistas, highlights how the discourse of rights and environmentalism has been a critical platform for neoliberal interventions in Chiapas. It shows that neoliberal commensurability with a hegemonic understanding of indigeneity as attachment to land has resulted in the exclusion of landless Indigenous communities from being recognized as Indigenous. This distinction, I argue, facilitates the reorganization of Indigenous communities and economies through livelihood changes and through different land uses and land tenures. Chapter 6 focuses on the contradictions that emerge from bringing together specific definitions of indigeneity, self-government, women's rights, and natural-resource management in Oaxaca state. By looking at the experiences of the Zapotecs of the Tehuantepec Isthmus, this chapter shows how the Oaxaca Indigenous Law provides no protection against the neoliberal strategies being implemented to drive Indigenous peasants off of their lands.

Finally, I offer some concluding thoughts on repossessing place and note four paradoxes: (1) global/state articulations of indigeneity unevenly empower Indigenous peoples; (2) not all landscapes are created equal; (3) Indigenous nationalism may lead to new internal divisions and further gender discrimination; and (4) struggles for rights increase state power.

# 1

# The Political Economy of Indigeneity Articulation

One of the significant global political features of the late twentieth century was the resurgence of Indigenous peoples as political actors claiming their right to self-determination. The most immediate manifestation of this resurgence was Indigenous peoples' assertion of nationhood. Although comprised of different Indigenous groups with different histories and aspirations, this Indigenous global movement ushered in a dynamic period of protest and international organizing, challenging notions of "national identity," history, sovereignty, and power. Jung (2003) and Harvey (1999) write that in Latin America, Indigenous subjects have moved from peasant to Indigenous identities. Tsing (2003) observes that in Southeast Asia, economically disadvantaged peasants have strategically adopted this label. Ramos (1998) points out how in the Amazon the term "Indigenous" helped rubber tappers to be represented as the people of the forest and to gain international support. It has been argued that the Zapatista movement in Chiapas, Mexico, caught national and international attention once it reframed itself as an Indigenous movement (Nugent 1995). The visibility of this global movement has been facilitated by a web of national and international networks (Niezen 2005), which has helped Indigenous peoples to be territorially bounded and transnationally articulated.

This chapter maps the different scales on which indigeneity formation is configured, the interactions between the global, the nation-state, and the local, as well as the hegemonic ideological framework shaping the construction of indigeneity and the inclusions and exclusions it engenders. This chapter asks: What are the political and social implications of diverse peoples using the term Indigenous? How is indigeneity mobilized in specific places and transnational spaces? What kinds of exclusions and inclusions and possibilities are facilitated through these articulations in place? What effects do different sites of articulation of indigeneity have on the negotiations between specific places and the global? How does gender inform visions of decolonized spaces? How do different colonial formations shape patterns of relations between Indigenous peoples and nation-states and the political actions of each?

Indigeneity is a product of the articulatory practices of Indigenous peoples and global discourse. To understand the dynamic character of indigeneity, we need to consider how struggles are grounded in specific locations where colonial entanglements have been implicated in shaping the political economy of indigeneity. Such articulations shape different meanings of what it is to be Indigenous in the contemporary world and subsume alternative understandings of self-determination and political autonomy in order to conform to the parameters of the capitalist states, resource rights, and self-governance. In this context, colonial strategies for containing/disavowing the "Other" are reproduced, limiting the possibilities of implementing alternatives based on local visions of place, identity, and knowledge systems (Gibson 1999).

The first section of this chapter explores how indigeneity constitutes a dynamic and complex field of governance where knowledge, discourse, power, and identity are produced, transformed, and contested. The second section proposes a historically grounded analysis comparing settler and extractive colonialism and the ways that these two colonial formations have been implicated in shaping the political economy of indigeneity. The third section discusses the relationship between place, Indigenous nationalism, and the discourse of rights. I attempt to show how indigeneity and the rights discourse are both mobilized and contested in place through a nationalist rhetoric. The final section analyzes Indigenous nationalism in relation to women and the discourse of rights, trying to reveal the contradictory ways that Indigenous women negotiate their "place" and their rights within their nations and imagine decolonized spaces. I argue that an analytical distinction is useful in revealing how specific colonial formations produce different political responses and possibilities and shape how society and the environment continue to be conceived and managed. However, this should not imply that these modes of governance did not overlap at times or evolve in practice.

Thus this chapter explores the continuing struggles of Indigenous peoples, their changing alliances, their engagement and disengagement with global discourses, the contested nature of their cultural and political positions, and the political contradictions inherent in constructing place. An analysis of these spaces of articulation of indigeneity helps us to understand the global process of producing indigeneity and the tensions and contradictions that arise due to the definition of Indigenous peoples by others and due to their negotiation of meanings, symbols, and projects across place and space.

## The Articulation of Indigeneity

Indigeneity is a complex concept and involves different dimensions. The concept has been used to refer to peoples who have been defined in "criterial" and "relational" ways (Merlan 2009, 305). Criterial definitions have insisted on the conditions and features that enable a multiplicity of peoples from around the world to identify as Indigenous. Although these criteria are represented as part of a self-evident category, they are informed by racialized constructions connected to colonial structures and government recognition. Similarly, relational definitions emphasize relationships between the "Indigenous" and the "non-Indigenous," and indigeneity acquires its meaning in relation to what is not Indigenous in specific colonial formations.

Indigeneity refers not only to definitions but also to the politics and the many actors that shape the collective social, political, cultural, and economic interests of Indigenous peoples. These politics develop on different scales, involve power relations, and raise questions about the processes that appropriate and transform global discourses in place. The articulated nature of indigeneity evokes a sense of the political as a process of consensus building, exclusion, alliance, and antagonism. If we consider these different dimensions of the concept, we can argue that indigeneity comprises a dynamic field of governance constituted by different actors on different scales producing knowledge, articulating discourses, exercising power, constructing and contesting identity, engaging in place-based struggles, and claiming ways of being in the world. How can we think of indigeneity as a dynamic and expansive field? How can we understand the tensions and contradictions in which indigeneity is embedded? Articulation is useful in characterizing indigeneity production, in understanding its structures, and in foregrounding power relations.

I understand articulation as the process of producing meanings, practices, and political possibilities. Articulation means that discourses and practices are shaped by place, economic structures, networks, and other interests that condition their possibilities. The theory of articulation emphasizes the need to move beyond interpretation to articulation as a critical project seeking to end oppression. Hall (1999) notes that articulation practices range from the local to the global and are useful in understanding contingency. He writes that at the global level, industrialism and capitalism, with their emphasis on technology and reason, temporally define the discursive field of "blackness" in terms of uncivilized and incapable. In Jamaica the rearticulation of "black" as signifying soul, beauty, and liberation has displaced this global meaning, transforming the essence of Jamaicanness. Laclau and Mouffe (1985, 94, 106), on the other hand, attempt to move beyond contingency and argue that in a world without foundations and given meanings, the concept of articulation is useful in explaining social struggles. They argue that the practice of articulation can be understood as a means to fix meanings and to define a reality temporally. They note that to live in a world without fixed meanings does not mean that all articulations are equally possible. In fact, articulation does not guarantee the success of any given discourse. Laclau and Mouffe observe that antagonism makes possible the disarticulation and rearticulation of hegemonic discourses. The practice of articulation establishes a relationship among elements by fixing certain meanings and contexts in ways that modify their identity. Social groups and organizations can construct identities based on rhetoric and social practices situated in place. From this point of view, discourses make certain forms of agency possible (DeLuca 1999, 341).

Although I draw on articulation theory to explain how meanings are produced, I do not think questions of knowledge, power, and Indigenous identity can be reduced to rhetoric and meanings. Critical geographers have emphasized the importance of contextualizing discourses and the role that spatialized images play in politics (Sidaway 1994; Agnew 2001). Tuathail (1996) and Gibson (1999) have expressed reservations about collapsing the social world to the field of difference and language. They argue, for instance, that capitalism, the state, and colonial structures are embedded in specific practices as well as material and historical contexts. I concur with these authors and insist that we must consider the historical and material contexts in which indigeneity is articulated if we are interested in demonstrating how systems of domination and subjugation are entrenched in temporally fixed (neo)colonial structures. Whereas articulations are characterized by their fluidity, colonial structures of domination are characterized by their continuities, making certain political actions (im)possible.

In this regard, Dodds and Sidaway (1994, 518) have stressed the role of "geo-optical support," or sites of production, which constitute the foundation for technologies of power. By privileging specific types of knowledge, maps, and ways of seeing the world, these technologies institutionalize the space-power-knowledge nexus of modern nation-states and inform political imaginations of space (Tuathail 1996, 73). Although Indigenous peoples themselves are agents shaping the articulation of indigeneity, other sites and actors are also involved in creating the complex field in which Indigenous peoples negotiate between local needs and global wants. They can be understood as the sites where power, social practices, knowledge, governance, and hierarchies are produced, contested, negotiated, and altered in the process of producing indigeneity. The state, networks, financial institutions, multilateral organizations, academia, environmental organizations, and the local are all examples of sites of articulation.

Because the articulation of indigeneity occurs in specific locations and geographic imaginations, it calls for a consideration of how political processes occur on scales other than the global. The different social groups included under the term "Indigenous peoples" do not have a unique trajectory, and their politics are motivated by different aspirations and shaped by different colonial entanglements. Since places are important loci of collective memories and political identities, the ability to mobilize different identities into forces of solidarity depends upon the specificities that determine the construction and maintenance of these identities (Harvey 1996). Whereas Indigenous peoples construct place as a bordered and self-enclosed space, international institutions such as the World Bank, the International Monetary Fund (IMF), and the state as well as other equally powerful sites of indigeneity production imagine the world as comprising "free unbounded space in which places are open to economic globalization" (Massey 1994, 15). In this sense, articulation and indigeneity production do not always involve radical contingency; political possibilities are historically constrained by fixed structural domination (Clifford 2001).

The increasing importance of the term "Indigenous peoples" is connected to the role of transnational networks, which have given different peoples a common platform of articulation. Networks help to construct, organize, and transmit material and symbolic resources that legitimize and produce indigeneity. Networks flow in multiple directions among the local, the state, and the global and at an unequal pace. If we think of indigeneity as articulated through a process that develops on different scales and is produced in different sites, we can distinguish between the global, the state, the local, the household, and the body. Global sites are the United Nations (UN), international nongovernmental organizations (NGOs), environmental NGOs, the World Bank, the IMF, human rights activist groups, and government policies that overlap with the other categories.

International financial institutions such as the World Bank and the IMF are powerful sites that have designed economic policies on Indigenous peoples and imposed them on place. States, in turn, have legitimized global discourses by embracing, reproducing, or co-opting them. At the same time, global discourses are mobilized and resignified by grassroots activists and local NGOs, thus facilitating new configurations of power beyond the state. Nongovernmental organizations are not only passive subjects of hegemonic forces and sites of articulation but also active subjects employing complex yet domesticated discourses of resistance and subversion to facilitate their goals in specific places. Like the different sites of articulation, networks also have different powers and resources and forge different relationships. Networks are in different conditions of participation, mobilize different discourses in different places, and foster exclusions and inclusions. This transnational process can be understood as the condition in which networks of relationships are forged on different geographic scales that transcend pre-existing boundaries of nation-states, markets, and civil society (Blaser 2004).

One of the most important issues in the articulation of indigeneity is the question of who is included and excluded. This process of inclusion and exclusion is influenced by place and by "the complex interactions of knowledge, power, history and geography that have variously shaped colonial and 'post-colonial' encounters" with Indigenous peoples (Rossiter and Wood 2005, 357). The politics of indigeneity make it impossible to design and implement Indigenous policies without actually defining who is Indigenous. As Thornberry (2002, 58-59) points out, the politics of definition are embedded in moral, political, and ontological considerations that have important implications for Indigenous peoples.

Thus who determines who is "Indigenous" and what rights are attached to such an identity are among the most contentious issues arising from these transnational interactions and the practices of articulation. Considerable thinking and debate have been devoted to defining objective standards for identifying Indigenous peoples versus acknowledging their right to self-identification. On the one hand, the formulation of strict definitional standards excludes some Indigenous groups who need protection.

On the other hand, the lack of a universal definition helps some host-states to continue denying the existence of Indigenous peoples within their territories (Colchester 2002).

Historically, colonial powers, nation-states, and international agencies have developed and imposed their own rigorous yet exclusionary definitions of who is Indigenous upon Indigenous populations. The formulation of exclusionary definitions has been one among many strategies that nation-states have used to systematically deny Indigenous rights. As a result of the many negative experiences Indigenous peoples and organizations have had with official definitions of Indigenous status, they have insisted that they know better "who is Indigenous" (Morkenstam 2005, 437).

Proponents of an objective definition of Indigenous peoples point out that a subjective theory of self-identification can be abused by those who do not need protection. These proponents of a universal definition argue that to qualify as "Indigenous," people should satisfy a set of objective criteria. From the International Labour Organization's Convention 107, later 169 (ILO 2003), to the United Nations Declaration on the Rights of Indigenous Peoples (UNDRIP) (United Nations 2007), international institutions have made serious attempts to establish a number of criteria by which Indigenous peoples can be characterized globally. One of the most cited working definitions of "Indigenous" communities, peoples, and nations was proposed by José R. Martínez Cobo, the first UN special rapporteur for the Sub-commission on Prevention of Discrimination and Protection of Minorities, in his famous *Study on the Problem of Discrimination against Indigenous Populations* (1986). This working definition offers a number of basic ideas for defining "Indigenous peoples" while recognizing their right to define themselves. The definition reads as follows: "Indigenous communities, peoples and nations are those which, having a historical continuity with pre-invasion and pre-colonial societies that developed on their territories, consider themselves distinct from other sectors of the societies now prevailing on those territories, or parts of them" (Martínez Cobo E/CN.4/Sub.2/ 1986/7, Addendum 4).

Moreover, this definition states that Indigenous peoples constitute "non-dominant sectors of society and are determined to preserve, develop and transmit to future generations their ancestral territories, and their ethnic identity, as the basis of their continued existence as peoples" (Martínez Cobo E/CN.4/Sub.2/1986/7, Addendum 4). Martínez Cobo establishes that historical continuity may consist of the endurance, for an extended period reaching into the present, of one or more of the following factors:

1  Occupation of ancestral lands, or part of them.
2  Common ancestry with the original occupants of these lands.
3  Cultural practices.
4  The use of language.
5  Residence in certain regions of the world.
6  Other relevant factors. (Martínez Cobo E/CN.4/Sub.2/1986/7,
   Addendum 4)

Despite the prevalence of this definition, some observers have rejected it on a variety of grounds, including the issue of historical continuity with pre-colonial societies and the assumption that all groups are in the position to preserve, develop, and transmit their ancestral lands to future generations in the way they are expected to. Moreover, the above definition assumes that European conquest and invasion, often by military means, are part of the historical legacy of all Indigenous peoples.

Another problem with Martínez Cobo's (1986) definition arises when identifying the descendants of the "original inhabitants." What exactly does this phrase mean? The issue of originality implies that someone was somewhere first. What about Indigenous travelling and migration patterns? When I think of the Americas, I think of stories about people being drawn from the landscape and migrating across the landscape; do such stories make us less Indigenous? An additional problem is that descendants of the original inhabitants have undergone transformation, sometimes resulting in different political entities. Has this process made the Métis of Canada or the Miskitos of Nicaragua non-Indigenous even though they identify otherwise? The focus on first and static conceptions of Indigenous habitation not only ignores movement and connections but also dissociates what it means to be Indigenous today from the "ideal Indigenous subject" located in a distant past.

Another relevant definition crafted in the late 1980s in the context of the General Conference of the International Labour Organization (ILO) can be found in Convention 169, a legal tool aimed at recognizing and protecting Indigenous rights. This instrument builds upon some of Martínez Cobo's criteria. Convention 169 applies to "tribal peoples in independent countries whose social, cultural and economic conditions distinguish them from other sections of the national community, and whose status is regulated wholly or partially by their own customs and traditions or by special laws or regulations" (ILO 2003, 7). Convention 169 also applies to "peoples in independent countries who are regarded as indigenous on account of their

descent from the populations which inhabited the country, or a geographical region to which the country belongs, at the time of conquest or colonisa-
tion or the establishment of present State boundaries" (ILO 2003, 7).

Although Convention 169 distinguishes between tribal and Indigenous
peoples, the difference between these two categories is not very clear. For
most countries, however, this issue has been extremely contentious because
the term "peoples" implies a difference in how international law should regard Indigenous rights. Arguably, the term "peoples" in international law
implies the right to self-determination and secession or the right to constitute a new nation-state.

Convention 169 has also faced criticism for its emphasis on the social,
cultural, and economic differences between Indigenous peoples and mainstream society. Since Indigenous peoples are considered to be at a disadvan-
tage, states are given an active role in deciding how to improve Indigenous
peoples' conditions of life. Indigenous peoples and NGOs have argued that
despite emphasizing the term "peoples," the convention fails to firmly recognize Indigenous peoples' rights to self-determination by giving states too
much residual authority over these peoples (Sanders 1995, 12-13; Anaya
1996, 73). Moreover, the convention emphasizes the need to protect a cultural identity, an approach that might be prone to essentialism.

In October 2007 the UNDRIP was ratified by Mexico and other countries and later by Canada. The UNDRIP expands land rights and states that
"Indigenous peoples have the right to maintain and strengthen their distinctive spiritual relationship with their traditionally owned or otherwise
used and occupied lands, territories, waters and coastal seas and other
resources" (United Nations 2007, Article 25). This declaration has defined a
legal concept of territory, which is designed to secure a place for Indigenous
peoples within the configuration of the modern state (Bryan 2009, 28-29).
Consistent with this definition, the UNDRIP also articulates a definition of
Indigenous citizenship that is business-driven. The declaration states that
"Indigenous peoples have the right to maintain and strengthen their distinct
political, legal, economic, social and cultural institutions, while retaining
their right to participate fully, if they so choose, in the political, economic,
social and cultural life of the State" (United Nations 2007, Article 5).

I argue that by securing a political place for Indigenous peoples, the
declaration recognizes an articulation of indigeneity in which the nation-
state plays a role in "accommodating" Indigenous cultural rights while encouraging Indigenous peoples to fully participate in the political, economic,
social, and cultural life of the state. Moreover, the combination of culture

and development restricts Indigenous peoples'. abilities to make autonomous decisions (Engle 2010, 7).

The notion of development has been connected to the articulation of indigeneity since the late 1960s and early 1970s, when international networks
on Indigenous rights were formed. Organizations such as the International
Work Group for Indigenous Affairs gave the Sami people a strong voice in
the international arena, and both Survival International and Cultural Survival specifically advanced Indigenous agendas based on difference, which
challenged dominant ideas of development and integration (Wilmer 1993,
141). Around this period, the Organization of American States, with influence in the Latin American region, established the Inter-American Court of
Human Rights in San José, Costa Rica. By the 1970s Indigenous advocacy
and Indigenous organizations had matched the internal developmental expansion of many nation-states as they engaged in the exploitation of natural
resources, including oil, minerals, and hydroelectricity through the construction of dams in "peripheral areas" in the global North (Saladin d'Anglure and
Morin 1992).

Although contemporary Indigenous movements are often traced back to
the 1960s and 1970s, this does not mean that Indigenous peoples were not
involved in struggles against development and land dispossession before this
period. Rather, it means that they used other banners and deployed other
discourses in pursuing their long-held interests and demands. Scholars who
have focused on Latin American countries, for example, have argued that
the ethnic groups that were once "peasants" struggling for land and facing
the impact of development are now being represented as "Indigenous" (Jung
2008). In my view, the absence of the label "Indigenous" means neither that
local understandings of indigeneity did not exist prior to its global articulations nor that indigeneity comes into existence only because it has been
named. The argument that indigeneity is only a contemporary phenomenon
is problematic and calls into question what we have in mind when we speak
of Indigenous peoples and the particular ways that we expect them to perform indigeneity in order to be recognized as Indigenous. Furthermore, the
struggle for land/territory is only one component of Indigenous identity.
Historically, Indigenous communities have revolted to defend their resources, territories, and political autonomy, but they have used different strategies as "defense mechanisms" to protect themselves from real or perceived
threats (Engle 2010, 8).

In Mexico, for example, some of the organizations that clearly identified as Indigenous were created and sponsored by the government itself,

which had been actively promoting bilingual education for Indigenous peoples since the 1930s and trying to integrate them into mainstream society. Indigenous bilingual teachers were among the first to clearly espouse the discourse of Indigenous cultural rights, making this concept apolitical for those Indigenous organizations that insisted on maintaining ideological independence from the government. Many organizations simultaneously claimed an Indigenous and class-based identity (Sánchez 1999). For example, the Zapotec Coalición de Obreros, Campesinos y Estudiantes del Istmo in the Tehuantepec Isthmus, Mexico, was one of the first Indigenous movements to articulate a Zapotec and a class identity in the struggle to maintain political autonomy. In Mexico, Indigenous movements have tended to follow an approach that has focused on discourses of democracy, political autonomy, and human rights.

In contrast, in Canada most Indigenous organizations that emerged to challenge the threats of encroachment and destruction posed by development expansion adopted a more international stance, stressing Indigenous sovereignty, treaties, and self-determination. The World Council of Indigenous Peoples (WCIP), formed in Port Alberni, Canada, included different Indigenous organizations from around the world. The WCIP maintained some alliances in Latin America, but its presence in Mexico was diluted in the early 1990s precisely because of a difference in strategies. The Inuit Circumpolar Conference is another transnational organization made up of Inuit from throughout the circumpolar world. This organization facilitated the construction of networks and a transnational Inuit polity that would emerge and participate in Arctic governance (Shadian 2007).

Indigenous activism and transnationalism have been neither homogeneous nor free of conflict. Indeed, one of the expressions of such conflicts has developed along a divide between Anglo and Spanish America that reflects Indigenous peoples' different experiences and strategies. Niezen (2003, 70-71) has observed that "northern Indigenous peoples" have had more resources and an "assimilation-oriented education," which have allowed them to participate in international conferences and to understand the bureaucratic intricacies of international organizations such as the UN and the ILO more easily than their counterparts in the global South.

Niezen is right in stressing education and a lack of resources in characterizing the North-South split; however, this cleavage is more complex. As an uneven practice of uniting and representing discourses and of creating meanings and political possibilities, the articulation of indigeneity is a struggle embedded in fixed colonial structures. The type of colonial formation and mode of governance developed in specific places has shaped Indigenous peoples' experiences and political actions. Furthermore, countries and places are also different because of their historical and contemporary linkages to broader political and economic processes. The questions of who intervenes where and what kinds of intervention are implemented for certain groups speak to the broader asymmetry of power relations shaping Indigenous peoples' struggles. Thus understanding the connection between colonial structures and the global economy involves realizing how the everyday enactments of development in the diverse landscapes of what are called the global North and the global South rest upon asymmetric relations and the contingent social, political, and economic exclusions Indigenous communities have experienced.

Transnational collaborations between North America and Latin America did occur in the 1980s. However, such collaborations were not exclusively between Indigenous peoples themselves but also between NGOs, academics, and Indigenous peoples (Sanders 1995; Anaya 1996). In Mexico earlier critiques of hegemonic discourses on development came from academics. In 1960, influenced by the Red Power movement in the United States, a group of radical non-Indigenous anthropologists launched a critique of "indigenism," or government Indigenous policy, as being a continuation of colonialism. This group of anthropologists was invited to join the National Institute of Indigenous Affairs in order to redesign Indigenous policy in Mexico. The institutionalization of this critical perspective, however, depoliticized indigeneity and reduced it to securing cultural rights.

By the second half of the 1980s, it was clear that Indigenous activism was booming and that new networks were being worked out. As Blaser, Feit, and McRae (2004) have rightly noted, different and at times contradictory positions, new relationships, and new concerns emerged as different organizations, institutions, NGOs, academics, and communities connected with each other. Concerns, issues, and approaches were incorporated into political agendas and also co-opted into developmental projects. Concepts such as "sustainable development" became popular and purposely ambiguous to allow for the pursuit of different agendas across different networks with opposing views (Adams 2001; Blaser, Feit, and McRae 2004).

Academics' interventions had unintentional results. In their critique of mainstream development, scholars advanced the idea that Indigenous peoples have a unique system of knowledge that could serve as the basis for more successful interventions. The concept of Indigenous knowledge was quickly invoked in the UN's 1992 Rio Declaration on Environment and Development and in different World Bank reports. The concept also emerged in conservation projects in which Indigenous peoples were constructed as the "noble savage" and in development projects committed to raising the standard of living in Indigenous communities close to development zones. Academics and NGOs engaged in collaborations that advocated an Indigenous resource-based approach, and Indigenous peoples themselves articulated this notion of indigeneity for the purpose of making political claims (Blaser 2004). Resource rights were translated differently in different areas. The World Bank, for example, brought this new concept into its policies, which specifically targeted Indigenous peoples in the global South. To this institution, Indigenous peoples comprised a distinct, vulnerable social and cultural group whose members needed assistance to be integrated into economic development. As I show in the next chapter, global discourse on economic development, the environment, rights, and difference provides important insights into the complexities, power dynamics, and contradictions surrounding the articulation of indigeneity.

## Geographies of Colonialism: Land and Labour

Earlier I argued that despite the emphasis on collaboration when we speak of Indigenous transnationalism, this process has been embedded in tensions and divisions not only along the North-South divide but also, I maintain, along the English-Spanish divide. I mentioned in the introduction that because of my Indigenous background, I was invited to participate in a research project focusing on the Fifth Centennial of Indigenous Resistance across the Americas at the National Autonomous University of Mexico. The project followed different hemispheric Indigenous gatherings, which culminated in Guatemala City on 12 October 1992. Among the things that struck me the most during these meetings were the political differences along the English-Spanish divide. I am referring not only to language but also to the colonial experience. Whereas some Indigenous participants and organizations located in Canada and the United States insisted on sovereignty claims and land title, Indigenous organizations in Spanish-speaking countries insisted on human rights, political autonomy, and dignity.

Besides the global North-South divide briefly discussed earlier, what else is behind these different claims and discourses? Are claims to sovereignty more expansive than claims to political autonomy? In my view, this cleavage is closely connected to different types of colonial formation. Drawing on the contributions of critical geographers, anthropologists, historians, and settler colonial studies, this section analytically distinguishes between settler and extractive colonialism. I show that different systems of domination and subjugation are crucial to understanding indigeneity articulation and how distinctive Indigenous demands, actions, and responses stem from structurally different colonial processes. Importantly, I do not see colonialism as a monolithic structure of oppression (Comaroff and Comaroff 1991, 183). For example, in some places, the validity of Indigenous laws and forms of governance were recognized and lands protected.

Colonialism remapped the discursive and physical spaces and places of Indigenous peoples through different strategies. However, not all empires wanted the same thing from their colonies, nor were all colonized spaces the same. British and Spanish imperial enterprises differed in important ways. Differences between these colonial projects have been studied; however, their spatial and economic operations as well as their specific forms of governance have not been extensively explored. Seed (2001, 2) contends that whereas the English conquered land and property, the Spaniards colonized people, allowing them to retain their lands in exchange for labour, resources, and social humiliation. These different approaches did not result simply from ecological accidents and historical encounters but also from different traditions about valuing, transferring, and allocating wealth that emerged in Europe before colonial quests.

Although Seed establishes an important distinction, I add two dimensions not sufficiently considered. First, conquering land presupposed that the land was symbolically empty (terra nullius) or inhabited by homo nullius (non-humans). However, most of Seed's arguments focus on the economic reasons driving dispossession. Framing Indigenous lands as wastelands, even in instances where lands were cultivated by Indigenous communities, implies that Indigenous peoples had to be disavowed and their territories emptied of presence. Settler colonialism is useful in exploring the different modalities employed to disavow Indigenous peoples. According to Wolfe (2006, 388), settler colonialism is characterized by its tendency to eliminate Indigenous peoples not as the rightful owners of the lands but as "Indians." Indigenous peoples were displaced, driven away, fenced in, their ancestry was regulated in an attempt to reduce numbers, and their children were abducted and resocialized in residential schools. From his perspective, not only *where* Indigenous peoples were but also *who* they were constituted the primary motive for elimination. Conquering people, in contrast, implies that people were recognized as being humans, as being *peoples,* who were subjugated for the purpose of exploiting labour. As opposed to viewing Indigenous peoples as obstructing access to land, extractive colonialism takes the view that the more subjugated people are, the more access there is to labour. Second, Indigenous labour was important to both British and Spanish colonialism, yet it had very different functions, which structured the conditions in which Indigenous peoples laboured and in which Indigenous labour became visible.

Labour involved more than just extracting or producing economic wealth from the colonies. Silliman's (2001, 380, original emphasis) definition of labour as practice is particularly useful in understanding Indigenous agency: "I define labor as the social and material relations surrounding any activities that are designed to produce, distribute or manipulate material items for personal use or for anyone else or any activities whether material or not that are *required or appropriated* for use by someone else." Thus labour was a colonial imposition and a form of discipline involving everyday life and embedded in social and power relations producing inequalities. As a set of practices, labour involves not only the modes of implementation but also the everyday practices of people's experiences, negotiation, appropriation, suffering, and living in a given labour regime. Thus labour can also be considered a locus of social agency (Silliman 2001, 381). Although colonizers used labour to extract wealth, Indigenous peoples maintained some degree of social agency to maintain continuity, exercise circumscribed autonomy, and reconstruct their identities. In the context of settler colonialism, Indigenous peoples may engage in unequal labour relations to guarantee their survival as distinctive peoples.

Because labour involves bodily experiences, it is also gendered. Colonialism and capitalism not only dispossessed Indigenous peoples but also rested on a gendered division of labour that specifically disadvantaged women through their exclusions from independent harvest, access to land, and in some instances, wage labour itself, transforming Indigenous gender relations. Although in many studies the terms "labour" and "work" are used interchangeably, I outline some useful distinctions here to understand the role of work in Indigenous economies. Both work and labour involve practices and activities that require energy and produce energy. What distinguishes labour and work is that labour is appropriated by someone else, whereas work is embedded in a horizon of communal and social power relations, is oriented toward the household as the basic productive unit, and is part of a cycle involving production, consumption, exchanges, storage, resource allocation, scarcity, and so on.

Land and labour involved spatialized practices that reorganized the self, the community, and the logic of Indigenous relations and that manipulated knowledge, ideas, norms, and laws. Human geographers (Kobayashi 1994; Delaney 2002) have argued that space is relevant to understanding disavowal, segregation, othering, dispossession, exploitation, and bodily experiences. Harris (2001, xxiii-xxiv) has examined the making of Indigenous space in British Columbia. He argues that making Indigenous space involved both the discursive adjudication of land and the material displacement of Indigenous peoples to smaller reserves. Making colonial space involved not only the confinement of Indigenous peoples to clear the vast land but also the conceptual and material transformation of the environment (Sluyter 2002). Colonialism was a structure with which to control land, labour, and resources and to transform space. Nevertheless, making colonial space involved different strategies in different colonial contexts. In settler colonialism, landscape transformation involved the physical and symbolic elimination of Indigenous peoples to accumulate land for settlers. Extractive colonialism, in contrast, involved practices that included reproductive labour, controlling resource and trade nodes, and labour distribution.

Colonial constructions of race, gender, the "Other," the "savage/hunter-gatherer," and the "pagan" structured the social-spatial segregation and colonial economy that functioned to support the project. Colonialism created gendered spatialized metaphors and dichotomies between people and nature, colonized and colonizer, settler and reserve, frontier and metropolis, and female/private and male/public. However, although the configuration of intimate colonial spaces disciplined bodies, the colonized also generated clandestine practices and strategies aimed at resisting, adapting, and remaking such spaces. In other words, although the colonized were dominated, their desires, visions, and strategies were not fully captured by the colonial system (de Certeau 1984, xviii).

Practices of the colonized – their transformation and reappropriation of space – contribute to our comprehension of the social construction of indigeneity, gender, space, and resistance. To understand the space of colonization, we must explore its effects, dispossessions, and repossessions (Harris 2004). Building upon this geographic understanding of colonial space, resistance, and labour as practice, this section of the chapter raises some broader historical issues that manifest in the divergent conditions of indigeneity in both Canada and Mexico. This approach is useful in analyzing the heterogeneity of Indigenous experiences, the geography of colonialism, the interconnection between practices producing domination and agency, and the different strategies of resistance. This approach is also useful in understanding how colonial landscape transformation continues to shape how the environment is conceived today. Importantly, although I distinguish between settler and extractive colonialism, I also attempt to shed light on how colonialism varied in practice, revealing the limits and contradictions of colonial rule.

I start with settler colonialism in Canada and the arguments Seed (2001) poses. She argues that because land was the very foundation of the British legal system and economic transactions, the central objective of English colonization was to own land and to separate people from their lands. The English used different means to secure land ownership. Until the seventeenth century, Seed notes, England did not require written documents for land ownership. Land could be owned as a result of exchanging goods and of labouring on vacant lands. Labour allowed the English settlers to legitimize dispossession and value themselves in opposition to the "savage" or "lazy Indian." In the so-called New World, settlers' actions, such as building a house or a fence, were considered sufficient to acquire land. Other means to own Indigenous lands included transforming them by bringing slaves to work there as well as purchasing the lands outright. Treaties also figured as a way of acquiring land. However, Seed notes, treaties were not agreements between nations. In the sixteenth century, English and, to some extent, French traders used treaties as a way to acquire everything from fur to sugar from Indigenous peoples. Because land is central to settler colonialism, when possible the English also encouraged the settlers to seize "unproductive" or "waste lands," which were considered unpopulated, uncultivated, or simply wilderness (Seed 2001, 50).

Although I believe Seed's account of British colonialism is correct, it is incomplete since it conceals Indigenous labour both before and during colonialism, reproducing the old binary between "traditional economies" and modern/European labour. Although labour was central to dispossession, colonialism involved other elements, including the separation of nature from society, the denigration of "unimproved" nature, and the construction of a moral economy based on the exclusive control of land and its unlimited accumulation by those who could transform it (McCarthy and Prudham 2004, 278). Indigenous peoples held different understandings of nature, and these understandings involved specific forms of work. Later Indigenous peoples not only adapted to the fur trade but also took entrenched skills and adapted them to new markets generated by land dispossession (Raibmon 2006, 26). They simultaneously participated in both the so-called traditional and capitalist economies. In engaging in unequal labour relations, Indigenous peoples guaranteed their survival as distinctive peoples (Veraccini 2011, 3). Customary participation in the wage economy helped Indigenous peoples to fulfil their responsibilities to their communities. In my view, this challenges the assumption – embraced by current neoliberal constructs – that Indigenous peoples live in the conditions they do because they have not participated in the capitalist economy. Thus it is important to pay attention not only to the specific colonial settings in which Indigenous labour has occurred but also to the current conditions under which Indigenous peoples engage with capitalist development and neoliberal institutional arrangements.

In the earliest stages of colonialism, both the British and the French were interested in the profitable fur trade, to which Indigenous labour was essential. The fur trade, one of the most important industries in North America, played a major role in the development of Canada for more than 300 years, with the Hudson's Bay Company playing a key role in this process. First Nations entered into treaties with both French and English settlers to secure the fur trade and to establish military alliances. These treaties had very different meanings for the English and the Indigenous peoples. For the latter, treaties were a way to establish friendship and co-operation between nations; for the former, treaties were another way to acquire land (Seed 2001, 53). Although treaties were important, not all Indigenous peoples signed them. In Indigenous jurisdictions such as the Arctic, where land was not necessarily a priority for European settlers, Indigenous governance systems were maintained to secure value from Indigenous economies (Howitt 2009, 146).

As the British Empire expanded through northern North America, tensions between settlers and Indigenous peoples became common, and the notion of the "primeval forest" became increasingly used to designate Indigenous lands. Although Indigenous territories were imprinted by human actions and inhabitants were governed by complex systems of land use and ownership, disavowing Indigenous peoples and constructing them as "hunter-gatherers" and their lands as being waste or "wilderness" corresponded to a practice of eliminating Indigenous peoples. Moreover, these constructions justified the civilizing action of English settlers and the rejection of Indigenous land ownership (Tennant 1990; Harris 2002).

In the logic of eliminating Indigenous peoples, settlers were characterized as being settled in permanent replicas of what they had left behind. In
contrast, Indigenous peoples were deemed fragile and in the process of dis-
appearing (Veraccini 2011, 6). By the late nineteenth century, colonial policy
had shifted to other practices of elimination of the Indigenous "Other." As
Brown (1993, 661) argues, through this shift, cultural difference became
political deviance and cultural representation became ideological domination. The invocation of the idea of progress, with its attendant binary of
barbarians versus civilizers, turned logical distinctions into moral hierarchies that targeted the existence of Indigenous bodies, law, and governance
systems. Throughout this process, discursive and legal practices were aimed
at transforming Indigenous peoples into something else.

In addition, anti-miscegenation discourses became an element of larger
processes of national self-definition on the basis of race. Exclusion and re-
straint provided the cement that held the confederation together. Once
dispossession was accomplished, Canada was constituted as having two
founding "races" or "nations" – the English and the tolerated French – which
completely ignored the existence of Indigenous peoples (Fairweather 2006,
204). Canada's own "national settler" essence was constituted in terms of
a transnational British kin bound together by racial ties. By the time of
Confederation, most of the government's informal "Indian" policy had taken
shape. After Confederation, the federal government assumed control over
Indigenous issues under Section 91(24) of the Constitution Act of 1867,
passing the Indian Act and later creating the reserve system. Through the
Indian Act, racial segregation and gender discrimination were formalized,
allowing for the colonial authority to reproduce itself as a settler society
(Brown 2001, 669). As a settler state, Canada retained permanent and indisputable sovereignty over the land by effectively limiting Indigenous
peoples and spaces through mapping, numbering, and surveillance (Harris
2002, 271).

The British imperial civilizing role marked a new stage in "Indian" policy,
one in which the church would be a key actor in implementing residential
schools. In addition, a legal definition of "Indian" was established, and
Indian Agents were put in charge of administrating all Native lands and
properties. In paternalistically defining who was and was not "Indian," the
government usurped the birthrights of First Nations women and their children (Green 2001), further eliminating the Indigenous "Other." Additional
early provisions of the Indian Act reinforced women's subjugation. Until

1951 women were excluded from the band electorate and public meetings, and Indian Agents exercised considerable discretionary powers over property inheritance, which usually benefited men (Fiske 1991).

When First Nations peoples resisted the Indian Act, disciplinary amendments were made. When Indian Agents did not approve of Indigenous leaders, provisions were introduced to give them the power to depose those considered "immoral or incompetent." When, in the view of missionaries, Indigenous traditional customs interfered with assimilation, provisions were also introduced to ban ceremonies such as the potlatch in British Columbia and the Sun Dance on the Prairies. Through residential schools and enfranchisement, assimilation policies were oriented to extinguish Indigenous status and rights. In retrospect, it can be noted that the Indian Act has remained a strong impediment to Indigenous citizenship. Voluntary or forced enfranchisement presupposed giving up Indian status and communal ownership (Tennant 1990).

Citizenship for "Indians" after the Second World War was part of a deliberate policy of dealing with a population perceived by the federal government to be potentially threatening by bringing its members into the Canadian mainstream (Bohaker and Iacovetta 2009, 429). This offer of citizenship was an exclusive choice between Indigenousness and Canadianness. Although Indigenous peoples were encouraged to adhere to Canadian citizenship, they paradoxically did not acquire full political rights to vote in both federal and provincial elections until the 1960s, Quebec being the last province to allow Indigenous peoples to vote in provincial elections. Moreover, the extension of political rights to "Indians" in 1960 masked these oppressive legacies of colonialism and racism (Youngblood Henderson 2002, 420). The complexities of Indigenous peoples' status suggest only the "settler versus Indigenous" experience. The historical socio-legal discourses attached to Canadian citizenship effectively maintained Indigenous peoples in their colonial, vulnerable space.

Although both settlers and colonizers moved across space to establish their dominance in specific places, their operations differed in important ways. In contrast to settler colonialism, extractive colonialism relied on labour, and unlike English settlers, Spanish colonizers thought the resources, particularly mineral resources and labour, of the New World were theirs. In the English tradition, land would not have been separated from resources. In the Iberian tradition, in contrast, land and subsurface resources were governed by different rules. Land could be governed under different modalities, but precious minerals could be governed only by a specific set of rules (Seed 2001, 58). In the Iberian tradition, the mineral resources of the subsoil were communally owned by members of the Catholic Church, not by "pagans." Spanish colonialism insisted on "surveying underground." According to Scott (2008, 1860), the knowledge, technologies, and practices that shaped the exploitation of the underground were extremely different from British colonial strategies in Canada in the nineteenth century. Indeed, Scott argues that colonizers' anxiety about what was underground shaped perceptions of what was on the surface. This is an important distinction that continues to shape relations between Indigenous peoples and the state in these two countries.

The search for and exploitation of mining resources drove Spanish colonization in Mexico and other regions of the Americas, but the colonizers needed labour to exploit such resources. The extraction of silver and gold had profound impacts on diverse social and cultural landscapes and provided Europe with the material it needed to secure its global position (Blaut 1993). Indigenous peoples were forced to operate within a specific work structure and were enslaved in silver mines. Only in the mid-sixteenth century did this exterminatory slavery practice start to erode. Once control was established and Indigenous leaders had accepted the Spanish presence, a modus vivendi based on relations of domination was institutionalized. Indigenous communities were allowed to retain their lands in exchange for a tax, or tribute, paid by each adult male. In Spanish the word "tribute" refers to more than simply paying taxes. *Rendir tributo* (rendering tribute) is also about deference and recognizing someone's social superiority (Seed 2001, 60). Certainly, the practice of paying taxes was very familiar to the many Indigenous peoples in Mexico, where extractive institutions were already in place when the Spaniards arrived. The Mexica (or Aztec) Empire had managed to subjugate different Indigenous regions in Mesoamerica. Unlike the Spaniards, the Aztecs were not interested in colonizing but in taxing; it was the community as a whole that was responsible for producing the goods and services paid to this Indigenous empire, not the individual males. Colonial administrators unquestionably exercised domination over the Indigenous population of New Spain; however, they also needed stability to maintain the colony (Florescano 1997, 161). Colonizers depended upon Indigenous self-governance to sustain labour exploitation.

Because extractive colonialism is driven by a determination to sustain subordination rather than elimination, Spanish colonizers allowed Indigenous communities to reproduce themselves based on the Aztec notion of *altepetl* (autonomous communities). They could maintain their own normative systems, including the rules for transmitting property and assigning lands within the República de Indios (which essentially comprised Indigenous subjugated communities), in return for paying tribute and accepting colonial rule (Florescano 1997, 186). The making of the colonial space rested on the parallel spaces of the República de Españoles and the República de Indios distinguishing between conquerors and colonized people. The República de Indios maintained different types of land, including lands for community celebrations and lands for communal and individual use (Florescano 1997, 190). These communities rested upon a moral economy of reciprocity, which can be defined as a set of social practices and relations based on a moral code aimed at fostering reciprocity and networks of security in the form of *tequio* (community work) among equal kin and hierarchical neighbours. Based on this moral logic of reciprocity, what is given (e.g., services, gifts, resources, and goods) must be returned in the form of something of "similar" value. These networks of support constitute a local mechanism for resisting exploitation and domination. Moreover, the community and the *comunal* provided Indigenous peoples with institutional organization and a strategy of resistance (Martínez Luna 2010).

The Leyes de Indias (Indigenous Law) also recognized Indigenous peoples' right to choose their authorities according to their own customary practices as long as the leader was responsible for collecting the tax. Unlike modern human rights, which are vested in the individual, Indigenous rights in the República de Indios were vested in the collective, or *pueblo* (people) (Seed 2001, 59). Indigenous peoples effectively used the longstanding Spanish notion of "from time immemorial" to defend their lands in colonial courts whenever conflicts among communities and individuals arose. For the sixteenth and seventeenth centuries, extensive evidence exists of Indigenous women using colonial courts for issues related to ownership and community conflicts. Some scholars, including Kellogg (1997) and Horn (1997), have argued, for instance, that the active participation of Indigenous women in litigations reflected the formal power and authority women had in Indigenous societies before colonization. This power and authority had started to decline by the end of the seventeenth century as women's identity became linked to that of their fathers and husbands and as their roles started to be restricted to the domestic realm.

Although some may be tempted to believe that Spanish colonization was subtler than British colonialism because the former did not seize Indigenous land, this situation needs to be contextualized. Although the Leyes de Indias gave Indigenous peoples local political and legal independence and title over surface lands, the Spanish colonizers did not follow such legislation everywhere, particularly in the midst of the introduction of the *repartimiento* system of forced labour and consumption. Even when they did, the República de Indios became the space associated with "inferior peoples" and also the space of survival and resistance to domination. The República de Indios shaped Indigenous peoples' social practices, relations, and political actions. The denial of the dignity of the Indigenous "Other," in some contexts, resulted in the perpetration of physical violence and the violation of personhood and rights.

As time went by, collecting tribute and forcing people to labour became excruciating tasks as illnesses and the burden of labour started to decimate Indigenous communities, which were not even in the position to produce to meet their needs. Initially, Indigenous authorities were incarcerated if they could not collect taxes from their people; we can imagine how reluctant community members may have been to be elected as leaders. Spaniards were forced to change some of their practices in order to appeal to potential leaders. For instance, Indigenous authorities were given certain prerogatives, such as wearing Spanish clothing, and were addressed as dignitaries in recognition of their hierarchical status. In the hierarchical and racialized colonial society, Indigenous peoples were not permitted to wear ornaments or any other kind of clothing that could make them look similar to the Spaniards. Similarly, riding horses and walking in the middle of the streets were privileges reserved only for the colonizers (Seed 2001, 122). Indigenous peoples were expected to be docile, obedient, servile, and humble in the presence of Spaniards. In other words, Indigenous peoples preserved their lands, legal systems, and traditional authorities in exchange for accepting their inferiority, subjugation, and degradation.

Although Indigenous peoples were considered to be humans, a crucial distinction between colonized and colonizer was maintained. Memmi (2003, 53) notes that although some colonized people were more privileged than others, colonizers ensured that the colonized never benefited from certain rights. Based on their faith, colonizers were conceived to be superior and to be people of reason in contrast to the pagan, heathen Indigenous "Other." However, as religion was extended and more and more Indigenous individuals were baptized, Spanish colonizers could not continue to rely exclusively on faith. At the end of the seventeenth century, to maintain moral boundaries, the Spaniards adopted the notion of purity of faith. Indigenous peoples were prevented from accessing religious education and the priesthood since they would "contaminate" the Spanish faith. Indigenous people, particularly women who mixed Indigenous rituals and traditional medicine practices with Catholic rituals, were prosecuted and executed in the name of purity of faith. Indigenous sexual practices, which had previously been tolerated by the Spaniards, were equated with sodomy. Two-spirited, or gay, people were targeted as serious political criminals (Seed 2001, 123).

Paradoxically, although colonial administrators were concerned with contamination, they never enforced physical separation between Indigenous and Spanish communities, unlike the English. Because Spaniards depended on Indigenous labour, they saw Indigenous mobility as a means to access cheap labour. At the end of the seventeenth century, mobility, contact, and reproductive labour led to the emergence of a new racialized classification of groups called *castas*. Colonial authorities not only tolerated the so-called miscegenation and intermixing but, in some circumstances, even promoted such practices among different social groups (Axtell 1992, 206). Intermixing was often not institutionalized through marriage, and unlike the intermixing that developed in Canada, the so-called miscegenation in Mexico eventually resulted in a single racial group with class distinctions and racial undertones (Esteva-Fabregat 1995, 57). Mestizos (mixed descendants of Indigenous people and Spaniards) eventually became the larger population.

Because extractive colonialism maintains the difference between metropolis and colony, Creoles (Spaniards born in New Spain) did not enjoy the same benefits as peninsular Spaniards. The latter's wealth and loyalty to the metropolis displaced Creoles from institutions and municipal levels of government. Over time, this distinction fuelled Creoles' resentment and desire for independence from the metropolis (Brading 1985, 40). Because Creoles were a minority, they had to include Mestizos in their nationalist movement (Wimmer 2002, 122). In addition, to differentiate themselves from the metropolis and to appeal to the Indigenous population, Creoles attempted to indigenize themselves by staking a claim to the great Indigenous past.

At the outset of Mexico's transition from colonial rule to independence, most of the country was characterized by legal pluralism, Indigenous land-tenure systems, and enclosed communities. In an effort to draw clear-cut distinctions between independence and the colonial past, the newly independent government looked at France and the United States as models upon which to construct the new nation. Drawing on these examples, a republic based on the notion of one people, one culture, and private property emerged. Creoles, Mestizos, Afromestizos, and all "pacified" Indigenous peoples were transformed into citizens. Although this legal uniformity facilitated the construction of a homogeneous national identity out of the regional, ethnic, and linguistic diversity that dominated the landscape, it erased Indigenous subjectivity.

The independence movement formally replaced the exogenous relation of domination, but decolonization had important limits. Seizure of political power merely transferred control to another social group that conceived of decolonization as European progress, a notion that afforded Indigenous peoples no place. In this context, liberation brought a new form of postcolonial authoritarianism in which the political elite secured privileges for themselves and turned the state into an instrument of control. Indigenous communal land-tenure systems, for instance, were seen as colonial privileges that no longer belonged in a liberal, independent, modern country. The Leyes de Reforma (Reform Laws) were passed to introduce private property. By this means, the political elite of the new country reproduced popular European economic prescriptions and charged Indigenous people with being unproductive and uneconomic. Thus the purpose of the Leyes de Reforma was to open both land and labour to capitalist transformation. Indigenous communities revolted against these laws and the attendant land encroachment. However, as Florescano (1997, 50-71) notes, the resulting movements were conveniently framed as racial struggles threatening Creoles and Mestizos rather than as movements against the unpopular Leyes de Reforma. This framework helped the political elite to justify actions aimed at depriving Indigenous people of their citizenship rights, including even the sale of Mayas in Yucatan as slaves to Cuban sugar plantations. In these circumstances, it can be argued that the independence movement indeed increased the domination of Indigenous peoples.

Despite the government's legal actions to undermine both Indigenous normative and communal land-tenure systems, Indigenous institutions were maintained as a strategy for resisting the nation-state. Indigenous uprisings against the loss of collective rights and land dispossession continued through the nineteenth century until they merged with the Mexican Revolution of 1910. The emergence of Indigenous leaders such as Emiliano Zapata and the Liberation Army of the South brought the issue of Indigenous collective land rights back to the political agenda. As will become apparent in the analysis of the Mexican cases, different levels of institutionalization, the contradictory presence of the nation-state in different regions, community

closeness, and different types of land tenure have shaped the different meanings of "Indigenous community" and of the relations between the nation-
state and Indigenous peoples.

The *ejido* system, a form of land tenure in which plots could be individ-
ually used but neither sold nor bought, was legalized with Article 27 of the
Mexican Constitution of 1917, opening new spaces for landless Indigenous communities to reclaim their lands. This article effectively shielded
about half of the Mexican territory from the land market and in a fashion
similar to the República de Indios, Article 27 also recognized communities'
rights to hold land communally, including woodlands and water. Nearly
one-quarter of communal lands and *ejidos* (plots) are still located in forest
communities, which effectively manage more that 50 percent of the country's forested areas. Although the creation of the *ejido* system protected the
integrity of lands, it strategically changed the source of rights for landless
communities. Article 27 granted only usufruct rights to Indigenous peoples,
and the nation-state retained indisputable sovereignty over subsurface rights
that the Spanish colonizers had once claimed for themselves. In doing so,
Article 27 entrenched state power. Communally owned land, on the other
hand, basically amounted to Indigenous land since it was recognized by the
Spanish Crown either as part of the República de Indios or through restitution. Unlike *ejidos,* communal lands function as social-security nets by providing community members with the means to diversify their sources of
income and to protect themselves against unexpected events. Cattle hus-
bandry and wood and food gathering for local consumption are important
sources of in-kind contributions and play an important social role in the
Indigenous mixed economy (Ita 2006, 157).

According to Jung (2006), Article 27 became the cornerstone of the social contract between the nation-state and the reimagined peasant identity
and created a point of access for a type of political organization that demanded development and redistribution. Although I agree with Jung that
the *campesino* (peasant) identity became the political framework through
which to demand land for landless Indigenous peoples, I argue that they did
not leave aside the spatialized social organization, practices, and normative
systems associated with their local understandings of being Indigenous. In
fact, in Mexico the term "Indian/Indigenous" invokes an old and backward
image, which is the other side of the construction of *mestizaje,* or the ideology of racial hybridity.

After the Mexican Revolution concluded, a new citizenship regime
based on the Mestizo nation was articulated. The integration of Indigenous

peoples into this homogeneous national identity became a national imperative that created different levels of institutionalization within Indigenous regions. Moreover, the Mexican state appropriated European notions of race and culture, which later became a mode of rationality and of cultural reification aimed at policing borders and collectivities (Altamirano-Jiménez 2008a).

Of course, although *mestizaje* celebrated the Indigenous past, living Indigenous peoples were constructed as the internal "Other." Anthropology was instrumental in reinventing Indigenous identity. The National Institute of Indigenous Affairs moved from assimilationist policies to integrationist policies to critical policies to multiculturalism (Gutiérrez Chong 2006). Nonetheless, the common ground has been the search for effective policies to incorporate Indigenous peoples into the Mestizo social, economic, political, and cultural configuration. In the same way that the Spanish colonizers had differentiated themselves from the colonized, "postcolonial" Mestizos established a similar classification that equated indigeneity with being premodern, poor, uneducated, and rural. This characterization still persists today.

In the term *campesino*, landless Indigenous communities found a new means to collectively demand the restitution of their stolen lands. *Campesinos* can be defined as the tenants of small subsistence plots who are existentially engaged in agricultural labour. Indigenous peoples' motivations are neither essential nor timeless. However, this does not mean that such motivations come into existence just because the opportunity emerges (Hale 1997, 571). Thus Indigenous peoples did not become *campesinos* to demand land distribution, as other rural communities did. To landless Indigenous communities, Article 27 and *ejidal* landholding became a means to recover the lands illegally taken away by the colonizers, government, and local strongmen alike. At the local level, Indigenous normative systems merged the *ejido* system into Indigenous communal land tenure and filled the justice vacuum left by the Mexican state's inability to penetrate remote Indigenous regions. In fact, the persistence of different land-tenure systems and the overlapping of the Indigenous normative order and the civil legal order have been at the centre of different territorial conflicts and illegal occupations of Indigenous lands. Moreover, against a monolithic, homogeneous understanding of community, we need to consider how gender is implicated in how resources are distributed. Because the Agrarian Law had been gender-biased since its conception, *ejido* rights were granted mainly to men because women were not seen as "heads of households" until at least

1971 (Baitenmann 1997, 297). Nonetheless, in the adaptation of dynamic Indigenous normative systems to new realities and convoluted situations, women's land rights were shaped by colonial dichotomies and gendered spatial divisions that have informed individual, family, and community daily life. In this regard, Zapotec anthropologist Jaime Martínez Luna (2010, 89) observes that, as Indigenous peoples, "we are the unique result of our own culture, but we are also colonized ... hence, contradictions are a daily occurrence." He sees resistance and action as means to address these colonial contradictions.

By distinguishing between settler and extractive colonialism, this section has shown how space, territory, and place were spatially remapped not by an event but by colonial structures that continue to shape present realities. By comparing Canada and Mexico, this section has shown that acknowledging colonial-specific formations is crucial to understanding the ways that states have relationally constituted indigeneity and to explaining how structurally different colonial formations have shaped economic development and different political reactions and demands.

## Place, Indigenous Nationalisms, and Articulation

Global articulations that ignore place emphasize transiency and diaspora. Although Indigenous migrations and diasporas focus on relations, trading routes, transborder Indigenous communities, urban Indigenous people, and other routed stories, what we all have in common is how we relate to one another and to the landscapes we inhabit, many of which were once Indigenous. Narratives connecting place and memory are integrated into larger landscapes of belonging and politics. Place is more or less a bounded space of face-to-face relationships among people and social and natural forces. As such, place is not an empty arena where people live but a meaningful habitat that has an effect on people and their struggles. "Although Indigenous peoples' senses of place have been worn by centuries of colonial-capitalist displacement, they still serve as an orienting framework that guides radical Indigenous activism today" (Coulthard 2010, 81). Indigenous peoples' struggles for self-determination are not based on marginalization, exploitation, or a colonial past. Rather, these struggles are aimed at defending a way of being in the world. As an ideology, Indigenous nationalism is aimed not only at building new relationships that break away from the colonial but also at re-establishing self-determined, ancient jurisdictions in place(s). Thus Indigenous nationalism is embedded in deeply specific notions of place, collective history, responsibility, and belonging.

People's conceptions of their struggles are embodied and placed in specific locations.

This section discusses the role that place has in Indigenous activism and nationalism. I put forward two interrelated arguments. First, place is not reducible to attachment to the land; place is a space of ontological relationships among people and between people and their environments. Second, to understand Indigenous nationalism, we need to move away from Eurocentric theories of nationalism, which argue nations and nationalism are European phenomena that emerged in modern human history. Reducing nations and nationalism to the European and North American modern experiences reduces Indigenous peoples' history, interconnections, and politics to "cultural practices." Third, although Indigenous nationhood is not a new phenomenon, it cannot be reduced to a "simple and singular-scale politics" (Howitt 2009, 141). Indigenous nationalism articulates forms of resistance to external threats aimed at destroying peoples' senses of place. Thus Indigenous nationalism is embedded in a dialogic tension between global articulations of both indigeneity and the rights discourse, on the one hand, and specific understandings of place and of being a *people* with a history and a distinctive legal order, on the other hand.

The question of when a social group is a *nation* has been extensively discussed in different theories of nationalism (Gellner 1983; Anderson 2000; Smith 2001; Connor 2004). These theoretical discussions have focused on the origins of the nation and have mainly centred on the European and North American experiences at the expense of non-Western and gendered experiences. These discussions have been debated either in terms of the nature and origins of nations and nationalism or in terms of the emergence of new nationalisms.

The first discussion is a continuation of the debate between primordialists and modernists. The former argue that nations are natural and organic and have always existed in human history. Geertz (1973), for instance, contends that ethnicity is more likely than nationalism to serve as the basis for building a nation. According to Geertz, theorists of nationalism conflate not only nation with state but also nation with loyalty, forgetting that identification with a created national identity occurs through domination. However, interactions and earlier collective and cultural experiences do not disappear. The distinction between ethnicity and nationalism allows us to ask critical questions regarding the relationship between the two and to be mindful of how ethnic bonds can serve to challenge state nationalism (Geertz 1973, 258). The relevance of this position derives from its emphasis on the continuity of cultural and ethnic commonalities within the context of historical national formations. In other words, state nationalism does not completely eliminate these affiliations.

The modernist position, in contrast, tends to undermine continuity and instead to emphasize social change. Gellner (1983, 6-7), for example, points out that in industrial societies the political elite use nationalism as a means to respond to economic conditions and needs. Like states, nations are contingent rather than a universal necessity. Gellner claims that nations and states could not have existed without each other, but their emergence was contingent and independent. From this perspective, "nationalism is not the awakening of a nation; rather nationalism invents nations where they do not exist" (Gellner 1994, 390). In pre-industrial societies, Gellner adds, peoples were richly endowed with cultural ties and potential ethnic difference. However, political nationalism is extremely rare in these societies. In the process of nation building, there are two complementary processes: the need of the political unit to be culturally homogeneous and the ability of the industrialization process to destroy the complex network of social differentiation that is expressed in differentiated speech and in code dressing, among other social practices that existed in pre-industrial societies (Gellner 1994, 36). In other words, differentiation is not viable in the context of modernization, nor is the premodern nation. Although many Indigenous states did not have a "state" in the contemporary sense, they had highly centralized or organized governments capable of widespread mobilizations. Otherwise, how can we explain the Aztecs' and Incas' imperial expansions or the political sophistication of the Iroquois Confederacy, to mention a few examples? To reduce Indigenous peoples to premodern cultural entities is to ignore their politics and their complexities.

Constructivists, on the other hand, undermine the role of culture and ethnicity altogether. Constructivists argue that neither cultural nor ethnic commonalities guarantee the formation of any sense of identity, let alone the ability of a given collectivity to reclaim nation status. Although Anderson (2000) acknowledges that all nations are modern creations, he does not think nationalism invents nations where they do not exist. Rather, all communities are imagined, and the imagining is a modern process based on imagined relations instead of on face-to-face interactions present in "premodern communities." From this point of view, nations are not the products of given sociological conditions such as language, religion, and ethnicity but are created through major modern institutions such as the print-capitalism put in place to imagine these communities as limited, sovereign, and exclusive (Anderson 2000, 54).

In this regard, Brennan (1990, 44) argues that we should remember that the term "nation" refers both to the nation-state and to something more diffuse and ancient, such as the local community and family, which create the conditions for belonging. Thus the issue is *what* is mobilized in the process of constructing nationalism. More specifically, what is the relevance of sociological conditions such as ethnicity, language, culture, and belonging in nationalist projects? Why do most nationalist projects make people identify with a specific language or way of being in the world? Why do some groups of people feel excluded?

Without rejecting the manipulative dimension of nationalism and without completely denying the modern status of nations, Smith (2001) adopts an intermediate standpoint, which he calls "ethno-symbolism." Focusing on the ethnic roots of modern nations, he argues that ethnic identity is not an invention. *Ethnies,* understood as human populations with shared ancestors, myths, histories, and cultures, can be traced in ancient history as the antecedents of modern nations. Central to Smith's delineation of *ethnie* is that it encompasses substantial elements of sharing and internal solidarity, leaving room for the inclusion of Indigenous nationalism. I concur with Smith's argument that nationalism can be understood as an ideological movement that seeks to attain and maintain autonomy, unity, and identity on behalf of the members of a determined social group (Smith 2001, 24-25). As an ideology, nationalism renarrates the past to serve the present, implying that the past is not just imagined. With regard to Indigenous peoples, it is possible to argue that shared memories, history, cultural practices, and more important, a sense of place are central to the formation of their collective identities. At the same time, we can note that the elements that bind people together can also be subject to political mobilization.

The second debate has focused on whether "new" assertions of nationhood are indeed nationalist. In the 1980s the world witnessed major political changes that questioned not only the homogeneous nature of historical national formations but also the assumption that state nationalism had been able to completely fragment ethnic and cultural ties. Theorists such as Hobsbawm (1992, 181) wrote that these expressions of nationalism would be short-lived because, after all, nationalism was an anachronism. Similarly, Kohn (2008, 4-5) and Gellner (1988, 57-61) argued that nationalism was a modern phenomenon and that any attempt on the part of nonstate parties to revive a historical culture was to be considered backward and essentially reactionary because culture was irrelevant to modernization. Smith (1995, 160) defended a different view. He argued that nations had not been transcended in the era of globalization. Rather, the wave of nationalism observed around the world had shown the enduring nature of the national idea. Similarly, Hutchinson (1999, 392) argued that the continuing vitality of autonomist movements among national minorities and ethnic national minorities revealed the multinational and contested nature of most nation-states. From this point of view, it was acknowledged that economic globalization was producing specific circumstances that challenged the sovereignty of the state and led to the resurgence of social groups claiming nation status.

Guibernau (1999, 1) has theorized about the types of nationalisms constructed by "nations without states." Stateless nations, she argues, can be understood as "cultural communities sharing a common past, attached to a clearly demarcated territory, wishing to decide upon their political future and lacking a state of their own. These communities are included within one or more states, which they regard as alien, and assert the right to self-determination, which is sometimes understood as further autonomy within the state or the right to secession." Guibernau (1999, 3) further argues that the combination of cultural identity with territorial identity and the emphasis on this composite identity over all others are what give nationalism much of its appeal and resilience. Thus both state and stateless nationalism share the notion of territorial attachment. As Guibernau (1999, 26) observes, most of these communities emphasize memories of a past when they used to enjoy autonomous institutions. In addition, they contest their current relationship with the state, which is based on political dependence, limited or nonexistent access to power and resources, and a lack of political power to recognize their rights.

Although scholars have paid attention to these expressions of stateless nationalism, most of the studies have continued to focus on Western national minorities at the expense of non-Western nations. In an attempt to be more inclusive, Guibernau (1999, 84) argues that Indigenous peoples can be considered to comprise a form of stateless nation. Thus they are conscious of forming a group with a proper name; they share a collective culture, which includes a common ancestry and a common myth of origin; they are attached to a specific homeland; they have a collective memory of historical events and memories of a time when the nation enjoyed independence; they are willing to take control of their political future. Guibernau argues that Indigenous peoples demand to be recognized as nations by claiming a position in the discourse of rights, an integral part of which is the issue of protection and promotion of Indigenous peoples' rights. Although Guibernau's effort to include Indigenous peoples in her theory of stateless nations is relevant, she seems to overestimate the promotion and protection offered by the discourse of rights. More important, although Indigenous nationalism shares important elements with other expressions of Western stateless nationalism, it is also different.

Kanienkehaka scholar Taiaiake Alfred (1995) states that the idea of "we" emphasizes not only community but also a collective responsibility to carry one's people – their history, traditional values, principles, and stories. From this perspective, the moral grounding for Indigenous nationalism is found within Indigenous experiences, connections to place, and responsibilities, and this nationalism is not only a reaction to domination. As an ideology, Indigenous nationalism shapes the construction and promotion of collectivities, the attitudes of members toward the nation, and the *actions* that members take in seeking to achieve and maintain self-determined visions. This means that a sense of being a self-determined nation exists prior to collective actions.

In a similar vein, Zapotec scholar Jaime Martínez Luna (2010) writes that the notion of "us" comes from a self-determining and action-oriented collective. It is through people's actions that a sense of us, of being a community, has been maintained up to the present day despite colonial and nation-state efforts to assimilate Indigenous peoples. In the case of the Zapotecs, these actions are encapsulated in the notion of communality. Martínez Luna defines "communality" as an experience, practice, attitude, and ethos that has four interrelated elements: territory, governance, work, and *fiestas* (community celebrations). The principles that hold these elements together are reciprocity and respect. These principles are crucial to expressing and deliberating upon disparate views, to consensus making, and to sharing efforts. The communal ethos, or communality, continues to drive the anticolonial struggles of Indigenous peoples (Martínez Luna 2010, 87-89). I agree with Alfred and Martínez Luna that the reproduction of community cannot occur without people's continuous actions and fulfilment of responsibilities *in* place.

Indigenous self-determination in this sense is intrinsically connected to Indigenous peoples' local efforts to maintain control over their territories and over their natural, social, economic, and cultural environments. Anthropologists, geographers, political ecologists, and Indigenous scholars have demonstrated that Indigenous peoples have different understandings of nature. These peoples signify, use, manage, and inhabit their natural environment in ways that are specific to their habitats and different from those of non-Indigenous societies. Although the meaning of nature varies across space, scholars have shown that Indigenous peoples have a set of practices and ways of thinking about, relating to, and managing the natural world. These practices are driven by place- and time-specific knowledge and by embodied capacities to perform tasks in social contexts based on cultural logics and gender expectations (Escobar 2005). For the Zapotecs, for example, territory, nature, land, resources, and a sense of the world are all connected to social practices and community. Although the community is the space of performance, the space where we are born, and the space where our ancestors (real or imaginary) were born and are buried, community is not separate from nature, which can be neither reduced to subsistence practices nor configured as something external to be managed and used.

Responsibility and interconnections are also crucial to Corntassel's (2003) understanding of Indigenous peoplehood and self-determination. By combining the approaches of ethno-nationalism, international law, and Indigenous rights, Corntassel emphasizes self-identification and four interrelated concepts: sacred history, ceremonial circles, language, and ancestral lands. These concepts are central to defining Indigenous identity. All of these elements are interlocked and have spiritual and relational values, which constitute the source of Indigenous peoplehood. Because these elements are relevant to Indigenous identity, they are neither alienable nor utilitarian. Rather, their interconnectedness is the source of our obligations to one another and our communities.

Although, as Coulthard (2010) has noted, this place-based ethos, or communality, has been affected by colonial displacement and structures, it continues to guide our political visions and relationships. In paraphrasing Peter Kulchinsky, Coulthard (2010, 81) argues that what distinguishes anti-colonial struggles from other struggles is a sense of dispossession, not exploitation. Following this line of argument, one sees that a sense of dispossession sets Indigenous nationalism apart from other forms of nationalism.

I find the perspectives of Alfred, Martínez Luna, Coulthard, and Corntassel useful in understanding the ways that Indigenous nationhood differs from other forms of stateless nationalism. A sense of place, action, responsibility, and communality are central to the collective ethos of being Indigenous. What I think these perspectives lack is a gender analysis revealing how some place-based practices are gendered and involve experiences with the body, household, community, and self-determination. Furthermore, because contemporary Indigenous nationalism is faced with increasing transnationalism and is embedded in a complex and contested dialogue that has developed between the local and the global and between different legal traditions, some concerns are not negotiated exclusively in place, such as what actions are taken, whose experiences are emphasized, who decides what is sacred, what ceremonies are valued, and how Indigenous peoples continue to relate to their lands and to each other.

The study of place has become an important field of inquiry in a number of disciplines. Place is a geographic space with particular meanings for particular people. Escobar (2001, 152) argues that place can be understood as the experience contained in a specific location, which is embedded in notions of belonging, power relations, and boundaries and is strongly linked to everyday practices. Similarly, Coulthard (2010, 80) points out that "place is a way of knowing, experiencing, and relating with the world." Escobar (2001, 154) also argues that place, body, and the environment are integrated into particular configurations. He contends that culture is carried out in places by bodies that, in turn, enact cultural practices. Greider and Garkovich (1994) note that place is produced through the use of cultural symbols that have and convey meaning. Interactions between individuals result in social understandings of place, and the meanings of a particular place are conveyed and created through discourses, practices, and ways of acting in the world.

The term "politics of place" was coined to describe the ways that politics are situated in a particular landscape and influenced by their locality (Kemmis 1990). Later, the term was defined as the process through which "particular territories are imbued with meanings, shaped by cultural practices, and reworked in the rough-and-tumble of rural politics" (Moore 1998, 349). These and other definitions conceptualize place not as a given but as a contested terrain (Harvey 1996; Gupta and Ferguson 1997). Accordingly, a sense of place is political and is based on difference as much as commonality. I understand "sense of Indigenous place" as the intersection of both common ground and contested meanings.

Global articulations of indigeneity reduce place to the selection of certain "cultural commonalities," which have the effect of undermining histories, roots, and routes as sources of diverse Indigenous experiences. In place, these universalized and fixed cultural representations of indigenity can exclude those who do not fit (Castree 2004, 135). These fixed representations do not mean that both Indigenous identity and nationalism emanate from a false heritage. Rather, the reification or essentialization of culture and tradition is part of the globally circulated politics that constrain Indigenous places and reassertions of nationhood. The idea that Indigenous peoples are just cultures and that indigeneity can be reduced to a specific form of attachment to the land depicts Indigenous peoples and places as residues of an ancient past and depoliticizes their claims in the present. However, it is through the language of nationalism that Indigenous peoples' places, histories, and territories are connected to their pasts, presents, and futures. It is through the assertion of peoplehood/nationhood that these aspects of Indigenous experience become political.

When Indigenous peoples claim self-determination and sovereignty, they reaffirm their sense of being a collective *in* place. At the same time, they engage with the global discourse of rights. Again, this is not to suggest that Indigenous nations and nationalism are a new phenomenon or that Indigenous politics are reducible to place. Rather, the point to be made is that contemporary Indigenous nationalism is embedded in spatialized strategies connecting different scales of politics and different discourses and practices. Indigenous identity has attained resonance to the extent that the state itself and other global actors use it as a marker of inclusion and exclusion. That some Indigenous peoples identify themselves in terms of their legal-political relationship with the state rather than in terms of any cultural or social ties to their communities is an example of this situation. Alfred and Corntassel (2005, 659) have argued that identification with colonial and state legal definitions pulls Indigenous peoples further and further away from their cultural practices and the community aspects of "being Indigenous" and toward a government-imposed legal-political construction. I agree in principle with this observation. However, it is important to note that Indigenous peoples' strategies and practices of articulation are complex and contradictory instead of unified and singular precisely because of the contested terrains in which indigeneity is constituted and because of the specific contexts in which it is deployed.

In different forums and using various strategies, diverse Indigenous peoples, in both rural and urban settings, have asserted their right to self-determination, understood as their right to determine their social, political, economic, environmental, and cultural well-being as nations/peoples without state interference. For many Indigenous peoples, their political strategies are strongly connected to place, territory, and the environment and are expressed in ways that build upon their own legal orders. In other circumstances, Indigenous peoples have articulated other understandings of indigeneity for the purpose of advancing their claims in transnational spaces and being recognized as Indigenous. Indigeneity, from this perspective, is not a homogeneous Indigenous response to social, political, environmental, economic, and cultural threats. Rather, the articulation of indigeneity is dynamic and diverse.

So how are globally circulated discourses mobilized and for what purposes? What effects do they produce in place? For example, the fact that many Indigenous communities appeal to the language of rights to achieve their political objectives and to resist the degradation of their environments, individualization, and market-driven policies implies that people already have a sense of its political legitimacy. This situation calls our attention to the tensions associated with the global discourse of rights. For example, the UNDRIP states that "Indigenous peoples have the right to maintain and strengthen their distinct political, legal, economic, social and cultural institutions, while retaining their right to participate fully, if they so choose, in the political, economic, social and cultural life of the State" (United Nations 2007, Article 5). The UNDRIP also protects the right of Indigenous peoples "to maintain and strengthen their distinctive spiritual relationship with their traditionally owned or otherwise used and occupied lands, territories, waters and coastal seas and other resources and to uphold their responsibilities to future generations in this regard" (United Nations 2007, Article 25). What kind of protection does the UNDRIP provide? What are the possible outcomes?

Although, as explained in the previous section, the discourse of rights is articulated and disseminated through different actors – including NGOs, the churches, the government, Indigenous organizations, and sites of articulation bridging different scales – this discourse, as Merry (2006a, 9) suggests, is localized within specific contexts of power relations, social practices, and understandings of local justice. In Mexico, for instance, some Indigenous peoples have adopted the discourse of rights, yet they have grounded it in their own legal systems and notions of community. Accordingly, people appropriate, negotiate, and translate general principles of rights according to specific situations, worldviews, needs, conceptions of justice, and ways of being in the world. Certainly, conflicts arise from the pretension of human rights to universality, which disregards the specificity of places. Resistance and local mobilization of the rights discourse are not only contextual but also contradictory. Local reappropriation of the discourse of rights in turn shapes people's identity, struggles, and understanding of place (Speed 2008, 19).

One of the most relevant examples of conflicts arising from the fact that the rights discourse disregards the specificity of places is the debate over the right to self-determination. Although international law recognizes self-determination as a right available to all *peoples,* Indigenous nationhood and self-determination have been very contentious. Governments have opposed the definition of this collective right. In fact, contention over the meaning of self-determination was a roadblock to the approval of the UNDRIP. Countries such as Australia were concerned with protecting the territorial integrity of states. Mexico, Chile, and Brazil also expressed concerns about using the very concept of self-determination in this declaration. Canada raised questions about the relationship between Indigenous groups and state sovereignty if the international right of self-determination was included in the declaration. The Canadian government supported the principle of self-determination for Indigenous peoples but only if it was limited to the framework of existing sovereign states and only if it meant giving Indigenous peoples more autonomy over their own affairs. From this perspective, Canada believed that the challenge was to design a concept of self-determination that obliged states and Indigenous peoples to work out arrangements for the sharing of power within the limits of the nation-state and existing institutions.

When the four countries that initially opposed the declaration reversed their position, they further qualified their support. The US government, for example, noted the importance of lending support but emphasized a particular interpretation of the UNDRIP with regard to the right to self-determination and the stipulation that Indigenous peoples' free, prior, and informed consent must be received when any actions are to be taken on Indigenous lands. The US government argued that it wanted to develop a new understanding of self-determination that was specific to Indigenous peoples and that could serve as the basis for recognizing "the inherent sovereign powers of self-governance." Regarding the requirement to obtain free, prior, and informed consent when contemplating actions on Indigenous lands, the US government stated that, in its view, the provisions included in the declaration "call for a process of meaningful consultation with Tribal leaders, but not necessarily the agreement of those leaders, before the actions addressed in those consultations are taken" (Obama 2011). The critical element here is "consultation," which diminishes the requirement of free, prior, and informed "consent" stipulated in the UNDRIP.

Similarly, the Canadian government noted that the declaration was an "aspirational" document that did not change Canadian laws or concerns. Canada noted that serious concerns remained regarding provisions dealing with lands, territories, and resources; free, prior, and informed consent when used as a veto; self-government without negotiation; intellectual property rights; military issues; and the need for balance among the rights and obligations of Indigenous peoples, the state, and third parties. Furthermore, the Canadian government stated that the declaration would be interpreted "in a manner" that was consistent with the Constitution and Canadian legal framework (Aboriginal Affairs and Northern Development Canada 2010). Although both Canada and the United States have now endorsed the declaration, these countries continue to object to its main tenets. This is a contradiction because the realization of Indigenous peoples' rights requires the creation of appropriate mechanisms and political will on the part of the state.

Although Indigenous peoples are agents involved in the articulation of indigeneity, their discourses and practices are challenged by concepts and definitions that replicate colonial structures. In other words, although Indigenous peoples are recognized as nations/peoples in the rights discourse, they are conceived of as lesser nations than non-Indigenous nations. In acquiescing to this diminished understanding of self-determination, Indigenous peoples and organizations have provided positive assurance that Indigenous peoples do not intend to dismember existing countries. Rather, they are pursuing their right to self-determination conceived of as some form of free association with the nation-states in which they live.

Contested visions of the right to self-determination exist. Many Indigenous peoples envision the right to control their territory, natural resources, social organization, and decision-making institutions and to maintain their ways of life. In this regard, Youngblood Henderson (2008, 71) has noted that self-determination is a prerequisite "for the exercise of spiritual, territorial, social, cultural, economic, and political rights, as well as for practical survival." From this point of view, well-being for Indigenous peoples is not possible without self-determination.

Many Indigenous nationalist struggles are aimed not only at cultural recognition but also at controlling place as the space that contains specific experiences that are embedded in notions of belonging and in relationships among people and between people and natural forces. Non-Indigenous groups, financial institutions, and other powerful sites that have a stake in the ecosystems claimed by Indigenous peoples and by the state itself may be willing to recognize Indigenous peoples' cultural distinctiveness. However, they are not willing to share control over resources and ecosystems.

As a product of different sites of articulation and multiscalar politics, indigeneity and the rights discourse have simultaneously helped Indigenous communities to legitimize claims over place and to limit their political imaginations. Tensions, frictions, and contradictions arise not only from who defines indigeneity and the rights associated with it but also from how power is exercised throughout sites and networks of articulation on different scales and throughout different geo-political regions. Contemporary Indigenous nationalist struggles can be understood partly, but not exclusively, as a response to these global articulations. The phenomena of self-identification as Indigenous and engagement with the rights discourse have been neither natural nor inevitable. They are products of Indigenous peoples' agency.

## Gender and Indigenous Nationalism

The previous section has discussed how a collective ethos and responsibility in place are central to Indigenous peoplehood and nationalism. However, not everybody experiences place in the same way. Men's and women's understandings of place are defined by their habitats, by their being in place, and by the practices that shape their livelihoods and identity. Factors that affect Indigenous women's bodies, homes, local habitats, and community relations constitute arenas that mobilize women and are often ignored by political ideologies (Harcourt and Escobar 2002, 8). From this perspective, a sense of Indigenous place is political and based on difference as much as commonality.

As an ideology, nationalism is about politics and borders. Indigenous nationalist rhetoric often uses given senses of place, cultural practices, tradition, gender roles, and sexuality as border guards aimed at maintaining unity and commonality. Thus the common assumption that Indigenous women should uncritically embrace Indigenous nationalism, even if it is embedded in sexism, is problematic and calls the relationship between Indigenous women, place, and nationalism into question. By using gender and nationalism as specific categories of analysis, this section reveals the contradictory ways that Indigenous women negotiate their "place" and their rights within their nations and nationalist projects. Two questions guide this analysis. First, if colonialism is central to indigeneity, how has Indigenous nationalist rhetoric of the nation and the self been affected by colonial conceptions of space? Second, how do Indigenous women define and imagine anti-colonial spaces and places? If local knowledge and power relations shape the appropriation of the global rights discourse, whose knowledge and whose understandings of place are taken into account have uneven consequences for people. As a result, Indigenous nationalism involves the contestation, reappropriation, and reconfiguration of place-based practices.

The "complex geographies of power" (Allen 2003, 2) in which indigeneity is articulated and Indigenous nationalism is deployed are embedded in a global-driven framework that continues to obscure hierarchical social organizations, including race, class, sexuality, and gender inequalities. I argue that Indigenous women's politics and engagement with nationalism and the rights discourse vary and serve to defend place, reinterpret their struggles, and critique naturalized notions of spatial belonging such as patriarchy, on-land versus off-land Indigenous, married-in versus married-out, and landless half-citizen versus landholder citizen. At the same time, Indigenous women's politics are read in complicated ways by the state and other non-Indigenous actors. State readings of women and indigeneity often disempower women's politics and their negotiation of their places within their nations and within Indigenous struggles. More important, these readings craft specific interventions around women's bodies and their rights. Thus, in examining the spatial dynamics of Indigenous nationalism, an Indigenous feminist critique calls for disorienting colonial narratives that continue to break the ties between the self and the collective, men and women, people and nature, family and community. To address the issues stated above, I draw upon the work of feminists who have challenged theories of nationalism for universalizing men's experiences and upon anti-colonial and Indigenous feminist scholars' contributions that extend colonizing strategies to nationalist projects. I do so in an attempt to make Indigenous women's politics central to Indigenous nationalism and to the politics of defending place.

As discussed in the previous section, theories of nationalism are diverse. What is missing in these theories is how the study of nationalism has ignored women. Although historically women have shaped and been shaped by nationalist and liberation movements, their voices and their roles have remained silent and invisible. In the construction of nationalisms, the idea of a "we" as a specific identity has been centred on male perceptions of the

world – that is, on a "masculine we" that is represented as something unified, as though women and men have the same place in this "we." In surveying the relationship between nationalism and women, Wilford (1998, 1)
argues that it is difficult to find a notion of nation and nationalism that is
not male-crafted because the intention of nationalism has been to distinguish between an "us" and a "them" rather than to focus on internal cleavages within the "us."

Nevertheless, gender and womanhood are often defined in relation to
the nation. Although nation has different meanings in terms of belonging,
myths of origin, and borders, all of these meanings are permeated with definitions of femininity and masculinity (Enloe 1993). As Ranchod-Nilsson
and Tétreault (2005, 1) write, "the centrality of gender to resurgent nationalist forces and discourses continues to be striking." Each nation assigns
gender roles to its members. By defining roles for men and women, nations
also deny the existence of a gender identity outside of the traditional male
or female identities. In theories of nationalism, the nation has been explored
either as a "natural" extension of the family and kinship relations (Geertz
1973) or as a constructed homeland that, nonetheless, has subsumed women
within a body-centred politics as a metaphor for the boundaries of the nation (Yuval-Davis 2002, 9). In cultural nationalist discourses, Yuval-Davis
continues, gendered bodies and sexuality are central to reproducing the
nation.

Gender relations are at the centre of nationalism and of constructions of
social identities. Yuval-Davis and Anthias (1989, 7) have identified five major ways in which women have been implicated in nationalist projects: (1) as
biological reproducers of the nation, (2) as reproducers of the nation's
boundaries through marital and sexual practices, (3) as transmitters and
reproducers of national cultures, (4) as symbolic signifiers of difference, and
(5) as participants in nationalist struggles. Because of the centrality of social
reproduction to culture, gender relations are often conceived of as the core
of cultures. The notion of home and the gendered roles played within it
become a naturalized basis for the reproduction of the nation (Yuval-Davis
2002, 17). Since women are often seen as the carriers of traditions and the
honour of the nation, they are policed and disciplined to ensure continuity
with an ancient past, whereas men can look forward to the future. In agreement with Yuval-Davis, I argue that culture must not be regarded as having
a homogeneous, fixed nature but must be understood within both its spatial and social contexts. Culture, tradition, and practices are political resources that are mobilized for different purposes at different times. As

political resources brought into nationalist ideologies, they are full of contradictions and contestations.

Although these feminist contributions to understanding nationalism as a gendered ideology deeply embedded in power relations are very important, they are not sufficient to explain Indigenous women's realities and support for nationalist movements. Additional categories of analysis need to be brought into the discussion. Postcolonial feminists have argued that to understand the depth of women's oppression, it is necessary to pay critical attention to the structures of race, colonialism, and ethnicity. Postcolonial feminists have been very critical of theories of nationalism for nominating Europe as the nation's original home and for blatantly ignoring Third World countries' experiences. McClintock (1993, 67) has noted that there is no single narrative of the nation; different genders, classes, ethnicities, and generations identify differently with the nationalist experience.

Often, Indigenous women have been subsumed within the "women of colour" category. However, Indigenous women's specific experiences remain undertheorized (Suzack et al. 2010, 1-2). Postcolonial feminists (Spivak 1989; Mohanty 1991; Stasiulis 1999) have contributed greatly to the discussion of women's "doubly marginal" status and have challenged Western feminists to consider intersections with other axes of difference. Intersectionality is crucial to understanding different dynamics of subordination and domination. The notion of intersectionality was first introduced by Crenshaw (1989) to deal with the specific realities of African American women. The concept starts with the analytical assumption that people's identities – including gender, race, sexuality, class, and nationality – are not exclusive but multilayered at all times, influencing people's unique social position in the world.

Although intersectionality is an important concept, Indigenous women's experiences differ in important ways from those of so-called Third World women analyzed by postcolonial feminism. In her influential essay "Cartographies of Struggles" (1991), Mohanty redefined the notion of Third World as having particular socio-historical conjectures and noted important commonalities between women in the global South and women of colour in the global North. Nevertheless, as Mohanram (2002, 51) has argued, such redefinition reproduces a homogeneous conception of the Third World that emphasizes the global economy as an organizing principle and that emphasizes women's alliances that develop in multicultural contexts. Although in the literature the term "Third World" has been superseded by the term "postcolonial," which encompasses different national-racial formations, this term continues to undermine Indigenous colonial experiences. More specifically, postcoloniality tends to bypass Indigenous struggles and to problematically position Indigenous peoples as being just like any other minority.

How can we understand Indigenous women in relation to struggles for self-determination? How do women construct anti-colonial spaces and places? Mohanty's (2003, 7) notion of decolonization is useful as a starting point: "decolonization involves transformations of the self, community and governance structures. It can be addressed only through active withdrawal of consent and resistance to structures of domination." In this definition, Mohanty makes clear that decolonization is both a historical and self-reflexive process. Furthermore, she insists that decolonization is achieved through self-reflection in the context of emancipatory collective politics. From her perspective, domination, whether real or perceived, rests on divisions that create and maintain borders on different levels and in different spaces.

Colonialism relied on spatialized governance practices that emphasized dichotomies between colonized and colonizer, private and public, reserve and city, frontier and metropolis, and female and male space, all of which constrained and shaped people's lives and practices of resistance. Indigenous women's experiences underline the continuation not only of gendered colonialism – even within the context of independent nation-states – but also of gender discrimination within self-determination projects. As a gendered ideology strongly connected to power, Indigenous nationalism has replicated power-based gender relations and relations of domination. Indigenous rhetoric has often constructed women's demands for inclusion as "inauthentic," "untraditional," or a threat to decolonization projects. Often, gendered struggles against colonialism have been framed as "women's issues" – as issues of membership, poverty, property rights, and/or individual versus collective rights – by the formal male leadership and then presented as a wholesale threat to Indigenous sovereignty (Lawrence and Anderson 2005, 3).

Indigenous women and scholars have challenged Indigenous male leadership and male-driven visions of self-determination. However, how Indigenous women withdraw consent from and critique structures of domination is a matter of great contestation within Indigenous communities and scholarship. It is possible to identify at least two approaches. The first draws on Indigenous constructions that honour and value womanhood; the second identifies with feminism. Whereas some Indigenous women and scholars have employed feminism to challenge domination, others have completely rejected it. Those who reject feminism espouse the view that Indigenous knowledge and traditions are more favourable for women and for challenging universalized unequal gender relations.

Indigenous scholars and activists who reject feminism warn us against being assimilated and against emphasizing a hierarchical relationship between nationhood and gender. Accordingly, feminism becomes a colonial project to domesticate Indigenous women. In this regard, Jaimes and Halsey (1992) claim that the national, regional, and global networking of transnational feminist practices must be seen in the context of global transnational colonialism, which targets Indigenous peoples worldwide. To these authors, Indigenous women are oppressed first and foremost as Indigenous people. Therefore, the survival of Indigenous peoples is ultimately the survival of all people belonging to these groups, whether man, child, or woman (Jaimes and Halsey 1992, 311).

Similarly, in analyzing feminism in the context of Hawaiian nationalism, Trask (1996, 910-11) points out that all feminisms are foreign to Indigenous peoples and that feminism is a threat to nationalist aspirations. From this point of view, Indigenous self-determination includes all people, not only women. Thus colonization traverses all aspects of Indigenous societies, including women's issues, domestic violence, and equal employment, among others. Indigenous women in these struggles fashion Indigenous-based views of what constitutes "women's issues" according to their own traditions. Indigenous traditions often emphasize women's roles as mothers and as reproducers of communities, families, and cultural practices. Representations based on tradition often portray past Indigenous women as symbols of power and strong matriarchs as worthy of regaining their past status.

Being particularly concerned with colonization and with finding ways to end oppression, this perspective distances itself from feminism, perceived as being concerned mainly with gender oppression. This distance does not mean that this perspective is not woman-centred; rather, this approach formulates a political discourse that draws upon the past roles of women within their nations (Sunseri 2010, 154). Kanienkehaka scholar Patricia Monture-Angus (1995) adopted the position that although feminist theories need careful scrutiny, we may take from them what is useful to our analysis and exclude ill-fitting solutions. Monture-Angus warned us that an Indigenous women's perspective is not a matter of privileging either a static vision of tradition or regressive perspectives. Although Indigenous women may embrace culture and tradition, and thereby support a nationalist project, they do not necessarily embrace the same vision of nationalism as men do – especially when doing so would mean perpetuating women's subordination.

In her analysis of Oneida women, Sunseri (2010, 156) adopts a similar standpoint, arguing that drawing upon Indigenous traditions involves "revitalizing and reaffirming our own ways of governing, free from impositions by the ... state, and reintroducing the founding principles of the Great Law of Peace in order to heal, to unite, and to re-establish 'good relations' ... 'Gender balancing' represents a core component of our system of governance." Sunseri acknowledges that although, historically, many Indigenous cultures were more egalitarian, these societies have been affected by different, interconnected colonial processes and social institutions. Thus contemporary attitudes toward and perceptions of Indigenous women are the result of an entangled combination of situations, policies, conditions, and time. Like other scholars, Sunseri argues that this drawing upon Indigenous traditions does not imply that Indigenous identity is frozen in a precontact, romanticized form. Like any other societies, Indigenous societies evolve. Thus she advocates drawing on Indigenous principles to solve internal divisions and to empower Indigenous women (Sunseri 2010, 157-58).

I find Sunseri's arguments appealing. However, they also raise some questions. How specific is the Oneida society? Could we extend this approach to other Indigenous societies even if they do not acknowledge the existence of past strong matriarchs? How do we deal with essentialized narrations of the nation? In many instances, women's demands for inclusion and equity are being diminished based on the argument that these are not authentic aspects of Indigenous societies. Culture and tradition are two factors that have often been used to determine who is "a real Indigenous woman."

Drawing on different epistemologies and practices, Indigenous scholars who identify as feminists have stressed the need to look for decolonizing possibilities that break away from colonial power structures and develop practices that resist forms of everyday exclusions and domination (Green 2001; Smith 2005; Suzack et al. 2010). In this sense, Indigenous feminists continue to be concerned with gendered experiences of colonialism and self-determination. Smith (2005, 118) has observed, for example, that colonization as a project is connected to the sexual violence perpetrated by white settlers against Indigenous female bodies. She has noted that in her formulations Kimberlé Crenshaw falls short in explaining how intersectionality may be useful in analyzing sexual and domestic violence. Smith argues that if sexual violence is a tool not only of patriarchy but also of colonialism and racism, entire Indigenous communities are victims of sexual violence. Thus, in Smith's view, to develop an Indigenous feminist politics focused on self-determination and sovereignty, we must start by critically exploring how colonialism is perpetuated through sexual violence and sexism within Indigenous communities. Indigenous women's experiences of colonialism cannot simply be reduced to an opposition between the feminist and the foreign, on the one hand, and Indigenous traditions and the insider, on the other. I argue that this division is one of the detrimental aspects of the spatial and metaphoric colonial distinctions between insiders and outsiders and between on-reserve and off-reserve status that mark gender and Indigenous identity.

Navajo scholar Renya Ramirez (2007, 23-25) also points out that Indigenous peoples' survival depends upon ending the violence and sexism women confront in their everyday life. She argues that criticism of feminism among Indigenous scholars and leaders is in fact related to the prevalent sexism in Indigenous politics and the fear that feminism may cause conflict between women and men. In this situation, it is generally assumed that Indigenous women cannot be both Indigenous and feminist because the risk of this intersection is ultimately seen as assimilation. Both Smith and Ramirez see decolonization as a process that requires unique strategies and critiques and involves targeting denials, exposing silences, and identifying colonial epistemologies that may be present in self-determination projects. From Smith's (2005) perspective, decolonization involves the rearticulation of indigeneity and self-determination in ways that move away from the nation-state's offer to recognize Indigenous peoples.

Indigenous legal scholar Val Napoleon (2005) and Gutiérrez and Palomo (1999) have argued that the most comprehensive discourses on self-determination start with self-reflection. Napoleon (2005, 31) has noted that individual self-determination is a prerequisite for a meaningful and inclusive self-determination: "The aboriginal political discourse regarding self-determination would be more useful to communities if it incorporated an understanding of the individual as relational, autonomous and self-determining. That is, a developed perspective of individual self-determination is necessary to move collective self-determination beyond rhetoric to a meaningful and practical political project that engages aboriginal peoples and is deliberately inclusive of aboriginal women."

From Napoleon's (2005) perspective, a person's self-determining autonomy is expressed through relationships with others. Individual, self-determining autonomy is not threatened by the collectivity but is constitutive of it. Similarly, Gutiérrez and Palomo (1999, 75-79) have argued that there cannot be autonomy for any Indigenous peoples if women are excluded.

They argue that in order to implement autonomy from a woman's perspective, a number of processes that start with the self must take precedent. Like Napoleon, Gutiérrez and Palomo insist that the self is not about individualism; rather, the self is interconnected with family, community, and the people. These authors emphasize the need to challenge the Western, patriarchal, unitary conception of self in order to reimagine difference. In centring the self of self-determination and personal autonomy, they complicate homogeneous notions of "we" and emphasize Indigenous women's agency. Indigenous women's relations to struggles for self-determination are not about prioritizing either gender or the nation but rather are about critically engaging with current sexist practices and withdrawing consent to structures of everyday domination. The primary source of domination of Indigenous women is not only their Indigenous status; they are both women and Indigenous, and their experiences of domination are multilayered. Gender, race, indigeneity, and nationalism create complex intersecting processes of exclusions and inclusions. An Indigenous feminist critique calls into question colonial narratives of "authentic" Indigenous subjectivities, bodies, and practices and encourages an understanding of place as both produced and productive.

In positioning myself as an Indigenous feminist, I recognize that there has been a history of feminist discourse used for colonial purposes to justify intervention to "better the lives" of colonized women (Mohanty 2003). In the literature and the media, violence against women and conflicts over gender discrimination have often been cast as cultural problems – as distinctive marks of the "backwardness" of Indigenous societies. These representations fail to understand the colonial roots of these instances of violence and conflict. These constructions elide the multiple social markers and power relations that have historically structured social, economic, legal, and political systems. Contrary to these colonial constructions, the circumstances facing Indigenous women are not only "cultural" and are not limited to the gender violence they confront within their communities. The state itself has victimized and perpetuated the victimization of Indigenous women.

In Canada, for instance, Indigenous women's activism gained attention in the late 1960s during the fight against the gender-discriminatory provisions of the Indian Act. Under these provisions, First Nations women lost their status when they married outside their bands. Indigenous women also had fewer rights regarding wills and estate property than those enjoyed by men and non-Indigenous women. In fact, the issues of inheritance of property, matrimonial property, and membership have produced more victimization for Indigenous women than any other issue. Particularly relevant was the Lavell case, which came before the Supreme Court of Canada in 1973. Jeannette Lavell, an Ojibwa woman who had married a non-Indian man, decided to contest the deletion of her name from the band list on the basis that this action contravened the Canadian Bill of Rights. Lavell's action faced strong opposition from most Indigenous organizations and government alike. In this context, the Office of the Attorney General of Canada, on behalf of several Native associations such as the Indian Association of Alberta, the Indians of Quebec Association, the Federation of Saskatchewan Indians, and the National Indian Brotherhood, rejected Lavell's claim, arguing that Native peoples were, in general, against Indigenous women's aspirations (Manuel and Posluns 1974; Cardinal 1977). The final decision of the Supreme Court was unfavourable to Lavell and was justified based on the following assumptions: the Indian Act could not be overruled by the Bill of Rights, the Indian Act did not discriminate against women, and discrimination was merely a legislative embodiment of Indigenous customary social and economic practices (Jamieson 1978, 84).

In representing Indigenous politics as being against women's aspirations, Indigenous organizations and leaders have reproduced colonial orders. For the Supreme Court, however, gender discrimination was not an outcome of colonialist legislation but an expression of Indigenous cultural practices. Instead of looking at the structural processes that had produced gendered discrimination, the Supreme Court left Indigenous women with no legal recourse in Canada; they would have to look for other options. The United Nations Human Rights Committee agreed to hear a complaint against Canada by Sandra Lovelace, a woman from the Tobique Reserve in New Brunswick. In July 1981 the committee finally rendered a verdict finding that Canada had indeed violated the International Covenant on Civil and Political Rights because the Indian Act denied women equal treatment under the law.

Because Canada was found in violation of international human rights accords in its treatment of Indigenous women prior to its adoption of the Charter of Rights and Freedoms of 1982, the Canadian government felt compelled to amend the Indian Act to address gender discrimination. Bill C-31 was passed in 1985 in a context of severe political differences between Parliament, the Department of Indian Affairs and Northern Development, the band governments, and Indigenous women's organizations. Indigenous leaders' simultaneous assertion of sovereignty and dismissal of gender as irrelevant to matters of self-government ironically reflected the same colonialist ideologies that Indigenous leaders had been criticizing in Canada for decades (Baker 2006, 142).

Because of these differences, Bill C-31 resulted in new policies that have continued to affect women. Since this bill was enacted, some bands have stopped providing services to nonstatus Indians and have refused to extend these same services to newly registered women and their children. Women have been denied fishing licences, and their children have not been admitted to reserve schools and have been denied medical services (Holmes 1987, 19). In addition, Bill C-31 has created two classes of Indian status: Section 6(1) refers to individuals who have two parents with Indian status, and Section 6(2) refers to individuals with only one registered parent. Women wanting to register their children must now disclose the father's identity and prove his Indian status. First Nations women have objected to this policy because it intrudes on their personal lives and does not eliminate sexist discrimination but merely defers it from one generation of women to their descendants. Moreover, Indigenous women have little legal recourse to seek redress of their situation. Borrows (2002) has argued that Bill C-31 limits Indigenous citizenship based on racialized grounds. Although the intentions behind these amendments might have been good, exclusions based on either blood or descent can too easily lead to racism. Membership has been vigorously contested. Some Indigenous communities restrict membership to protect the value of benefits; some believe strength is gained by increasing the number of Indigenous persons, which is in decline because of blood-quantum requirements.

Unlike in Canada, Indigenous women's activism in Mexico became visible only with the Zapatista uprising. Historical records show that Indigenous women have organized for centuries to defend their lands and maintain their communities' autonomy. Since the 1970s they have also created women-driven spaces to reflect on their own experience of exclusion as women and as Indigenous. As a result of economic crises, Indigenous men migrated and Indigenous women started to play additional roles. However, women's participation and experiences remained invisible (Hernández Castillo 2001). Almost simultaneously with the Zapatista movement, a powerful Indigenous women's movement emerged to challenge state discriminatory policies as well as reified conceptions of Indigenous legal orders and traditions. The demand for the democratization of gender relations within the family, the community, organizations, and the state reveals how domination occurs on different scales and has multiple effects on Indigenous women.

Indigenous women's demands for rights and their challenges to Indigenous peoples' legal traditions have been used by the Mexican state to recast culture and gender discrimination as impediments to democracy and development. In this situation, gender identity becomes a site of liberation and state intervention, which obscures Indigenous women's agency. The process of transforming a colonial and neocolonial state into a "caring" and "compassionate" one has important limits. In practice, this intervention has served to conceal inequalities and to blame different groups of people for deviating from the "ideal, moral subject" (Altamirano-Jiménez 2011).

In both Canada and Mexico, Indigenous women have used specific discourses of rights to frame their struggles and advance their aspirations as Indigenous persons and as women. In doing so, women have appropriated place and rights discourses in ways that have transformed their meanings. An Indigenous feminist analysis of women's politics starts by considering how the body, home, place, the environment, and self-determination are implicated in politics. The body, however, should not be understood as exclusively bound to the private. As discussed earlier, the body is linked to the materiality of the self, family, community, and the environment. The body is the first place where women experience exploitation as well as sexual and domestic violence. Home is also a contested political space. It is the space where Indigenous women exercise power through their traditional roles as mothers, caregivers, and wives. At the same time, it is the space where they are dominated, exploited, and subjected to violence (Harcourt and Escobar 2002, 9). Place is the space containing relations to nature and to people. Harcourt and Escobar (2002, 9) rightly note that place and the environment are connected to people's survival, livelihood, justice, sense of place, and self-determination.

In asserting nationhood, Indigenous nationalism mobilizes narratives and the rights discourse to represent place as a homogeneous space where women's concerns and aspirations are not evident. In addition, the state itself mobilizes a human rights framework that disempowers Indigenous women because they are constructed as "victims of their own culture" rather than as subjects challenging racism, prejudice, patriarchy, and inequitable social and economic circumstances. These divergent uses of the rights discourse result from how nations are imagined, how indigeneity is defined, and how power is exercised in different places and on different scales. I challenge the idea that the "marginal" is exclusive to the global South and to nonindustrialized places in the global North and argue instead that constructions of the passive, victimized "Other/woman" are based upon the different scales and places that have been socially and politically constructed as open to state intervention. Thus the female Indigenous body becomes a site where discourses and political strategies are borne and contested.

## Conclusion

This chapter has mapped how indigeneity is produced. By looking at indigeneity as a field of governance, this chapter has shown how knowledge, power, identity, local experiences, resistance, and ways of thinking and acting in the world are produced and contested. Indigeneity has enabled different groups of people to assert nationhood and self-determination, but at the same time, it has constrained their possibilities. Although the articulation of indigeneity involves fluidity, discourses, and the apparent freedom of Indigenous peoples to exercise their agency, this chapter has demonstrated that systems of domination and subjugation are entrenched in spatial and temporally fixed colonial structures, which are characterized by continuities that make certain political possibilities and inclusions (im)possible.

The historical comparative analysis in this chapter has shown how colonial structures and modes of governance produced the roots of gendered Indigenous material inequities, displacement, and containment. Specifically, this chapter has established a historical and analytical distinction between settler and extractive colonialism. Whereas the former was characterized by an insistence on disavowing the Indigenous presence, the latter exhibited a determination to sustain exploitation and the subordination of the colonized. As a contested field of governance, indigeneity is strongly linked to these colonial formations.

# 2

## Indigeneity, Nature, and Neoliberalism

The previous chapter shows that the articulation of indigeneity is shaped by colonial structures, by sites of articulation, by economic, social, and political interests, and by gendered senses of place, all of which operate on different scales and make certain political visions (im)possible. The chapter argues that the articulation of indigeneity is neither homogeneous nor the only Indigenous response. Global discourses on rights and development are locally engaged, contested, and transformed through articulatory practices that produce diverse understandings of indigeneity that both challenge hegemonic views and are modified by them.

This chapter explores how neoliberal understandings of the self, difference, and the market are grounded in the colonial legacy and have shaped state practices and articulations of indigeneity. Specifically, this chapter asks what kinds of configurations result from the intersection of Indigenous identity, rights, and the environment under neoliberalism? How do indigeneity articulations shape Indigenous political (im)possibilities and gender inequalities? Do the structural differences between settler and extractive colonialism have an impact on how neoliberalism, identity, and the environment are articulated in Canada and Mexico?

Building on the work of scholars from different disciplines, including anthropology, critical geography, and political science, I analyze the connection between indigeneity, nature, gender, and neoliberalism. I argue that by articulating essentialized understandings of indigeneity and by defining the economic opportunities open to Indigenous communities, the state and multiple sites of articulation naturalize colonial spaces. Unlike in the past, current economic strategies shaping the spatial and social reconfiguration of place and indigeneity rest not only on the liberalization of the natural environment per se but also on schemes aimed at commodifying "saved" environments. The neoliberalization of the environment incorporates Indigenous peoples into the market and intensifies commodity production as a way to encourage Indigenous peoples to abandon their land-dependent livelihoods and practices. Moreover, although the emphasis is on preservation, the extraction of resources such as oil, gas, and minerals is concomitant with conservation. Exploring the types of economic initiatives being promoted for Indigenous peoples requires paying attention to power relations between the global economy, the state, and place as well as the specific outcomes. Thus the contingent expressions of neoliberalism are shaped by the state, local histories, and the livelihoods of Indigenous communities. Moreover, the dynamic nature of indigeneity articulation and the socioeconomic changes shaping and being shaped by Indigenous peoples are relevant to comprehending these peoples' place-based struggles.

One theoretical theme that runs throughout the arguments made in this chapter is that a critical approach to neoliberalism must start by considering how its processes unfold in specific locations in which neocolonial power is exercised. A second theme is that although examining neoliberalism in practice is helpful in revealing the contradictions and unevenness of this project, substantial commonalities of process and outcomes occur throughout difference. A third theme is that neoliberalism is a qualitatively distinct phenomenon organized around difference, rights, the environment, the self, and the market. I see these intersections as being useful in analyzing the specific discursive, social, and material effects of how indigeneity is defined, policies are framed, economic possibilities are envisioned, and gender hierarchies are reproduced.

In the following sections, I first discuss neoliberalism as a governance project connected to difference, the market, the global discourse of rights, the self, and the environment. Second, I explore the relationship between rights and the ways that Indigenous places are reconfigured through "intelligible" articulations of indigeneity, which have important implications for women. Third, I analyze how neoliberalism has shaped responses to Indigenous claims.

## Theorizing Neoliberalism

In recent decades, there has been a considerable expansion of the literature on neoliberalism. From a political-economy perspective, debates have focused on either conceptual discussions or contrasting research agendas along the global North-South divide. In the global North, particularly North America, research on neoliberalism has focused on economic development, urban settings, and the transformation of citizenship regimes. In contrast, in regions of the global South, particularly Latin America, debates about neoliberalism have centred on rural contexts, Indigenous peoples, the environment, and the well-known Washington Consensus.

Some studies have noted that neoliberalism produces both constraints and opportunities for Indigenous peoples. This understanding of neoliberalism assumes that this project is progressive because it focuses mainly on institutional change and ignores "spatial and territorial implications" (Keil and Mahon 2010, 3). Similarly, Massey (1994, 279) argues that it is important to pay attention to how spatial constructions are embedded in "power geometries." Stories of progress, development, and modernization reorganize difference into a time sequence in which place is detached from space. However, neither space nor place is separate from time, context, and power.

In the literature, neoliberalism has also been represented as a monolithic force that has the capacity to transform all spaces, reconfigure freedom and choice, and redistribute wealth (Martin 2005; Bargh and Otter 2009). From this perspective, resistance is not only futile but also backward. For many, however, this meta-narrative is inaccurate (Lewis 2009, 113). Do these divergent accounts of neoliberalism mean that scholars ask some questions and use some concepts in some parts of the world but not in others (Young and Matthews 2007, 176)? Do these accounts mean that we use the term "neoliberalism" to explain different processes? How can we interrogate neoliberalism?

Larner (2003) points out that the diversity of accounts suggests that there is no single or unitary neoliberalism. Rather, we can understand neoliberalism as a process that involves a multiplicity of often contradictory effects and practices. However, if neoliberalism is so diverse and diffuse, how do we know we are studying the same phenomenon? Other scholars (Peck 2004; Howitt 2009) have noted that although local contexts determine outcomes, it is important to identify the commonalities within the apparent differences. Although the general forces and discourses through

which neoliberalism has been implemented have deserved much theoriza-
tion, more research is needed to explain how spaces, places, and economies
are neoliberalized (Peck 2004; Young and Matthews 2007). Neoliberal policies emerge from and are rooted in specific colonial, social, political, cultural, and economic contexts. Accordingly, it is important to take this spatial
element into account when explaining neoliberalism's locally contingent
form (Perreault and Martin 2005; Magnusson 2009).

Neoliberalism is not driven by an external, invisible hand but by specific
actors, sites, institutions, networks, the state, and discourses, all of which
have material effects in different places. Although neoliberalism has usually
been treated exclusively as an economic project involving deregulation,
privatization, individualization, and transformation of the state-citizen relationship, neoliberalism also shapes the constitution of identity and the
commodification of nature (Laurie, Andolina, and Radcliffe 2002; Bakker
2010). Brown (2001, 39-40) argues that despite "foregrounding the market,
neo-liberalism is not only or even primarily focused on the economy"; rather,
it has "cultural, social and political effects that exceed its surface." From this
perspective, neoliberalism involves not only deregulation but also the re-
regulation of nature. Thus neoliberalism involves practices, knowledge, and
ways of inhabiting the world that emphasize the market, individual rationality, and the responsibility of entrepreneurial subjects (Hale 2002).

In his analysis of Indigenous peoples in Central America, Hale (2005)
notes that neoliberalism involves the reorganization of society along the
lines of decentralization, the reduction of the state, the affirmation of basic
human rights, the redirection of social policy, and the development of civil
society. According to Hale, the recognition of cultural difference and the
granting of compensatory collective rights to "disadvantaged" social groups
are integral to neoliberalism. These cultural rights, along with their socio-
economic components, distinguish neoliberalism as a specific form of governance that shapes, delimits, and produces difference. Hale (2005, 12-13)
has rightly noted that when difference is carefully produced as cultural
rights, it poses little challenge to the neoliberal project.

In Hale's (2005) account, governance refers to the project of governing
society and entails a fundamental organizational and institutional reconfiguration. The concept of governance seeks to capture how economic and so-
cietal issues are governed by networked interactions between states and
nongovernmental organizations (Jessop 2002, 199). Scholars from other
disciplines, including critical geography and political ecology, have extended the use of the concept of governance to explore how neoliberalism

involves complex relations between nature and society, which affect access to and control over resources and property regimes (Watts and Peet 2004). Scholars have detailed how the complex connection between ecological systems and property rights over resources is reworked through colonialism, capitalist development, and neoliberalism (Robbins 2004).

Although management of the environment has often been considered an apolitical exercise, it is implicated in relations of power and in economic systems, and it is informed by hegemonic knowledge that authorizes who has the "truth" about how nature is to be understood and the environment managed. This approach suggests that it is possible to examine claims about the environment in terms of its status not as a true object but as historically produced. This approach is useful in analyzing how gender and the inequalities between men and women are closely connected to how nature is produced. Claims about the environment, the economy, conservation, wilderness, and cultural rights are crucial to interrogating how power is exercised, social groups are enrolled, and networks are forged and maintained.

## The Neoliberalization of Nature and Indigeneity

As a project that reorganizes relations between society and nature, neoliberalism draws on liberalism. Heynen and Robbins (2005, 6) characterize the neoliberalization of nature as comprising governance, privatization, enclosure, and valuation. Governance refers to the institutional and political compromises through which capitalism is negotiated; privatization, a technology of governance, involves the commodification of natural resources; enclosure implies the appropriation of common resources and the exclusion of the communities to which they are connected; and valuation refers to the process by which complex ecosystems are transformed into resources/commodities through pricing. McCarthy and Prudham (2004) argue that this is not new. Classical liberalism and the dissemination of free market capitalism rested upon the liberalization of the natural environment. The liberal dispossession of nonhuman nature occurred through the transformation of human nature, the denigration of "unimproved" nature, and the construction of an economy based on the exclusive control of land and its unlimited accumulation by those who could transform it (McCarthy and Prudham 2004, 278). As discussed in the previous chapter, in Canada the myth of emptiness and "unimproved" land, for example, not only validated Indigenous dispossession but also shaped the political and legal corollaries that constructed this country as a settler space.

Neoliberalism is distinct because it brings together global discourses of rights and the environment, thereby opening up space for the recognition of Indigenous rights as well as for management practices that have uneven implications for Indigenous places and senses of place (Swyngedouw 2009, 122-23). As a mode of governance, neoliberalism expands the scope of nature to include relationships between the human and nonhuman worlds, moving from nature as a resource to socio-natures. Swyngedouw (2009) and Bakker (2010) point out that the concept of socio-natures is central to accounting for how human genomes, genetically modified organisms, pet love, knowledge, and environmental services are transformed into commodities. From their point of view, moving beyond an anthropocentric understanding of nature helps us to address the full range of strategies and socio-natural entities being subsumed within processes of neoliberalization. In agreement with Bakker (2010, 717), it is possible to argue that neoliberalization strategies vary depending on the target, whether property rights, governance practices, or different types of socio-natures.

Because Indigenous people's lives unfold in specific locations and environments that are socially constructed, we need to consider what meanings people attribute to place and what relationships they build with place (Benwell and Stokoe 2006). The neoliberalization of socio-natures socially and ecologically decontextualizes these relationships and meanings. Through this process, people's relationships with place are emptied of meaning and transformed into isolated cultural practices or quasi hobbies, and the nonhuman world is broken down into units of value within the economic realm. Although dynamic relationships are crucial to Indigenous ontologies, stereotypical constructions transform indigeneity into a "primordial artifact" whose expressions are reflected through a "primitivist relation to nature" (Sylvain 2005, 357-58).

The promotion of a peculiar understanding of indigeneity mediates development by emphasizing a "primordial identity" and "fixed attachments to land," which are not inclusive of Indigenous social complexities. Moreover, the representation of Indigenous peoples as part of pristine nature and the alignment of their activities with the conservation of nature effectively deny the territorial claims of these peoples (Rossiter 2004). When environmental discourses of scarcity and conservation are based on a construction of the "noble indigene," they have a disciplinary effect that disregards issues of equity and the historical dispossession of Indigenous peoples. Performances outside of these oppositional constructs render Indigenous subjectivities unintelligible (Braun 2002, 71). Because territorial and resource conflicts are one of the most pressing issues for Indigenous peoples, it is crucial that we analyze how nature is produced and gender reinscribed.

Indigenous peoples' responses to neoliberal policies have been diverse and apparently contradictory. In their demands for recognition, equality, territory, and self-determination, Indigenous peoples have articulated meanings of indigeneity and cultural difference that are intelligible to the state and other transnational sites. In doing so, they have also reproduced problematic processes of differentiating between "intelligible" and "inauthentic" forms of indigeneity that perpetuate structural inequalities (Hale 2002; Povinelli 2002). At the same time, Indigenous movements opposed to the neoliberal project have stood against the grid of intelligibility that neoliberalism has imposed on indigeneity. As Valdivia (2005, 285) notes, meanings of indigeneity – whether used to resist or to justify integration into the neoliberal project – are important to understanding the complexity of Indigenous peoples' struggles and to questioning fixed notions of indigeneity articulation.

## Neoliberalization Strategies and Environmentalism

In the current neoliberal context, nature is valued not only for its resources but also for the services it provides, which we have taken for granted, such as clean air, water sources, carbon storage, biodiversity, and other socionatural entities that both people and the global economy now depend upon. These ecological services, or gifts, are regarded as "natural capital" and create economic opportunities for conservation around the world. Natural capital is more valuable preserved than dead. Environmental knowledge has been crucial to shaping the disciplinary mechanisms of a globalized environmentalism (Goldman 2001, 193) that is often underpinned by a "one-world" discourse that claims we are all globally connected through our intertwined ecological fate (King 1997). What emerges is a hegemonic story of the "fragile earth," which is under stress from human action and in need of care and protection from an "imagined, homogeneous global community" (Macnaghten 2003, 65). This way of producing nature and its resources as bounded has elicited a discourse about the limits of the earth, a central tenet of environmental politics (Dobson 1990).

Because the context for conservation has changed, new approaches have been envisioned to secure capitalist expansion. This has required unprecedented global co-operation in which the state, environmentalists, financial institutions, corporations, citizens, and Indigenous peoples alike have different roles to play. For example, consumers have sought to ensure the products they buy come from healthy and sustainable practices. To remain competitive in the global market, corporations have embarked on "new practices" and now act as environmental funding agencies that "support" communities' efforts to take care of their ecosystems. Environmental nongovernmental organizations have provided society with tips on how, as individuals, we can all protect the environment and reduce our footprint on the earth (Rutherford 2007, 295). Rural communities, particularly Indigenous communities, on the other hand, have been made accountable for their places' ecological degradation. Unlike colonial administrators, who did not value resource-dependent communities, neoliberalism values Indigenous territories both for the services locked up in their ecosystems and for the natural resources they contain.

Internationally, Indigenous peoples have raised concerns that these conservation market initiatives could result in large-scale forest plantation to create forest sinks and in further loss of Indigenous traditional livelihoods; that they are based on hegemonic worldviews regarding territory that reduce forest, lands, seascapes, and sacred sites to their ability to absorb carbon; and that they disregard Indigenous collective rights (Gerrard 2008, 943).

If colonial constructions of Indigenous peoples in terms of race, the "Other," the "savage" living in the wilderness, and the unreasoning pagan structured the processes by which Indigenous peoples were dispossessed and exploited in the past, we can ask what material effects the intersection of indigeneity, rights, and nature produces in the present under neoliberalism? I argue that the processes and mechanisms through which the economy is organized, indigeneity is recognized, and the environment is regulated reinscribe patterns of colonial racial and gender inequalities.

In the context of economic development, Indigenous peoples are constructed as having a "special interest" in issues related to climate change. In many parts of the world, Indigenous peoples have felt compelled to embrace the opportunities provided by conservation in order to articulate a version of indigeneity that highlights the guardianship of environmental patrimony and biodiversity. However, Indigenous peoples are vulnerable not only to the impacts of climate change but also to government responses to this important issue. Moreover, although conservation and terms such as "efficient" and "green" may be driving economic development, the neoliberalization of socio-natures is implemented unevenly, with the exploitation of primary commodities such as oil, gas, and minerals remaining unchanged.

Why are some types of socio-natures neoliberalized in some places but not in others? As mentioned earlier, Bakker (2010, 722-24) offers a useful typology for exploring how different processes of neoliberalization are applied to different kinds of socio-natures depending on their biophysical characteristics, their articulation of labour and consumption practices, and the effectiveness of existing property regimes. For instance, in some cases, privatizing and commercializing primary commodities such as minerals, gas, and oil are more effective and profitable approaches than providing environmental services. In forested communities, in contrast, reducing emissions is central to the provision of environmental services. The identification of neoliberalization strategies is useful in understanding how variation is mediated through the uneven production of nature and conservation. Specific processes and strategies have different trajectories and different impacts on people.

The valuation of socio-natures requires at least three elements: first, the institutionalization of deliberate land-management practices to ensure services; second, the alienation of affective relationships to place; and third, the granting of rights to forests, biodiversity, and primary natural resources (Wunder 2005). In this approach, economic opportunities open for Indigenous peoples may involve receiving payment for providing ecosystem services such as carbon sequestration, knowledge on biodiversity, ecotourism, and watershed protection. In many circumstances, land-use changes and the elimination of Indigenous livelihoods are a precondition for nature to be labelled for export. Ecosystem services can be bought by corporations, donors, governments, and tourists. The premise is that nature is better protected by managing the nonhuman world as a commodity. Promoters of this approach contend that by transforming into commodities some aspects of nature that were previously regarded as separate from the economy, the conservation economy serves the dual purpose of improving the welfare of the poor and fostering greener economic growth (McAfee and Shapiro 2010, 2).

Whereas the liberalization of nature resulted in the dispossession of Indigenous lands, under neoliberalism a double dispossession occurs through the recognition of a reified version of indigeneity and through a bundle of rights based on the alienation of Indigenous peoples' relations and responsibilities to place. The rescripting of indigeneity is embedded in notions of entrepreneurialism, the self, and the economy. I argue that Indigenous peoples' articulations of indigeneity both as environmentalists and as

entrepreneurs, although apparently contradictory, facilitate capital circulation. The articulation of indigeneity and territorial struggles are deeply connected to Indigenous peoples' livelihoods, ownership of natural resources,
and wider development policies threatening their sense of place (Nightingale
2002; Escobar 2005).

## Comparing Neoliberalization Strategies

Although there is a sizable body of literature that deals with gender and resources, relatively little of it explicitly interrogates how gender and the inequalities between men and women are closely connected to how nature is
produced under neoliberalism. This section examines how gender becomes
salient and reproduced. I ask what kinds of imperatives and political
(im)possibilities are created when fixed articulations of indigeneity, the neoliberalization of socio-natures, and the rights discourse are brought together? How does the production of nature reinscribe gender? Does the structural
difference between settler and extractive colonialism have an impact on
how neoliberalism, indigeneity, and the environment are articulated in Canada and Mexico? I argue that indigeneity, the framework of rights, and the
neoliberalization of nature have coercive gendered effects. Specifically, I
suggest that as a social construct, gender is reproduced through struggles to
control place, through indigeneity articulation, and through the neoliberalization of the environment, all of which have uneven outcomes in different
locations. As Larner (2003) states, the analysis of neoliberalism can benefit
from thinking about this governance project as involving processes that
produce spaces, states, and subjects in complex ways.

　　Feminist ecologists have focused on the material practices that bring
women closer to the environment (Agrawal 1994). Scholars have shown
how access to and control over resources, gendered knowledge production,
and local environmental struggles are embedded in the global political
economy (Schroeder 1997). These contributions consider gender to be a
category of analysis that is relevant beyond the household and is salient
within policies, legislation, and practices related to the production of nature. This approach is significant because it shifts the direction and emphasis of analysis. Rather than seeing gender as structuring people's interactions
with the environment, this approach emphasizes how the production of
nature brings into existence categories of social difference, including gender
(Nightingale 2009, 166). From this point of view, gender itself is reinscribed
in and through practices, policies, and responses associated with specific

knowledge. By examining the implementation of neoliberal policies in rela-tion to the production of nature in Canada and Mexico, I illustrate how the production of knowledge and the relationships between people, markets, and nature are fundamentally gendered.

In Canada land claims have been used to resolve, once and for all, Indigenous territorial disputes. By burying the colonial past, this approach perpetuates the imperative of settler colonialism to eliminate and subsume Indigenous peoples. Land claims are based on the liberal discourse of rights and on colonial narratives of land title, "improvement," and "traditional" economic activities in which financial compensation is provided in ex-change for land. In Canada Indigenous peoples wishing to secure land rights and resources must prove the authenticity of their claims by demonstrating historical continuity with a precolonial past anchored in land-use patterns. In this framework, Indigenous peoples' economies are reduced to subsist-ence activities. As "hunter-gatherers," they only appropriated the fruits of the land for the purpose of feeding their families and eventually trading with Europeans.

In Mexico, in contrast, although decolonization in theory terminated colonial rule, in practice structural inequalities and neocolonial arrange-ments have been reinserted by the postcolonial state. This continuity is driven in such a way that Indigenous peoples remain dominated. In these neocolonial arrangements, the state maintains the colonial notion that it has rights to the subsoil, or subsurface, ensuring that Indigenous peoples never benefit from subsurface resource exploitation. Because in many re-gions Indigenous peoples effectively continue to communally own and control their lands, neoliberal policies and environmental governance have aimed at liberalizing some Indigenous peoples' control over their lands and at re-regulating other peoples' land uses. As I show in the last two chap-ters of this book, this spatial reorganization shapes who is recognized as Indigenous.

Let us start with Canada. In this country the concept of terra nullius has given way to a policy that recognizes Indigenous rights and that has adapted to neoliberalism. Changes to Canadian social citizenship experienced in the 1980s were dramatic because they altered the state-society relationship. Like many other Western countries, Canada underwent a period of neo-liberal government budget cuts, which were detrimental to the welfare state and the social fabric. Social policy was reoriented toward the goals of economic integration and privatization, which were seen as the keys to domestic well-being (Banting 1996; Brodie 2010). The neoliberal transformation undermined universality in favour of major reductions in social programs and the transfer of social welfare responsibilities from the federal government to the provinces. Moreover, a shift occurred from viewing social support as an entitlement of citizenship to developing policies that emphasize individual responsibility and economic independence, regardless of peoples' status in society (Bashevkin 2002).

Under neoliberalism, a new Indigenous citizenship was also configured. Historically excluded Indigenous peoples were encouraged to integrate into the global market in order to realize their collective rights to self-government and cultural difference (Altamirano-Jiménez 2004). In this context, Indigenous self-government was framed in terms of producing wealth and enabling "Indians, Inuit, and Métis to play their full roles as active and important contributors to the national economy" (Mulroney 1985, 163). Self-government was envisioned as promoting Indigenous "entrepreneurship" and "productive," "happy lives" (Mulroney 1985, 161). In this vision, self-government was translated into the transfer of some administrative responsibility from the state to Indigenous governments. Neoliberal discourses emphasized self-governance and control over locally delivered services and one's personal well-being. Although Indigenous self-government has produced a degree of autonomy and the devolution of some services, state and provincial control over the terms of Indigenous development has been maintained (Alfred 1999). Tripartite action – or the active participation of the federal and provincial governments and Indigenous leaders – has become the major tenet of this policy.

Although land claims have been considered a process to redress the dispossession of Indigenous lands, the Government of Canada continues to define the rules and subject Indigenous claimants to Canadian sovereignty (Alfred 2005, 29-30). For example, Indigenous peoples seeking to secure land rights and self-government have to prove the authenticity of their land claims by demonstrating the historical continuity of their land-use patterns. Interest in the power of maps as tools to secure territorial rights, manage resources, and strengthen cultures started in northern Canada and Alaska in the late 1960s and resulted in intellectual productions that included multivolume studies, atlases, guidebooks, and historical-analytical studies. Nietschmann (1995) and others made the case for Indigenous peoples mapping their own lands to assert title based on patterns of historical use and occupancy. In the Canadian Arctic, Freeman (1979) examined the advantages of involving Indigenous peoples as environmental researchers in social and ecological impact analysis. Similarly, Rundstrom (1991) underscored the importance of process over product and emphasized Indigenous mapping as a long-term negotiation process.

The codification of rights into human rights law, first in Canada and later internationally, informed efforts to use participatory methods in mapping Indigenous lands and produced legal victories. Yet mapping has opened up new forms of co-optation by constructing indigeneity as territorially bounded. Like the validity of Indigenous knowledge, the validity of cartographic representations is based on their ability to fit Western knowledge and modern forms of governance. Because of the political interests shaping the negotiations of land claims, emphasis is on the types of knowledge that actually enhance the state's capacity to govern, not on Indigenous knowledge that could potentially counteract hierarchical and colonial power relations (Bryan 2009, 25). Bryan (2009) explains, for example, that indigeneity is triangulated like points plotted on a map according to Indigenous peoples' close relation to nature and according to the continuation of their "traditional practices." Indigenous peoples' specific livelihoods and the knowledge they have of their habitats are valued in relation to how far removed they are from "civilized" modern societies. From this perspective, Bryan continues, Indigenous mapping and the mobilization of Indigenous identity are measured in terms of their ability to confine Indigenous peoples to the position of "savage," which configures them as living outside of modernity (Bryan 2009, 25, 27). As Peluso (1995) has noted, land-use mapping has created new ideas of territoriality, tradition, and customary law that affect Indigenous peoples' access to and control over resources. Moreover, Natcher (2001, 118) warns that this incomplete picture of land use can produce use patterns that "appear historic, static and unrefined," contributing to the belief that "traditional" land use is being abandoned in favour of participation in the neoliberal economy.

In these processes, place-based spatiality and knowledge are translated into a "universal" framework of modern space in which alternative views are not possible. For example, Indigenous peoples continuously negotiated landscape. Interests and ownership were recognized, and responsibilities were constantly adapted to dynamic social and political contexts, including population growth and decentralization of authority. Indigenous territories were imprinted by human actions, and their inhabitants were governed by complex legal systems that regulated land ownership, social organization, and resource allocation. However, under neoliberalism, the unequal power relations embedded in land-use studies and land claims negotiations not only reduce these ontological differences but also *indigenize* settler society.

The construction of Indigenous peoples as "hunter-gatherers" and their lands as "wilderness" corresponds to a conveniently constructed dichotomy between "Indigenous savages" and the settlers who actually transformed the land. Even though society's understandings of nature and wilderness have evolved over time in response to trends and ideas, this colonial construction continues to serve the needs of the hegemonic group at the expense of Indigenous peoples. By representing them as "hunter-gatherers" who lived *in* nature, the settler ontology prevents these peoples from fulfilling their aspirations in relation to their ancestral territories (Palmer 2007, 37). In this colonial narrative, Indigenous peoples used to perform economic activities that did not involve *profiting* from the land. Rather, they were "hunter-gatherers" who eventually traded with Europeans. By requiring diverse Indigenous peoples, regardless of their social organization, to prove they were exclusively involved in subsistence activities and by equating *hunting* with notions of land title, the state undermines difference and ownership of other landscapes, further erasing the diversity of Indigenous peoples and places.

Furthermore, most land-use studies in Canada have focused on the activities often associated with men and with subsistence production, namely hunting, fishing, and trapping. Natcher (2001) explains that if only men's activities are considered, areas on the land that are used sporadically by men may in fact be used more consistently by women. Thus decisions about land management and planning might be based on maps that present an incomplete picture of Indigenous economies. This practice of focusing on male activity disenfranchises Indigenous women and erases their roles in and contributions to their economies and societies. From this perspective, women's "traditional" activities – or work within the production cycle – are often deemed to be of secondary importance and limited to the household if they are included at all.

However, a comprehensive understanding of land ownership is incomplete without making reference to gendered experiences of place. As argued in Chapter 1, men's and women's understandings of place are defined by their habitats, by their being in place, and by the practices that shape their livelihoods, being, and identity. Not only do women contribute to their communities' economies and social organization, but their practices and livelihoods also require an elaborate knowledge of their communities' environments. Women were, and many continue to be, skilful harvesters. They harvested a rich variety of country food, displaying knowledge of the seasons, harvest sites, preparation, consumption, and storage. Although hunting and, to a lesser extent, fishing have been masculinized, scholars have shown that Indigenous women are extremely involved in these activities through specific tasks that ensure the productive acquisition of game and fish (Bodenhorn 1990; Frink 2002; Parlee et al. 2005).

Although gendered, demarcated participation in and control over the production cycle in Indigenous societies began in the household, it did not end here. To gain prestige or status as well as to survive, men and women had to have access to those ecological spaces and resources that enabled them to fulfil their duties. In this regard, Desbiens (2007) highlights how the division of labour is a function of the constructed division of space on the land. Spatial frameworks create divisions between the public and private spheres and between different forms of labour. However, these spheres are not rigidly separated. In practice, men and women cross the gender barriers to overcome unforeseen obstacles, including resource scarcity, illness, injury, and death, thereby ensuring that their families are properly sustained.

Not only did the colonial depiction of women as "landless" and confined to the household serve to legitimize gender inequalities, but such inequalities also continue to be embedded in the bundle of rights associated with male subsistence activities. As Desbiens (2007, 366) notes, land-use studies not only impose a Western understanding of land and nature on Indigenous communities but also continue the process of excluding women from the land, a process that started with colonization. The production of nature and the use of natural resources shape identity and territory (Desbiens 2004).

Furthermore, by translating Indigenous relationships and obligations to the land into a bundle of rights and Western notions of property, the Canadian state is able to control Indigenous peoples and their land and resources more completely and to secure development. Rights to continue engaging in Indigenous land-based practices, such as hunting, are protected only to the extent that development and environmental concerns allow. Thus property and rights are fundamental to free market policies and models of development (Bryan 2009, 30). By connecting "traditional economic activities" to the free market and by reducing self-government to the devolution of responsibilities, the neoliberal agenda gives Indigenous peoples specific roles to play and rights to enjoy in the process of neoliberalizing nature.

For instance, the National Round Table on the Environment and the Economy has released a report entitled *Securing Canada's Natural Capital: A Vision for Nature Conservation in the 21st Century,* which states that "the case for nature conservation in Canada is more than simply environmental, aesthetic or spiritual: it is increasingly economic. The growing case for con-servation goes beyond the direct contribution of our natural resources to the economy to take into account the economic value of the *services* our ecosystems provide" (National Round Table on the Environment and the Economy 2003, 9, original emphasis). The report notes that Indigenous peoples play an important role in harnessing the economic power of con-servation because of the specific knowledge they have of their ecosystems, which can be used to protect areas through co-management agreements negotiated as part of land claims. Moreover, the report states that conserv-ation needs to be envisioned in ways that bring incentives and benefits to the stewards of land in the form of outdoor recreation, ecotourism, non-wood forest products, and the provision of forest services, including carbon storage.

Although some Indigenous peoples are encouraged to participate in the conservation economy and to maintain a "pristine" environment for the fu-ture, industrial development and resource extraction continue to exist on Indigenous peoples' lands. To emphasize the irony of this contradiction, we might argue that although environmental considerations have created an opportunity for Indigenous peoples to govern themselves, neoliberal poli-cies determining the framework and the terms of self-government actually constrain this opportunity.

In colonial contexts, property regimes and improvement of the land dispossessed Indigenous peoples and undermined their legal systems. In contemporary contexts, colonial structures, environmental concerns, and the rights discourse restrict Indigenous peoples' access to their territories. The extent to which articulations of indigeneity construct the Indigenous subject in relation to the colonial experience influences not only how in-digeneity and place are reinterpreted but also how Indigenous futures are envisioned.

In nonsettler societies with an extractive colonial legacy such as Mexico, the state has maintained the colonial notion that it has rights to the subsoil, or subsurface, thus limiting the ways that Indigenous peoples can use the land. Because in many regions Indigenous peoples' ownership is recog-nized, neoliberal policies have deliberately targeted Indigenous peoples' control over their territories and their livelihoods so that subsoil resources can be integrated into the global market. In the early 1990s, as the North American Free Trade Agreement was being negotiated, the Mexican government, following the World Bank's recommendation, initiated a series of policies aimed at stabilizing the property regime and creating a land market.

Neoliberal agrarian reforms involved changes to Article 27 of the Mexican Constitution of 1917 in order to liberalize *ejidos* (land plots) and to re-regulate communal, forested lands. The approval of the Agrarian Law gave *ejidatarios* (*ejido* shareholders) legal rights to sell, rent, use, or purchase as collateral individual *ejidos* when entering new forms of association with private investors (Foley 1995). Under this law, private companies were allowed to purchase land up to twenty-five times the size permitted to individual shareholders and could potentially have access to over half of the Mexican territory. Whereas *ejido* lands were liberalized, forested lands were carefully maintained as communal lands as long as forest dwellers continued to be ruled by Indigenous laws. In a context where ownership of most forests is claimed by the state, forest dwellers must maintain their indigeneity in order to maintain their lands. Furthermore, even though the agrarian counter-reforms in Mexico were aimed at promoting private ownership, the government neither provided the joint titling of land for married or conjugal partners nor prioritized the claims of single female households, as other Latin American countries did. Rather, the modifications to Article 27 eliminated the inheritance rights enjoyed by Indigenous women in Mexico before the reform (Deere and León 2000; Hamilton 2002). Women's responsibilities and lack of access to capital are reasons why they are less likely to secure land rights in a privatized scheme, even when this ability may be legally and theoretically sanctioned (Ahlers 2005). In many Indigenous communities, land determines a person's citizenship rights; people with access either to communal land or to *ejidos* are considered full members of the community.

Although Indigenous men and women have been central to the maintenance of Indigenous lands and livelihoods, they engage differently with the land and Indigenous economy. Through centuries of interactions with their environments, women have created a rich reservoir and an elaborate knowledge of medicinal plants whose value is intrinsically linked to their societies. Even though many Indigenous women do not own land, they do have access to it and harvest and produce plants for family consumption. These activities occur in spaces located between or on land controlled by men or along bush-lines separating homesteads. In many Indigenous societies in Mexico, besides harvesting plants and raising animals, women's responsibilities and knowledge also include farming. Often, however, Indigenous women's contributions to their local economies are minimized. I argue that women are constructed as mere consumers rather than as knowers and producers who take part in complex governance systems. Indigenous women's central role within this framework is essential to maintaining Indigenous economies, to promoting spiritual understandings of the environment, and to protecting the resources that are crucial to their people's collective, emotional, and physical well-being. Thus the gendered difference in landholding rights does not necessarily mean that women do not have direct access to land. However, this difference conceals women's contribution to their local economies and hinders women's ability to negotiate horizontal gender relations within their households and communities.

Almost at the same time as the modification of Article 27, the International Labour Organization's Convention 169 (ILO 2003) was ratified by Mexico. To show its commitment and follow the World Bank's revised Operational Policy on Indigenous Peoples, the federal government reformed Article 4 of the Constitution to recognize the "pluricultural" nature of the Mexican society as well as Indigenous peoples' right to self-determination. It did not, however, go beyond this nominal recognition to specify the nature of such a right. Instead, self-determination was reduced to self-government. As it was, this recognition fell into the neoliberal multicultural trap (Stahler-Sholk 2007) of atomizing communities and weakening Indigenous economies and kin systems, which determine access to land and the moral economy of reciprocity.

Hale's (2005) concept of neoliberal multiculturalism is useful in explaining this nominal recognition. The separation of territorial rights from self-determination allowed Indigenous peoples some degree of self-government based on their normative systems as long as land tenure did not contradict the tenets of long-term economic development. Even though the Mexican government actively pursued the titling of *ejidos* through the Programa de Certificación de Derechos Ejidales y Titulación de Solares (PROCEDE) (Program for the Certification of Ejido Rights and Titling of House Plots), the program failed to create the expected land market. Many Indigenous communities, particularly in the southern states, did certify their lands. However, contrary to government expectations, they did not certify their lands as private property but as communal lands. In a context of neoliberal policies, cuts in expenditures, the elimination of credit, and reduced support for agriculture-related activities, Indigenous communities struggle to reproduce their ways of life.

Around the same time as the National Round Table on the Environment and the Economy released its report *Securing Canada's Natural Capital: A Vision for Nature Conservation in the 21st Century* (2003), the World Bank issued a report entitled *Mexico: Southern States Development Strategy* (2003). This report outlines a development plan that unevenly targets Indigenous communities. Whereas forest communities are encouraged to reduce emissions and participate in the conservation economy, peasant communities are blamed for their unproductive, unsustainable livelihoods. In this report, Indigenous peasants' livelihoods are constructed as a problem whose solution requires change and innovation, which are the pillars of this approach to development. In Mexico the economic opportunities envisioned for forested communities fall into categories similar to those in the Canadian case: ecotourism and cuisine sites, exploitation of nonwood forest resources (including biodiversity, resins, and mineral waters), and sustainable resource management in the form of carbon credits that polluters from the north can buy. Like in Canada, narratives of change and innovation in Mexico represent Indigenous livelihoods as "unrefined" and "static," contributing to the belief that some "traditional" land use must be abandoned in favour of participation in the neoliberal economy. Unlike in Canada, neoliberal strategies in Mexico have changed from exclusively targeting Indigenous peoples' land ownership to unevenly targeting their governance practices.

Government policies based on the World Bank strategies could potentially drive approximately 22 million people, 40 percent of whom are Indigenous, out of land-related activities. For Indigenous peoples whose very existence and sense of place are connected to their livelihood, reducing agriculture to an old, inefficient practice that is no longer sustainable suggests that to benefit from the economy, they must adapt or perish.

Ironically, corporations and northern countries actively pursue improved breeding materials derived from Indigenous varieties of corn and other agricultural produce as well as Indigenous peoples' – specifically women's – knowledge of medicinal and food plants. Moreover, although Indigenous peoples are "encouraged" to preserve some of their resources and commodify their cultural artifacts, these are not for local use. The overall goal in the southern regions of Mexico is to create nodes of networked production, development clusters, and communication infrastructure. Whether economic interests pursue bioprospecting, carbon trade, mining, or wind power, Indigenous livelihoods are reorganized to assist these endeavours or at least not to interfere with them (Finley-Brook 2007, 104). As part of this process, some Indigenous municipalities and communities are being reorganized in ways that contain them in small areas by claiming to reduce environmental impacts. Simultaneously, this process is encouraging unimpeded access to the natural resources in the rest of the region. Opponents have been vocal about the implications for national sovereignty, local autonomy, and food sovereignty.

So what kinds of dilemmas arise when Indigenous peoples' identities, cultures, and habitats are legally and economically defined by transnational agendas? Because neoliberalism threatens to alienate Indigenous peoples' places and senses of place, they have responded in different ways. Resistance, negotiation, and adaptation are features of indigeneity articulation. Reclaiming certain rights and engaging with specific political actions in the present are opportunities that come not only from a globally articulated discourse of rights but also from the economic, social, political, and cultural structures that are embedded in the colonial past.

## Conclusion

The extent to which articulations of indigeneity construct the Indigenous subject in relation to the colonial experience influences not only how place is reinterpreted but also how Indigenous futures are envisioned. Although places are configured differently in diverse parts of the world, the politics of indigeneity, the framework of Indigenous rights, and environmentalism as organizing principles have had similar coercive effects. The incorporation of "hinterlands," "marginalized places," and "frontiers" into the global economy has become part of an "optimistic," "viable" world in which Indigenous economic dependency and inefficiency can be reversed. This choice between adapting or perishing forecloses the possibility of asking how we might envision the viability and autonomy of Indigenous societies and economies while allowing space for self-determined change.

Contrary to the claim that increasing Indigenous people's cultural rights affords them an opportunity to address past injustices, this chapter shows how these rights are framed in ways that reproduce injustices. Unlike in the past, current geo-economic strategies rest not only on the liberalization of the natural environment per se but also on schemes aimed at commodifying Indigenous peoples' relations to nature. Under neoliberal governance, there is no issue of a dichotomy between individual and collective rights or between cultural and material local needs. Rather, the issue is how Indigenous laws, relationships, place, and gender are reframed to serve capitalist growth.

# 3

# Nunavut
————————  Arctic Homeland and Frontier

In December 2005, on behalf of the Inuit Circumpolar Conference, a team of lawyers filed a petition with the Inter-American Commission on Human Rights seeking relief from violations resulting from global warming caused by acts and omissions of the United States, one of the major polluters in the world. Three years later, in 2008, Canadian prime minister Stephen Harper responded to a series of questions sent by Mary Simon to party leaders. In his response to a question related to a bold new path that partners government with Inuit to close gaps in housing, health, economic development, and education needs by 2015, Harper stated that "Canada's success in the next century depends on the ability to create the right conditions for flourishing Northern development that properly balance the importance of growth with our responsibility to keep the North pristine for future generations" (cited in Inuit Tapiriit Kanatami 2008). In February 2011 the president of Inuit Tapiriit Kanatami, Mary Simon, said the Inuit were ready for oil and gas drilling in the Arctic offshore and that there were conditions attached to their support (Inuit Tapiriit Kanatami 2011).

At the heart of these events are questions such as: How have the Inuit negotiated different understandings of the Arctic? How have processes, contexts, and relationships shaped the articulation of indigeneity in Nunavut? What are the discursive, social, and material effects of how indigeneity is defined, how policies are framed, how political and economic possibilities are envisioned, and how gender hierarchies are reproduced in the Canadian Arctic?

This chapter explores these questions. I argue that the Arctic has been embedded in competing processes of identity construction. On the one hand, the Inuit have articulated a notion of indigeneity to assert control over their homeland. On the other hand, Canadian settler nationalism has constructed and asserted sovereignty over the Arctic frontier to provide a mythical reference that *indigenizes* the settler society. Through a complex combination of worldviews, place-based experiences, economic development, and environmentalism, different understandings of Inuitness have been produced either to challenge or to negotiate with Canadian sovereignty. Although the deployment of Inuit polar identity was successful in creating Nunavut, contestation over how Inuitness is lived, over what constitutes the "true, sovereign North," and over who gets to define how Arctic resources are used continues to exist.

As northern temperatures rise dramatically with global warming and excitement to navigate the Northwest Passage increases, debates over jurisdiction, notions of place, climate change, and sovereignty dominate the discussion of how the Arctic is imagined. The Arctic, however, is not an empty frontier. It is home to Indigenous peoples whose lives, laws, and society predate colonial history. The creation of Nunavut and the political, social, economic, and environmental challenges the Inuit face today need to be understood in terms of the context of Canada's colonial domination and economic and political interests in the Arctic (Hicks and White 2000, 45). First, I discuss how colonialism has shaped the two competing visions of the Arctic home and frontier. Second, I critically analyze the Nunavut Land Claims Agreement and show how this "modern treaty" does not alter the settler imperative to subsume the Indigenous "Other." Third, I explore the ways that gender relations are being negotiated in Nunavut. Last, I analyze the social and material effects of how development and environmentalism are understood in the region.

### Home or Frontier: Whose North?

The previous chapters have argued that two important components of colonialism are displacement and unequal relations. They have also argued that colonialism involved different strategies and modes of operation. The environment as something separate from society is a colonial construct that has dispossessed Indigenous peoples and alienated their relationships to place. More recently, the global response to climate change is another example of how colonialism continues to be implicated in how places and nature are produced. Reflecting on how Canada has historically asserted sovereignty in the Arctic and dealt with circumpolar Indigenous peoples is useful in interrogating the nature of settler colonialism in contemporary politics and the role of the state in shaping an exclusionary model of economic development that erases the Inuit's presence in the North.

There has been a great deal of discussion of the meaning and role of sovereignty in the modern world. For the purposes of this discussion, I am interested in how this concept functions. Sovereignty has been understood as the state's supreme authority over a given territory. It involves questions of borders, control over people's legal status, and the set of legal practices and principles that determine a state's scope of authority. Thus sovereignty has been understood as "a constitutive process of power construction" (Shadian 2010, 487). Following Butler (1999, 96), we can argue that the performance of sovereignty also entails managing things and people through specific practices that far exceed the legal field.

As a specific type of colonial project, settler colonialism was embedded in an inherent ambiguity (Wolfe 1999, 30). It relied on both the land and the notion of frontier. Land responded to the need to transform nature in order to dispossess Indigenous peoples. Frontiers, on the other hand, provided the spaces for indigenizing settler society while maintaining the settlers' distinctiveness. Both land and frontiers have been central components in undermining places of Indigenous self-determination. The concept of frontier assumes that for the settler state to claim sovereignty, the sovereignty of Indigenous peoples must not only be denied in international law but also transformed through dispossession within the field of domestic law (Evans 2009).

The assertion of sovereignty over Indigenous places and domains involved the creation of different scales of control that attempted to construct Indigenous peoples as having no history (Dodson 1994, 7). At the level of the body, Indigenous people's personal names were replaced by numbers, children were separated from their families, and their languages were outlawed. At the level of the extended family, Indigenous peoples were disciplined through displacement, relocation, and the creation of new settlements. At the level of their nations, Indigenous peoples were misrecognized and their ancient laws and jurisdictions denied. At the international level, nation-states have created rules and legislation by which Indigenous peoples' concerns and jurisdictions have been undermined (Howitt 2003, 148). The history of colonialism in the eastern Arctic is complex and has involved these forms of control.

Encroachment in the Arctic occurred slowly and later than in other parts of Canada because neither land nor environmental enclosure were initially a priority. Prior to contact between the Inuit and Euro-Canadian institutions, the basis of Inuit identity was the extended family unit. It was the family that made decisions about where to set up camp, fish, and hunt, and people identified with the places in which they lived and travelled. The extended family was organized along a gendered and complementary division of work. The extensive anthropological literature that is focused on gender dynamics in the North reveals consistent patterns: females assumed responsibility for childcare, household management, food gathering, and small-game hunting, whereas males were responsible for warfare and subsistence activities such as hunting and trapping (Guemple 1986; Bodenhorn 1990; Brumbach and Jarvenpa 2002). According to Guemple (1986), since gender was constantly reproduced through the repetition of actions, the allocation of work was based on people's ability to engage in the work assigned to a given gender. In precolonial Inuit society, neither gender infringed on the other's work, but when necessary, women and men had a working knowledge of the other's tasks. The different activities men and women performed were closely related to their habitat. The Inuit system of governance was based on consensus and discussion and did not involve a centralized territorial government; leadership rested on the older men of numerous small camps. In her analysis of Bering Strait "Eskimos," anthropologist Dorothy Jean Ray (1976) noted that every Indigenous nation she studied was aware of its borders as though fences had been erected. Yet boundaries between Arctic Indigenous nations were porous.

British sovereignty over the Arctic was asserted long before the region was properly known. In 1670 King Charles II issued a royal charter that granted a huge chunk of land, comprising the lands of the entire Hudson Bay, to the Governor and Company of Adventurers of England Trading into Hudson's Bay. Known as the Hudson's Bay Company, this venture was established to take advantage of commercial whaling and later, the fur trade. Through nodes and transport corridors, the Hudson's Bay Company effectively extracted dispersed furs through trading posts, waterways, and portages. By the 1850s trading posts had been set up throughout the Arctic that relied on the Inuit's knowledge, extended family structure, and self-governance. The royal charter, however, was consistently challenged until it was transferred to the Dominion of Canada in 1870. The dominion, however, continued to have difficulty in obtaining international recognition of its assertion of sovereignty. The "discovery" doctrine was considered insufficient for Canada to retain territorial rights over the Arctic, forcing this country to seek recognition through "effective occupation" instead (Loukacheva 2007, 19).

At the beginning of the twentieth century, as foreign states challenged Canada's sovereignty over the Arctic, government officials tried to fix the fluid boundaries of Inuit communities, and efforts were undertaken to make this nomadic people more sedentary. Settlements in the Arctic simultaneously undermined Inuit control over their land and served to mark Canadian sovereignty (Loukacheva 2007). Although the Inuit were forced to settle, Canada continued to disavow Indigenous peoples, recognizing them as legal persons only in 1939. Enforced sedentarization would enable both the assimilation of the Inuit and the management of northern frontier resources in a new and profitable way. The Inuit were simultaneously pulled to the settlements by their complete dependence on some services provided by the government and "pushed" off the land by the drastic reduction in livestock and low fur prices. This dramatic transformation affected the Inuit's practices by limiting their daily and seasonal access to ecological spaces and by separating them from their landscape. The accelerated sedentarization of a formerly nomadic people increased the number of social interactions among different clans and changed the composition of the family from extended to nuclear (Mitchell 1996).

These dramatic social and cultural changes accelerated toward the end of the Second World War due to the United States' and Canada's interests in energy resources. Sedentarization of the Inuit had opened up an immense "empty" frontier full of natural resources ready to be extracted. The United States initiated an aggressive exploration of natural gas in Alaska and built an exploration infrastructure in the Canadian Arctic with the intention of exploiting oil from the Beaufort Sea. Nevertheless, Canadian interest in the Arctic continued to be sporadic and did not consider the interests of the Inuit (Loukacheva 2007, 25). By the 1960s the number system for identifying Inuit had been replaced by family names, producing changes in how the self was perceived and how social relations were experienced. During field research conducted in Iqaluit in 2003, several research participants spoke of a "broken generation" of Inuit, who were lost between two worlds without belonging to either. This sense of desperation was attributed not only to the huge transformations the Inuit had experienced but also to their inability to control the pace of further changes and the symptoms of social distress caused by their alienation from their environment and governance systems.

Although many people felt helpless facing these abrupt transformations, local leadership started to be aware of the damage being inflicted and to respond to it. Slowly, the Inuit began to perceive themselves as a people who shared more similarities among themselves than with others. Mitchell (1996, 134) contends that the co-operative movement in the Arctic was particularly important to shaping the Inuit's labour relations and the construction of their collective identity. This artistic movement, however, was also important to the construction of a national Canadian identity. For most of the second half of the twentieth century, Inuit art was a crucial resource mobilized for the purpose of constructing a Canadian northern identity. Often, the government relied on a rhetorical identification with the frontier landscape and Inuit art to express Canada's identity (Stuart Pupcheck 2001, 191-92).

Although Canada mobilized Inuit art for the purpose of constructing its own identity, the artistic movement also shaped the Inuit's resistance and their collective sense of being, linking them to wider social, cultural, and economic networks. These networks soon influenced the creation of the Inuit Cultural Institute, which focused on Inuit stories and elders' traditional knowledge. The key factor that allowed for the politicization of the Inuit identity was the creation in 1971 of Inuit Tapirisat of Canada (ITC), later Inuit Tapiriit Kanatami. ITC was strategically created as a nongovernmental organization linked to a wider circumpolar network. As mentioned in Chapter 1, the Inuit Circumpolar Conference (ICC) is a transnational organization representing the Inuit and Inuvialuit of Canada, the Kalaallit of Greenland, the Iñupiat and Yupik of Alaska, and the Arctic Council, a partnership between government representatives and Indigenous peoples. As Howitt (2003, 148) states, multiscalar politics are not a given but a political response.

ITC enabled the Inuit to speak with one voice on issues concerning development in the North and the preservation of Inuit culture at a time when major resource-extraction projects were being developed on Arctic lands and offshore. To the Inuit, these projects represented major threats to their already challenged habitat and way of life, so ITC took on the responsibility of addressing these concerns with the federal government. ITC was extremely important to politicizing the Inuit's self-perception and to linking their shared identity to notions such as "land claims" and "collective rights."

A young generation of educated Inuit leaders who were knowledgeable of similar Indigenous struggles for land rights in other Canadian regions and circumpolar countries decided to make the case for the Inuit. When asked to elaborate on this generation of Inuit leaders, a research participant stated: "The leadership of our people before us, they were gentle people, very polite people and, in many ways, very timid. Our generation started to change that. We were not timid, we were a generation that started to say that things had to change, that things could not stay the same and that we were prepared to stand up for our rights" (Iqaluit, Nunavut, August 2003). Here, this participant refers to the changes embodied by a new generation of Inuit leaders. Unlike Inuit elders, who had difficulty understanding the need to "claim" their homeland and to have "rights," the new generation was able to speak the language that power would understand. Unlike some First Nations that draw upon treaty rights and coexistence, Inuit leaders, who never signed treaties, adopted a language of indigeneity, self-determination, and peoplehood. In contrast to Canadian sovereignty and the vision of the Arctic as a storehouse of resources, Inuit rhetoric connected place, the environment, and identity to construct the Inuit as the stewards of the Arctic.

The Inuit were among the first peoples in Canada to collaborate with academics and environmentalists to produce land-use and occupancy maps based on information provided by the "traditional knowledge" of Indigenous land users, mostly men (Freeman 1979). Indigenous cognitive maps were delineated verbally by using place names that conveyed cultural, historical, and spatial orientations. Through the public invocation of toponyms, cultural landscapes, and mapping, the Inuit demonstrated a historical and legal basis for ownership and occupancy. Kusugaq (2000, 20) notes that through this highly political process, the Inuit became inseparable from the landscape, and the landscape became inseparable from the Inuit.

Through this connection to the land, place has two sources of power for people: it includes all of the basic elements necessary for human survival, and it is a source of emotional power when the landscape and its physical attributes become part of the human experience (Penrose 2002, 278-79). Thus place is not only about a particular type of resource or landscape that exists on its own. Anything affecting the landscape has inevitable consequences for material, spiritual, and emotional human survival. These elements of survival and relationships with the land are precisely what distinguish the idea of the North as a "homeland" from the idea of the North as a "frontier." Although the Inuit have constructed place as bordered and self-enclosed space, the vision of the Arctic as a frontier imagines it as an open, free space ready for economic development. This has been a struggle over different understandings of geography and spatial organization.

That ITC was part of the ICC provided the Inuit of eastern Canada with a well-knit web of national and international networks, which helped them to be both territorially bounded and transnationally linked to different sites of indigeneity production, including the Working Group on Indigenous Peoples, the Economic and Social Council, and the United Nations Human Rights Council. What is interesting about the ICC is that it constructed Inuit identity as a collective identity that goes beyond the borders of the nation-state to include the circumpolar world. As a pan-Arctic nongovernmental organization, the ICC increased the Inuit's collective influence over both national and international Arctic governance. Eben Hopson (1978), founder of this transnational organization, once declared, "We Inuit are an international community of some 100,000 residing mostly in small villages along the Arctic coasts of Alaska, Canada, and Greenland. We are loyal citizens of the United States, Canada, and Greenland, but we are Inuit, or Eskimo, first and foremost ... We Inuit are hunters ... As the indigenous, native people of the Arctic, we enjoy certain native rights and entitlements."

In the 1970s Indigenous activism increased in Canada with the failure of the so-called White Paper, the policy of Prime Minister Pierre Elliott Trudeau's government to eliminate the Indian Act and further assimilate Indigenous peoples. In this context, renewed multinational interests in the North's resources prompted a heated debate over who owned them and who had the right to pursue economic development in the Arctic. The Canadian government adopted a new strategy with regard to the Inuit with the intention of affirming its sovereignty in the Arctic and representing itself as a moral international player that advocated sustainable development and Indigenous rights. In addition, Canadian nationalism embraced its northern-frontier identity, the "true North," which provided a means to legitimize Canada's interests and investments in the Arctic. Both ITC and the ICC embraced and promoted the idea of Canada's "northern" identity and continually represented their relationship with the Canadian government as a role model for co-operation and sustainable development in the international community (Shadian 2007, 324). In doing so, they signalled the Inuit's acceptance of Canadian sovereignty and helped this country to become a key Arctic player.

However, the Inuit-Canada relationship was not free of conflict and contestation. Canada's assertion of sovereignty depended upon the Inuit's immemorial occupation of the Arctic, and the Inuit wanted their land and sea rights recognized. According to Inuit leaders, the recognition of off-shore interests justified Canada's claim to the Northwest Passage rather than merely to the North's internal waters. The Canadian branch of the ICC maintained that recognition of Inuit offshore rights meant the Inuit's inclusion in how marine and environmental resources were managed in the Arctic. Canada, in contrast, maintained a colonial perception of the coast as an ontological division between sea and land, water and earth. According to Mulrennan and Scott (2000, 683), from the seventeenth century onward, this division worked to suppress customary marine rights among European populations and to affirm the monarch's authority.

In 1976 ITC finally submitted a proposal to the Government of Canada that suggested the division of the Northwest Territories into two territories. With this proposal, the incipient Inuit nationalism went further in its attempt to draw lines of inclusion and exclusion and to define Inuitness (Mitchell 1996, 342). Given the legal and political complexity of the Arctic, the ITC also urged the Canadian government to develop an Arctic foreign policy that recognized Inuit economic and cultural values and concerns, including seawater interests. Ten years later, in 1986, the House of Commons International Relations Committee issued a recommendation to the Canadian government stating the need to protect Inuit interests through the signing of a land claims agreement. The recommendation also stated the need to promote Inuit self-government in the Arctic and sustainable development. As the links between the Arctic and the outside world became stronger and were traversed by different networks and framed by different sites, discourses, and visions, the Inuit's search for control over their homeland was intersected by a wide spectrum of power relations.

## Nunavut: The Road to Self-Determination

Place is embedded in a complex relationship between memory and power. Nationalist narratives link place and memory and aim not only to build new relationships that break away from the colonial but also to re-establish self-determined, ancient jurisdictions in place(s). Thus Indigenous nationalism is embedded in deeply specific notions of place, collective history, responsibility, and belonging. Self-determination is about how people signify, use, and manage their natural and social environments in ways that are specific to them. However, although Indigenous self-determination is recognized by the state, it has been refashioned in a way that reproduces basic colonial structures and behaviours (Tully 2004, 201).

This section explores the social and material effects of how Inuitness has been defined, self-government has been framed, and political and economic possibilities have been envisioned in Nunavut. I argue that the separation of self-government from the environment has reduced the Inuit's right to self-determination to a set of "cultural interests" and replaced it with a devolution of responsibilities, thus undermining the Inuit's human presence in the North and their relationships to land and sea.

In 1993, following years of negotiations, the *Agreement between the Inuit of the Nunavut Settlement Area and Her Majesty the Queen in Right of Canada* (Government of Nunavut 1993) was signed, which divided the Northwest Territories and created the territory of Nunavut. On 1 April 1999 the eastern Arctic north of the sixtieth parallel and above the treeline, an area equivalent to one-fifth of Canada's landmass, became the new territory of Nunavut ("Our Land" in Inuktitut), in which 85 percent of the population is Inuit. This event resulted from the nationalist movement and transnational activism of the Inuit. Although this people constitutes the majority of the population, the Government of Nunavut is a public government in which both Inuit and non-Inuit are represented – the term "public government" referring to a nonethnic model of government. The fundamental idea behind the land claims was that the territorial institutions, state structures, and political process would reflect the nature of Inuit society. As nations are imagined to be extended families occupying specific homelands, key issues in the politics of this territory have centred on who should control place and its resources and how relations with the land should be codified.

When the Inuit were heading toward achieving a homeland, they faced the challenge of negotiating the terms and conditions of self-government and control over their land within a Western framework. Although the ideas of "homeland" and Inuitness were central to the struggle for self-determination, the land claims agreement was carefully designed to assert Canada's control over the territory and to provide Inuit some political space within this country's structure of government and political traditions. What exactly did this mean? How did the Inuit see themselves in this picture?

This agreement includes forty articles defining the powers and jurisdictions relating to membership, development, fauna, environmental policies, institutions, and self-government granted to the Inuit. Article 4, the shortest and most important article of this agreement, establishes the creation of a new territory called Nunavut, its Legislative Assembly, and the public nature of its government, which represents both Inuit and non-Inuit. The capital of this territory is Iqaluit, and its government is composed of an

Executive Council elected by the members of the Legislative Assembly (MLAs).

The Nunavut Land Claims Agreement (NLCA), the first modern treaty entrenched under Section 35 of the Constitution Act of 1982, has four basic objectives:

> to provide for certainty and clarity of rights to ownership and use of lands and resources, and of rights for Inuit to participate in decision-making concerning the use, management and conservation of land, water and resources, including the offshore;
>
> to provide Inuit with wildlife harvesting rights and rights to participate in decision-making concerning wildlife harvesting;
>
> to provide Inuit with financial compensation and means of participating in economic opportunities;
>
> to encourage self-reliance and the cultural and social well-being of Inuit. (Government of Nunavut 1993, 1)

The Inuit surrendered any land claims and title rights held anywhere else in Canada, including the Nunavut settlement area, in exchange for the following constitutionally protected rights and benefits: (1) collective title to approximately 350,000 square kilometres of land, 10 percent of which includes surface mineral rights; (2) priority rights to harvest wildlife for domestic, sports, and commercial purposes; (3) establishment of co-management boards to oversee wildlife and harvesting management as well as economic opportunities; (4) capital transfer payments of $1.148 billion to be paid over a fourteen-year period and to be administered by Nunavut Tunngavik, the Inuit corporation responsible for overseeing the claim; (5) a series of commitments to increase Inuit employment in the government, to give preference to Inuit-owned businesses in government contracts, to give the Inuit a share of royalties for nonrenewable resources, a $13 million fund, and to create three Nunavut parks; and (6) the commitment to create Nunavut (Government of Nunavut 1993). At first sight, this package seems very generous, but let us unpack some of its contents.

Although the NLCA gave the Inuit control over their territory, it also limited such control since they surrendered their Aboriginal rights in exchange for the creation of a homeland (Hicks and White 2000, 33). The surrender of these rights, in practice, meant that the agreement excluded all the traditional lands used by the Inuit for hunting, fishing, and other traditional activities, which are not only "cultural" institutions but also important components of the household's mixed economy. This type of economy combines land-based contributions from food and materials obtained through traditional economic activities with cash income from part-time or full-time wage-paying work. This mixed economy is considered a cultural adaptation to the dynamic yet uneven economic opportunities the Inuit have faced (Hicks and White 2000, 34).

Moreover, since the NLCA did not stipulate the incorporation of Inuit values and approaches to governance per se, the Indigenous elements brought into self-governance were incorporated only into different regulatory bodies responsible for Nunavut's co-management of wildlife, fishery, water, and land resources. The Inuit participate in these bodies, yet decisions are made jointly with the federal government and its bureaucrats. Because of the Inuit's advisory role, their actual capacity to build Indigenous autonomy is controversial. For instance, White (2006) suggests that the allocation of government functions in the realm of lands and resources can be considered self-governance. In contrast, other scholars argue that co-management is a process of co-optation that does not result in power sharing but in the strengthening of the state's control over resource policies (Castro and Nielsen 2001; Nadasdy 2005).

Moreover, although the creation of a recognized Inuit homeland included a devolution of powers from the federal government to the territorial government and the exercise of regional autonomy housed in the notion of self-determination, the federal government has not completely fulfilled its obligations. Loukacheva (2007, 3) argues that the scope of Nunavut's regional autonomy is still evolving and that the final result will depend on the Inuit's consciousness, their effective political participation, and the federal government's commitment to accommodating Indigenous claims and expanding Indigenous powers. In my view, there are other factors affecting the fulfilment of the NLCA and the Inuit's demand for greater autonomy. Some of these factors have to do with Canada's new strategy regarding its sovereignty in the Arctic and the continuation of a neoliberal approach in which autonomy as devolution is conceived as the ability of a self-governed entity to fulfil its responsibilities to deliver services.

Nunavut's exercise of its autonomy is also preconditioned by the adoption of a public model of government. Although the creation of this territory has been represented as an Inuit dream come true, its non-Inuit-centred institutions have reinforced a range of different visions that have framed Arctic issues and the interests of diverse groups. At the same time, this situation has secured the Inuit's right to self-determination only in a formal sense. This conflict is constantly manifested in different fields. During field research in Iqaluit, I asked a male interview participant whether Nunavut was what he envisioned. He responded,

> In those early days, we did not have a clear vision of what we liked. We knew we wanted a new government, but we could not describe it in detail. We knew we would have a territorial government, which is less than a province, but we decided that was the level we would start at. We did not have a clear vision of what Nunavut would be. That vision became clearer over the years. Does Nunavut fit that vision? No, not at the moment. (Iqaluit, Nunavut, August 2003)

This statement illustrates how the making of Nunavut has been part of a complex political process in which the meanings of autonomy and self-governance have occupied an expansive yet contested semantic field where people's everyday practices and visions clash with how the state responds to claims and exercises authority.

The Nunavut Implementation Commission (NIC) is another good example of these limitations. Created after the agreement was signed, the NIC was in charge of making recommendations on the political and administrative attributes of the territorial government. The NIC's proposals have had profound implications for Nunavut's politics. First, this commission recommended the adoption of a public government, as opposed to an ethnic government, and the integration of Inuit beliefs and values into the government. For example, all residents are entitled to run for office and to elect members of the Legislative Assembly on an individual rather than on a partisan basis. Second, this commission is mandated to serve Inuit interests by identifying and defining what traditional Inuit values and approaches can be integrated into the territorial government. This has been a very difficult task. To start, tradition and culture are fluid, contingent, and embedded in specific ontologies. Furthermore, national Inuit identity is relatively new. In this regard, White (2006, 15) observes that historically there were substantial differences among the various regional groupings of Inuit. Whereas some groups had powerful, authoritative camp bosses, others had looser political structures.

White (2006, 16), however, identifies a general set of values that are relevant to the Inuit, including harmony, teamwork, noninterference with individual choices, respect for elders, and demonstrated competency for leadership, all of which are values included in Canadian parliamentary democracy. The Nunavut variation of the Westminster model of responsible government lacks political parties and features consensus government, so co-operation and effective leadership are essential attributes. Compared to decisions driven by party discipline, decision making in a consensus government requires longer deliberations, teamwork, and the willingness to prioritize the needs of the group.

The concept of Inuit Qaujimajatuqangit (IQ) encapsulates Inuit ways of doing things, values, and beliefs. Although the use of Inuktitut is extensive in the Legislative Assembly and although language is interconnected with IQ, the opportunity for Inuit MLAs to express themselves in their own language does not necessarily enable them to imbue the operation of the territorial government with Inuit worldviews and traditions. Generally defined, IQ refers to what has been long known to the Inuit. This knowledge is part of the territorial government's vision statement even though this statement provides no clear guidelines for how IQ should operate in everyday decision making. For example, although Inuit values are incorporated as guiding principles for service delivery, their implementation in practice has been difficult. When asked to identify what IQ values had been incorporated into the territorial government's administration, several research participants had trouble identifying any. Thus the actual impact of IQ depends largely on this people's ability to influence government rather than on the agreement itself. In the words of one participant,

> There was nothing wrong with Nunavut adopting structures and politics from the Northwest Territories because at the time we thought there was still a lot of room the government could do to make it culturally relevant to the people. But nothing is happening because most of the staff the government has is from the South; I think they are not trained to be culture-oriented so they can understand our culture and southern culture. (Iqaluit, Nunavut, August 2003)

That Inuit knowledge has not been fully incorporated into Western government structures raises questions about whether this is actually possible within the current framework and existing power asymmetries between Inuit and Western knowledge and between Inuit and non-Inuit bureaucrats. In reference to co-management, Nadasdy (2005, 216) notes that the incorporation of Indigenous knowledge into existing institutional structures has resulted in a series of technical problems, including how to gather traditional knowledge rather than how to integrate alternative views into the existing state's structures and management practices. He argues that this situation prevents the changes that Indigenous peoples want to see.

Another proposal of the NIC was decentralization of government. Decentralization was perceived to be an expression of traditional Inuit political culture based on dispersed camps. Decentralization was dictated by various realities, including the availability of female clerks in small villages and the opportunity to shift the Northwest Territories' focus away from the capital city in order to bring the government closer to its people (Nunavut Implementation Commission 1994). Decentralization has occurred very slowly over the years, partly because of the complexity of the process and the high cost of establishing and operating government agencies across one-fifth of Canada's land mass. When I conducted fieldwork in Nunavut, several non-Inuit workers expressed their unwillingness to be relocated to smaller towns, further complicating the matter of decentralization.

In addition, although Inuit hiring has had positive results, some of the job descriptions for the decentralized positions have not been adapted to the local labour market. Most Inuit outside of Iqaluit do not have the necessary qualifications to apply. When the NLCA was signed, in exchange for the Inuit relinquishing their claim to Aboriginal land title, the federal government made several commitments related to the transfer of funding for training and education programs. However, the implementation of the land claims agreement has not focused on these broad objectives but on specific technicalities of the federal government's obligations (Dewar 2009, 79). Not only has the federal government remained unwilling to fulfil its promises, but neoliberal policies implemented throughout the Canadian Arctic have also restricted employment insurance and social assistance and have resulted in important cuts to healthcare, education, and social housing (Arctic Council 2009, 81), making the task of self-governing an enormous challenge. In 2006 the Government of Nunavut sued the Government of Canada for its failure to provide Nunavut the means to ensure its economic, social, and cultural development. In 2008 the Inuit and other members of the Land Claims Agreements Coalition submitted a complaint to the United Nations Human Rights Council concerning the ongoing failure of the Government of Canada to fully implement twenty modern treaties signed since 1975 (Nunavut Tunngavik 2006).

Arguably, land claims have been a mechanism through which Canada has attempted to recognize Indigenous peoples and establish a new partnership; however, its unwillingness to unlock the promises and synergies contained in these claims suggests otherwise. During my stay in Iqaluit, one of the things that attracted my attention was the number of people who had relocated there from other provinces. When asked to reflect on this situation, an Inuit woman working for the government said,

"Southerners" come to work to Nunavut because it is better paid and because they can have this in their resume, but after two years they leave. They are not committed to integrate, or try to understand our culture or what is happening here. Regarding our language? We should be speaking our language, but what do you see? It is not happening. (Iqaluit, Nunavut, August 2003)

The frustration expressed by this research participant was related to the slow pace of progress in implementing the land claims. More specifically, people have been frustrated with the lack of political will to address the challenges facing the Inuit population. Housing shortages in Nunavut are a severe social problem and have affected the pace of decentralization and increased the separation between "southerners" and Inuit. For example, the separation of new staff housing from the community's housing has created the perception among Inuit and residents that the best housing is reserved for outsiders. Southerners have become part of an elite community of public servants who have no connection with the Inuit community (Millennium Partners 2002; North Sky Consulting Group 2009). Unlike the provinces, territories like Nunavut have fewer sources of revenue to deal with these social problems, making self-governance a very difficult right to exercise. Moreover, as key land claims provisions remain unimplemented, at stake is whether or not the NLCA will continue to be central to improving the lives of the Inuit.

### Inuitness, Place, and Gender

Chapter 1 argued that place is a locale embedded in a wider spectrum of power relations, memory, and meaning production. However, not everyone experiences place in the same way. Men's and women's understandings of place are defined by their habitats, their being in place, and the practices that shape their livelihoods, being, and identity. Colonial experiences, changes in the economy, and political institutions are social processes related to how gender relations are negotiated and contradictions produced in place through complex geographical differences. The politics that unfold in place are constituted beyond the public sphere and are implicated in complex processes involving kinship and community relations, which contribute to the production of place. By using gender and indigeneity as specific categories of analysis, this section asks how the Inuit resist Canada's assertion of sovereignty and how gender is implicated in reimagining decolonized spaces and places? The following analyzes two instances in which gender is implicated in the construction of a collective identity: the gender-parity proposal and hunting as a social, male-driven institution.

In 1994 the NIC released a document recommending that the new government be gender-balanced by creating two-person constituencies, each with one male and one female representative. The proposal recognized the systemic barriers to women's participation in political processes and in the governance structure of contemporary Inuit society and outlined the need to eliminate such barriers in order to create balance and mutual respect between men and women in the decision-making process (Nunavut Implementation Commission 1994). In 1996 in a meeting sponsored by the NIC, 72 percent of the delegates approved the proposal in principle and called for a referendum on the proposal before it was submitted to the federal government. As I will show, the gender-parity proposal failed in the middle of a heated debate about the meaning of tradition and gender roles in contemporary Inuit society.

John Amagoalik (1997), considered the founding father of Nunavut and one of the proponents of the gender-parity proposal, wrote that "this [gender-parity] vote will reveal what kind of society we are." The referendum resulted in the rejection of the proposal for gender parity, with 57 percent against it and 43 percent in favour. The voter turnout, however, was only 39 percent, in comparison to the voter turnout of 88 percent during the later election of the new Government of Nunavut (Bourgeois 1997; Laghi 1997). Prior to the referendum on 26 May 1997, the proposal was discussed in an intense debate. Initially, the NIC highlighted only systemic barriers to Inuit women's participation and avoided cultural references in the proposal. However, the debate ended up in the sphere of the nationalist narrative for imagining the new nationality, its symbols, and who gets to speak for the nation.

Four arguments were put forth during the debate regarding the gender-parity proposal: (1) gender parity would help to restore the traditional equal value between women and men; (2) gender equality is foreign to Inuit society; (3) the proposal was against the "Inuit spirit," which is based on commonality, not on individualism; and (4) equality is best ensured by ignoring gender and racial differences.

The Inuit male and female leaders who had negotiated the land claims endorsed the first argument. During the weeks leading up to the referendum, members of Nunavut Tunngavik (which acts as the legal representative of the Inuit of Nunavut), the NIC, and Pauktuutit (the Inuit women's organization) ran a short campaign and visited a number of communities in the extensive territory. These parties argued that Inuit traditional society had been gender-balanced. According to this argument, gender roles were different yet complementary. Therefore, gender equality in the Legislative Assembly would best reflect such a division of work and the equal sharing of responsibility between women and men in precolonial Inuit society.

Amagoalik (1997) went so far as to parallel a family home with the Legislative Assembly, or the "house of the nation," in order to convey that Nunavut could not be run by a single parent because most people wanted to see both a father and mother working together in the assembly. However, the parallel between the house and the assembly proved to be problematic because it did not reflect the traditional different yet equal relationship between men and women, particularly within the context of non-Inuit institutions.

As the referendum results showed, the campaign mounted by the proponents of the proposal had failed. In fact, many people felt intimidated by what they perceived as a one-sided campaign, for the NIC had allocated resources to various Inuit and women's organizations such as Pauktuutit and the Northwest Territories' Status of Women Council in order to promote and defend the gender-parity proposal. In addition, leaders who supported the proposal could have been perceived as being "too bossy" and thus as violating the value of noninterference (Gombay 2000, 139).

Opponents, on the other hand, claimed that the notion of equality between the sexes was foreign to traditional Inuit society, where gender roles had clearly been defined and different. Manitok Thompson (cited in Laghi 1997), a high-profile female MLA, argued that "women performed as much work as men, but rarely had an input in major decisions of the nomadic life. Just because we have gender parity does not mean we will have gender equality." In Thompson's view, good laws and public policy were the proper means to secure equal opportunity for all individuals wishing to compete for the role of representing Inuit society at large.

Steele and Tremblay (2005) have argued that equal representation was, in this argument, measured in terms of the procedural equality of competition. That a prominent Inuit female advanced this view and the idea that the proposal was discriminatory against both men (by reserving seats for women) and women (by assuming women could not win without representational guarantees) helped to ensure that the proposal for gender parity would be defeated. Moreover, this argument increased the confusion about who constituted the legitimate voice of women's concerns and aspirations.

As well, the proposal's opponents used the third argument to claim that women could not be seen as a separate collectivity because such a perception jeopardized the viability of the whole. According to this point of view, the Inuit spirit requires that community decisions be geared toward unanimous consensus even if doing so means exercising strong forms of discipline among the members of the community. Since individuals cannot be abstracted from the community, the whole goal of statecraft is to transcend individual interests and to work for the community's public good. The ideas of unity, Inuit spirit, and teamwork are usually used to explain why the proposal for gender parity failed, and the literature on gender and nationalism reveals that these ideas are often invoked in nationalist movements.

No doubt, the presence of other actors further complicated the landscape. A vocal Christian minority used whatever means it had to mount a strong campaign defending women's traditional roles with regard to the family and home. Since the 1990s Christianity had played a major role in redefining Inuit "tradition," such that being a "real Inuk" was somehow bound up with Christian values. Thus a conservative interpretation of Christianity was used as a basis to oppose gender parity under the argument that this proposal was an instrument aimed at preventing women from fulfilling their duties to their families (Dahl 1997; Gombay 2000). In the words of an Inuit research participant, the failure occurred because "our leaders were not able to establish bridges with the people. Some were confused; others supported the proposal in private but were afraid of being misjudged" (Iqaluit, Nunavut, August 2003).

The gender-parity proposal – which would have been a revolutionary proposal almost anywhere in the world – failed. Since this defeat, different explanations for the failure have been presented. In their study of the development of equity policies and programs in Nunavut, Kobayashi and Bakan (2003, 21) provide different tentative explanations. First, they argue that Inuit society makes decisions through consensus and that major changes require a great deal of discussion and consultation. Second, they note that the rejection of the gender-parity proposal can be seen as a rejection of a nontraditional expression of tradition. They observe that supporters of the proposal used tradition and its centrality within the nation's past to reinforce gender equality within the conditions of modern life and political and institutional culture.

In contrast, Dahl (1997, 46) notes that the drastic transformations in the Arctic have produced identity insecurity in men and that this insecurity contributed greatly to the rejection of the proposal. He argues that men used to go out and return with food and with information about the outside world to pass on to the women at home. During recent decades, these traditional roles have changed dramatically. Condon and Stern (1991, 391) note that whereas the woman's role has been expanded, the man's role has been diminished. In traditional times, they argue, men were more nomadic than women. Men left the camps for hunting, whereas women took care of the household and children. After moving into permanent settlements, it was harder for men to reach their familiar hunting grounds. By stepping into the wage economy, women expanded their roles and started to subsidize men's traditional roles as food providers (Condon and Stern 1991, 412). Dahl's study and that of Condon and Stern make a compelling argument that changing conditions and gender roles had an impact on how the gender-parity proposal was received.

When asked why the gender-parity proposal failed, some male research participants expressed concern that Inuit women were already better positioned than men. A few female participants noted that women had had no choice but to become wage earners and to pursue an education. One female resident noted that "women are graduating, getting jobs, and still have to keep it steady at home" (Iqaluit, Nunavut, August 2003).

There was a perception among participants that men were facing higher unemployment rates and more difficulties maintaining their role as providers. A look at the numbers supports this perception. The Government of Nunavut is the main employer in Nunavut, and seven out of ten government employees are women. The 2001 national census reported that Nunavummiut (Inuit and non-Inuit) women earned more than other Canadian women but that Nunavummiut men earned less than other Canadian men (Minogue 2005). Statistics show that Inuit women are better off in terms of education and jobs. We could argue that the debate on the gender-parity proposal was a battleground not only over what culture and symbols better represent Inuitness but also over how changing roles are being negotiated and contested among the Inuit.

Since the creation of Nunavut, women have made some political gains. In Nunavut's second election, in February 2004, ten women ran, a number representing no real change from the 1999 election, in which eleven women ran, and only one was elected. In the second territorial election, only two women were elected in a highly polarized campaign in which women's voices and concerns were poorly represented. In 2008 Eva Aariak replaced Paul Okalik as government leader, becoming the first female premier in this territory. Nancy Karetak-Lindell, one of the few female Nunavut members of the Canadian Parliament, explained that in Nunavut Inuit women are discouraged by the community from occupying high political positions:

> I ran for KIA [Kivalliq Inuit Association] president and lost by 63 votes because I knew they [sic] were some men out there who absolutely did not want to see a woman in the KIA presidency ... I proved that by running the next time for secretary-treasurer and I won that overwhelmingly because there were some people in the community who felt that [the] secretary-treasurer position was a woman's job, but not the presidency. (cited in "A Seat of One's Own" 2001)

However, the observation that Inuit women have a role in politics that is more constrained and more informal than that of Inuit men is not exclusive to Nunavut. Women are usually more involved in informal spheres of politics in both Indigenous and non-Indigenous societies. Moreover, understanding Indigenous women's politics and relation to self-determination projects requires us to think critically about the different scales of politics. The body, the home, the community, the environment, and self-determination are crucial to Indigenous women's politics. These different scales of politics resonate with colonial strategies for managing people, things, and places.

At the local level, Inuit women are involved in school boards, councils, and other community-run initiatives, including measures to address violence against women. Inuit women have also been very active in transnational politics and have held prominent positions within national and international Inuit organizations, including the Inuit Circumpolar Conference and Inuit Tapiriit Kanatami. This suggests that Inuit women have taken on greater responsibilities and continue to expand their roles.

The negotiation and contestation of gender roles goes beyond the gender-parity proposal; it is also expressed in other spheres, such as hunting. In Nunavut hunting is considered essential to the social fabric and thus deserves our attention. The following analyzes hunting as a social institution. I argue that through the land claims agreement and the centrality of hunting, both Inuit men and women have been differently disenfranchised. Women's contemporary contributions are devalued within Inuit society, and hunting is devalued as an occupation.

Chapter 2 argued that in Canada land claims have been used to solve, once and for all, Indigenous territorial claims. Indigenous peoples wishing to secure land and resource rights must demonstrate historical continuity of land use and occupation. Mapping has been an important strategy for protecting Indigenous lands, yet it has produced important limitations in terms of what Indigenous peoples can actually secure. Customary use provides the basis for Indigenous rights, and maps locate an Indigenous people in a given space and demonstrate long-standing customary practices tied to the land. The strategy of locating culturally relevant practices without expressing their spatial ontological meanings and interrelationships freezes and decontextualizes such practices.

Land-use and land-occupancy studies of "hunter-gatherer" societies have remained largely male-centred and have excluded other procurement-related activities. In this cartographic-legal strategy, access to land is secured in terms of what is deemed essential to indigeneity. However, this strategy fails to secure the integrity of Indigenous lands. Moreover, while cartographic-legal representations disempower Indigenous peoples, they also disempower women in relation to men. Women's involvement is often limited because they are not considered knowers; bearers of geographic knowledge are usually elder men. In addition, cartographic representations of "cultural practices" usually focus on the spaces used by men to hunt or fish, without considering the extent to which women have been involved in making these activities a success.

The political movement that gave birth to Nunavut emphasized the Inuit's collective right to exercise control over the land, and the economic and political focus on the land and its resources positioned men's concerns at the centre of the nation-building process (Cassidy 1993). The indirect consequences of the land claims negotiations extend beyond the actual contents of the land claims. The bodies in charge of dealing with wildlife and distributing the compensation funds did not guarantee the equal representation of men and women and did not ensure women had equal access to these funds. For example, the Tunngavik Federation of Nunavut (TFN) negotiated wildlife-income support with the Northwest Territories government. The TFN agreed to narrow the focus of the program from the "household" to the "hunter," as this focus fitted within existing government initiatives that provided hunters with small amounts of money to subsidize the cost of gas and repairs to machines used for harvesting (Archibald and Crnkovich 1999, 8).

The Nunavut Wildlife Management Board was established in 1993 to maintain a balance between the protection of Arctic wildlife and the "cultural needs" of the Inuit. The board acts as a mediator between hunter and trapper associations and government regulators. Because hunting is the Inuit's most important subsistence practice, the board is a mechanism that men can use to voice their right to hunt and that the government can use to regulate this right. This governing structure does not recognize Inuit women's contributions within their society and does not provide a space for them to voice their concerns regarding, for instance, food and food safety. When a female research participant was asked to reflect on Inuit tradition and traditional activities, she said, "Tradition has a manipulative aspect. What is considered 'tradition' are those aspects related to the environment, hunting, bird migration patterns. That is to say basically what men do or know" (Iqaluit, Nunavut, August 2003).

This limited understanding of "hunter-gatherer" societies' engagement with the land does not look at women's contribution and how it has changed in Nunavut. Shannon (2006) points out that although some aspects of Inuit daily life matched the model of a gendered and complementary division of work, other procurement activities such as fishing were not divided along gender lines. She argues for extending the definition of "traditional activities" beyond hunting to better understand Indigenous economies. In "hunter-gatherer" societies, the organization of the household was more than a reflection of society; it was the society itself (Brumbach and Jarvenpa 2002, 202).

Similarly, Frink (2007) argues that for a broader understanding of how gender relations were constructed among the original peoples of the North, we must shift from the notion of work to that of a cycle of production. In her view, noting that men's and women's work was different yet complementary is not enough to account for how women contribute to their local economies in the North. In her archaeological study of the Inuit in Alaska, Frink suggests that storage facilities can be used to measure the economic authority women had. Gendered spheres were closely linked to the construction of identity. If hunting production brought men prestige, women's activities also brought women significant status. In addition, as a form of gender-demarcated control, storage played a significant role in an environment of scarcity such as the Arctic. Effective management of storage was particularly important since an individual's sense of identity arises from the skills and behaviours necessary for human survival. Although balanced gender relations existed, Frink argues, this did not necessarily eliminate the tensions and need for negotiations between men and women. Rather, gender relations were embedded in competition for status through economic strategies that produced prestige and authority. Furthermore, although in a "hunter-gatherer" society the activities of both men and women may have been consistent over time, the meanings and value of such activities were socially constructed and historically positioned (Frink 2007, 349).

Colonialism and its many agents, including the church, traders, merchants, government officials, and non-Inuit slowly redefined the meaning of gender production. Because men and women did not experience colonialism equally, this process changed the complementary relations between the sexes by favouring the participation of Inuit males in trading and leadership positions and by transforming women from producers into merely auxiliary processors in the colonial market economy. The emphasis on women's roles as "givers of life" and "transmitters of culture and language" further distanced the household from the public sphere – the Western space of politics. More important, this reflects the devaluation of female activities and roles, as such activities are not considered "productive."

Nuttall (1992) argues that all of these conditions contributed to relegating Inuit women to a less valued position than that of men, erasing the many ways that women contribute to their societies. In this context, the shift of wildlife-income support from the "household" to the "hunter" values men's activities to the extent that it conceals important economic and social transformations experienced by Inuit society. For example, since hunting has become mechanized and more expensive, family members with steady incomes now subsidize this practice. Although many female wage earners are willing to make the space for men to go hunting so that they can provide families with healthy food, hunting has increasingly been devalued as an occupation – as an economic activity. In an interview, an Inuit woman working for the Nunavut government expressed concern over how hunting is considered a leisure activity and how hunters are being perceived as unproductive. This conception puts pressure not only on full-time hunters to abandon this occupation but also on women who support hunters because the co-operative arrangement between them is not fully understood. Contrary to what Western feminists have argued about the category of "woman" signifying a connection to tradition and the past, male hunters seem to carry the burden of maintaining Inuit identity and traditions.

The "alienation" (Marx and Engels 1978) Inuit hunters face in Nunavut, on the one hand, and the high value attached to Inuit traditions and food, on the other, are creating the space for new practices, including the commodi-fication of country food (Chabot 2003; Gombay 2005). In a context of high rates of unemployment and scarcity, sharing, a value completely ingrained in Inuit society, is becoming a source of prestige for those who share and a source of stigma for those who do not. For example, full-time hunters valor-ize Inuit food and question the nutritive and moral value of non-Inuit food. Even if they have no money, they have skills to obtain valuable food. Women who fully participate in the wage economy, on the other hand, provide the means to support their hunter relatives. Full-time employees are also stigma-tized for not sharing non-Inuit food, whereas those who do share gain status (Searles 2002, 61). Sharing has extended to non-Inuit food; however, Inuit food continues to be accorded greater value, forcing Inuit to adapt their belief in sharing to the demands of the market economy (Gombay 2005, 119). During one of my visits to a research participant's house, she was very proud to offer me Arctic char soup. She said to me, "Eat, this is good for you, this is not the garbage you buy at the supermarket" (Iqaluit, Nunavut, August 2003).

This comment was not an isolated one and is part of a wider debate re-garding Indigenous human rights to traditional food. Indigenous food is a central element of Indigenous identity and livelihoods and involves many dif-ferent practices related to harvesting, storage, preparation, preservation, and consumption. Food and place are intrinsically connected (Feagan 2007). The valuation of country food is not separate from place. Rather, it can be seen as a strategy of resistance to processes aimed at deterritorializing place. When Indigenous self-determination is reduced to colonizing practices and institu-tions, Indigenous peoples have little control over their environments and live-lihoods. In this context, hunting and Inuit traditional food remain symbols differentiating between "real Inuit" and non-Inuit, symbols of indigeneity, and metaphors for the exercise of some control at home and over the land.

As a place of ethnic and cultural intersection, Iqaluit remains a town where the symbolic representation of identity and its contestation are very visible and marked by the diversity of people leaving and arriving. Despite the nation-building process in Nunavut, non-Inuit still fill many of the im-portant positions, including those in government, healthcare, education, social services, and business. Therefore, the push for autonomy and the ex-pansion of government bureaucracy have intensified the Inuit's invocation of difference and tradition (Searles 2002, 57). This invocation has produced alternative symbolic capital, which not only asserts the right to land use but also constructs a set of meanings and practices that distinguish between "real Inuit" and non-Inuit.

Nevertheless, the process of constructing Inuit narratives is immersed in constant renegotiations of the past, present, future, tradition, and gender relations. Referring to the past in the process of reaffirming a collective identity does not mean returning to the past. Rather, it is a selective reactivation of cultural symbols whose functions in the current context are related to a struggle over who controls Nunavut.

## Expanding the Grid of Intelligible Indigeneity?

Christie (2011) argues that as the Arctic is being opened to exploration and economic development, a new wave of colonization is unfolding in this region. In this new stage, sovereignty is once again a keystone shaping state policies, actions, and narratives. Indigeneity, he maintains, serves to resist this new wave of colonialism and to challenge state sovereignty. I agree in part with this argument. I believe that the politics surrounding the Arctic require us to consider how nature and climate are implicated in the new process of accumulation emerging in the region. In this final section of the chapter, I do not exhaustively analyze recent discussions on Arctic geopolitics. Instead, I reflect on the connection between indigeneity, nature, and neoliberalism in Nunavut. I argue that although indigeneity and place have the potential to challenge colonial narratives of Arctic sovereignty, the signing of the NLCA circumscribed Inuit political possibilities and the contingent character of the northern frontier.

Let us recall some of the discussion developed in Chapter 2, which noted that the success of environmental movements in the 1960s and 1970s influenced the conception of a new logic of accumulation based on the valuation of environmental commons. Environmental legislation and regulation developed unevenly across different places and countries and have led to the emergence of a new market of ecological goods and green capitalism. Unlike the previous means of commodifying nature, the new conservation economy also values ecosystems for being "untouched." Chapter 2 also noted that this type of economic accumulation both plunders available natural resources and produces socio-natures, which are the basis of natural capital. The intensified commodification and marketization of nature are integral components of neoliberalism and its insistence that anything of social worth must be tradable in the global market.

Although this type of economy is aligned with the notion that our knowledge and understanding of the environment are globally bounded, green capitalism is embedded in contradictions. First, the fate of capitalism is more dependent on nature than ever before (Smith 2009, 15). Second, neo-liberalism redefines the environment in a way that both conservation and environmental crises provide market opportunities (Johnson 2010, 831). As this model of capitalist accumulation intensifies, a new range of environmental questions arises. For example, which forms of pollution are acceptable and unacceptable? Where is environmental degradation a possibility, and where is the conservation economy more profitable?

Because sea ice is declining in the Arctic, circumpolar states have launched scientific expeditions, expanded territorial claims, and started military activity in the region aimed at taking material advantage of how climate change is unlocking hydrocarbons. As Johnson (2010, 829) argues, the effects of climate change are producing the conditions for "accumulation by degradation," which can be understood as the process through which the altered properties of a territory offer new economic opportunities. Interest in the region's enormous economic potential has revived discussions about expanding resource exploration, disputed subsurface resources, environmental degradation, control and regulation of shipping activities, and, of course, sovereignty.

Because new economic prospects are being anticipated by governments and corporations, we must ask what role the Inuit play in this vision. Who bears the costs of this type of development? Studies have shown how racial, ethnic, and class inequalities increase the risk of exposure to environmental degradation and, in turn, shape environmental activism (Dhillon and Young 2010). Historically, industrial development in the Arctic has produced considerable wealth, but most Inuit communities have not enjoyed the benefits. Resource extraction has created few sustainable, downstream links with the local economy and has generated little in the way of technology transfer and local employment. Moreover, exclusive reliance on resource exploitation and external markets has made this type of development highly vulnerable to the fluctuation of the global market.

Although studies have noted connections between environmental racism and activism, the Inuit have not consistently opposed development. For example, the chair of the Inuit Circumpolar Conference, Jimmy Stotts, notes that a "fair, enforceable and balanced agreement is needed to save the north from climate change" (cited in Henheffer 2009). However, he also warns that emissions targets could undermine the Inuit's interests now that they have finally started to take advantage of oil, gas, and minerals on their land. Previously, in October 2003, the ICC had pointed out that the destruction of the Inuit's culture and economy as a result of human-induced climate change was a violation of their human rights. In a similar vein, Inuit environmentalist Sheila Watt-Cloutier notes that "there is no justification for further eroding the northern climate by excavating for natural resources" (cited in Henheffer 2009).

Although concerned with climate change, Inuit leaders have pushed for expanding their Indigenous rights and government jurisdiction to further benefit from development. In 1993, when the NLCA was signed, the Inuit transferred their Aboriginal title over one-fifth of Canada to the government of Canada, and the federal government made several commitments related to the transfer of funding for training and education programs and for the devolution of greater governance powers, including offshore rights, to publicly elected leaders. Because seabed resources are considered part of the offshore territory, the Canadian government has argued they fall under federal jurisdiction (Mifflin 2008, 88). This is just one example of the Canadian government's approach of searching for "irreconcilable legal disagreements" as an excuse for not fulfilling promises it made during the land claims negotiations. Mifflin (2008) has noted that in failing to fulfil its promise to the Inuit, Canada is seriously compromising its most compelling legal argument for asserting sovereignty in the Arctic: Inuit historical title based on continuous occupation. Although I agree with Mifflin's observation, I do not think this discussion is limited to state sovereignty; rather, it extends to how the Inuit seek to expand notions of indigeneity. Failure to recognize Indigenous spatial constructions of the land and sea as comprising a continuum has limited Indigenous resource rights. Although the NLCA's wildlife provisions integrate marine and terrestrial species, Inuit lands are located at the ordinary high-water mark, excluding marine areas (Government of Nunavut 1993, Article 19.2.6). According to Mulrennan and Scott (2000, 699), this means that state recognition of Indigenous rights is limited to rights to land and that state jurisdiction over sea areas remains paramount.

Because the Inuit have a limited economic base and rely on a subsistence economy, the reduction of their resource rights introduced serious challenges. Pressures on the subsistence economy come from different places. For example, international legislation banning the trade of seal pelts had a major impact on Inuit communities in the early 1980s. More recently, in July 2008, the US decision to protect polar bears resulted in the banning of polar bear hunting, another source of revenue for Inuit communities. Conservationists generally agree that Indigenous peoples should be excluded from these bans as long as they are engaged in subsistence hunting. Wildlife management began in Arctic Canada in the 1960s and was concerned with controlling human consumption of animals. The introduction of sport fishing and hunting in coastal communities brought the imposition of harvest quotas, which have now been redefined with the restrictive conservation policies banning polar bear hunting. Conservation policies, together with the neo-liberal tightening of admission criteria for social benefits, are having negative consequences for northern peoples (Arctic Council 2009, 81).

Thus, although the Inuit are struggling to maintain their identity and subsistence practices and are concerned with climate change, they can no longer depend exclusively on their subsistence economy, let alone on a fragmented understanding of their economy as being limited to the land. The Arctic economy is divided into four streams: the subsistence economy; large-scale development; government, which is the largest employer; and social assistance (Conference Board of Canada 2001, 51). Unemployment is a major concern in Nunavut. To meet the challenges, Inuit are demanding a fair share of the resource development unfolding in their homeland and more control over how development is conducted on their land. In 2005 "more than 1,000 permits" were "issued to companies to explore for minerals on more than 150 million acres of land in Nunavut" (Buell 2006, 10, citing CBC North 2005). In some instances, the exploration and discovery phase disrupts subsistence activities without creating long-term opportunities for the Inuit.

Despite the 2007 federal throne speech related to northern governance, Nunavut has continuously been prevented from generating its own means of providing its citizens with basic infrastructure and services (Mifflin 2008, 88). The government's decision to assert sovereignty in the Arctic has focused on the region as a frontier that needs to be protected by increasing military surveillance through aircraft overflights, naval manoeuvres, and the construction of icebreakers. By emphasizing the role of the military, Prime Minister Stephen Harper's Arctic policy has reverted to a Cold War military rhetoric in order to respond to potential sovereignty challenges (Mifflin 2008, 87).

As expected, the Inuit have openly challenged this posture. Inuit Tapiriit Kanatami (2009) argues that, apart from a military display, an effective Arctic strategy requires a federal government willing to address elements of sovereignty that have to do with the social and economic development and environmental stewardship of the Arctic. Accordingly, an integrated approach in the Arctic should be based on a high and sustainable level of intergovernmental relations as well as on Inuit-government co-operation.

Mary Simon, president of ITK, has noted that establishing meaningful sovereignty in the Arctic should begin with recognizing Inuit use and occupancy of the Arctic land and sea and should include a power-sharing partnership between the federal government and the territorial government regarding research, environmental monitoring, and enforcement of sovereignty, in addition to a new deal for narrowing the wide gaps separating the Inuit from Euro-Canadians (Inuit Tapiriit Kanatami 2009).

In supporting Nunavut's preferred approach to ensuring Canada's sovereignty in the Arctic, the ICC has advanced a proposal based on the concept of "sustainable security" as an alternative to militarization (cited in Loukacheva 2004, 3). This proposal puts emphasis on asserting the right of local authorities to be informed about all issues related to the security policies within Nunavut, including issues affecting this territory's waters, offshore resources, air space, and ice; the protection of game and other limited vulnerable renewable and nonrenewable resources from any sort of military activity or its consequences; protection from any past, present, and future results of military actions in the Inuit territories; the right of Nunavut authorities to participate in decision-making regarding national defence; and the possibility for Nunavut to influence Canada's security policy when appropriate (Loukacheva 2004, 3).

Because the Inuit have emphasized these demands, they have been perceived as less Indigenous and less concerned with conservation and the reproduction of their identity. I argue, however, that it is important to consider how a particular slice of the debate on climate change – "accumulation by degradation" in the eastern Arctic – enacts a form of environmental racism by denying the heterogeneity of Indigenous peoples. Climate change is not only about unfolding a benign type of green capitalism but also about taking economic advantage of the conditions that the impact of climate change is producing. In my view, at the core of climate change and global environmentalism are questions about who can destroy the environment and who should bear the costs of protecting it. Drawing attention to this contradiction raises important issues regarding the tenets of green capitalism, conservation practices, and the continuation of colonialism more broadly.

Inuit rhetoric about reclaiming the Arctic/homeland is no longer based on securing land rights and resources for traditional activities but on Inuit self-sufficiency and autonomy in the modern context. From this perspective, "self-sufficiency" means not only having the right to continue to use the land as it was supposedly used before contact but also being able to meet contemporary challenges. In this regard, Loukacheva (2007) argues that in the Nunavut system of governance, success depends not only on defence matters and sovereignty but also on securing the economic viability of this territory. A model of development based exclusively on the southern idea of the Arctic frontier, although productive for Canada's economy, will not be sustainable in the long term. In the Inuit discourse, sovereignty policies are being closely linked to the local economy, the environment, employment opportunities, hunting, game profits, fishing, climate change, renewable and nonrenewable resources, and the impact of the military on the territory.

Local concerns like housing, suicide, substance abuse, violence against women, and the exorbitant cost of living in Nunavut are more pressing for people than are threats to sovereignty (Henderson 2007). For the Inuit, solving these urgent social concerns can be achieved only by gaining a share of northern economic development. This position is shared by the governments of Canada's three northern territories, which released a document in 2007 titled *A Northern Vision: A Stronger North and a Better Canada.* This document discusses sovereignty, sustainable communities, climate change, and circumpolar relations. In addition, the document asserts that northerners should be "the primary beneficiaries of northern resource development."

Inuit rights have become part of a rhetoric that reclaims Inuit stewardship over Arctic development – including oil exploration, hunting, and fishing – and that asserts control over the lands and seas in which these activities take place (Shadian 2006, 252). The signing of the NLCA has provided the Inuit political elite with an opportunity to transcend the notion of Inuit rights as a local concern and to develop a broader notion involving overall Arctic economic development and environmental protection. At the same time, however, the NLCA constrains the Inuit to work within the context of the Canadian state's sovereignty.

**Conclusion**
Earlier, I posed the questions: Who has the right to define people's environmental future? How have the Inuit negotiated different understandings of the Arctic? What are the discursive, social, and material effects of how indigeneity is defined, how policies are framed, how political and economic possibilities are envisioned, and how gender hierarchies are reproduced in the Canadian Arctic? Who has the right to develop or preserve Arctic resources? In the case of Nunavut, Inuit nationalism has been embedded in unbounded politics that seek to restructure rights within the

Arctic hinterland. The linking of global articulations of indigeneity and the geo-economics of this region have leveraged Inuit rights away from resource sovereignty and toward a state-mediated model of land claims centred on economic development and neoliberal self-government. In the context of the institutionalization of Inuit politics and the deep socio-economic changes that have further differentiated between Inuit and non-Inuit, among Inuit themselves, and between men and women, competing understandings of Inuitness reveal the complex arena in which the Inuit struggle to maintain control over their homeland unfolds.

Understanding the legacies of settler colonialism in the Arctic is useful in interrogating how Canada continues to assert its sovereignty over the region and how this notion operates to legitimize or delegitimize certain environmental practices, forms of difference, and political possibilities. In addition, colonialism helps us to understand the specific ways that the Inuit's bodies, identities, homes, and gender relations were controlled in the process of the Canadian state's assertion of sovereignty. The intersection of nature, indigeneity, and gender is useful in problematizing what gets to be read as "ecological" and "sustainable" and in foregrounding what new forms of epistemic violence are being enacted when Indigenous peoples are defined in ways that limit indigeneity to the "Indian slot."

At the same time, these conditions create the space for Indigenous peoples' agency and politics as they attempt to expand constraining definitions of indigeneity and to challenge the role of the nation-state as a broker of the global economy. For this latter possibility to exist, it is crucial that non-Inuit leaders and Nunavummiut alike develop their own understanding of how the Inuit want to live in the contemporary world by paying greater attention to what the Inuit have to say and how they represent themselves.

# 4
# The Nisga'a "Common Bowl," Gender, and Property Rights
---

Eleven years after the Nisga'a nation signed its final agreement with the Canadian government, it became the first Indigenous nation to take the agreement a step further by legalizing private ownership on Nisga'a land. This move potentially allows Nisga'a citizens to mortgage, sell, lease, or transfer their property to anyone they wish. The centralized Nisga'a government argued that the introduction of private property was a significant step toward true self-government. Consistent with neoliberal practices and understandings of the self and the market, the move toward private property was framed in terms of enabling the Nisga'a to fulfil their roles as active and important contributors to the national economy. The Nisga'a agreement and, later, privatization of Indigenous land stirred up a division among Indigenous peoples in British Columbia. Those who support the move see it as a way to end dependency. Those who oppose private landholding see it as a cultural sellout. This means that the Nisga'a were judged for being neither modern nor Indigenous enough by non-Indigenous and Indigenous parties respectively. Although the Nisga'a have been praised by some think-tanks and political commentators for their individualistic and entrepreneurial approach, they have also been criticized for their understanding of differentiated citizenship.

The case of private property highlights the contradictory character of indigeneity articulation as it intersects with neoliberalism. As a form of governance, neoliberalism disarticulates established meanings and establishes new ones. Scholars have explored how in settler societies Indigenous peoples are driven to fit certain preconceived criteria in order to achieve recognition. At the same time, such recognition is shaped by imperatives that fail to maintain such difference. In this regard, Povinelli (2002, 39) argues that recognition "constitutes Indigenous persons as failures of indigeneity ... And this is the point."

This chapter examines how the Nisga'a's economy, politics, and cultural difference have been shaped by the settler society in ways that link an intelligible understanding of indigeneity with entrepreneurialism. Specifically, I ask what kinds of imperatives and political possibilities are created when Indigenous knowledge is politically mobilized to fit Western legal systems and Western notions of property and rights? What happens to the stories that are not told and to those holding such knowledge? I suggest that the colonial resource economy and environmentalism offer some insights into what visions have been successfully articulated in British Columbia under neoliberalism. Although indigeneity as a bundle of rights is grounded in notions of the "Indian slot," people produce other subjectivities through the interaction between local experiences and neoliberal understandings of the self, the market, environmentalism, and rights. Underlining this practice are political, socio-economic, and colonial structures and cultural transformations that shape Indigenous everyday geographies in place. Thus place is crucial to considering the specific and local ways that people have been dispossessed. Building on the work of scholars of colonialism, Indigenous geographies, and the governance of nature, I emphasize that the production of nature is closely connected to the making of the settler colonial identity.

First, I discuss Nisga'a articulation of indigeneity and the relationship among place, resources, and labour. Second, I illustrate how articulations of indigeneity are shaped, negotiated, and contested by a dynamic process of self-identification, belonging, borders, and gendered senses of place. Third, I examine the Nisga'a land claims agreement in relation to the limits, contradictions, and ambiguities intrinsic to the engagement of indigeneity and neoliberalism. Finally, I draw some conclusions.

## Settler Colonialism, Land, or Labour?

This section explores the relationships between colonial capitalism and nature in the process of creating settler colonial space in the Nisga'a territory. I argue that although it is relevant to take into account the ways that specific colonial formations shaped historical geographies, we need to consider how these modalities were reworked in the face of local conditions. The experience of settler colonialism is grounded in dispossession. The coveting, colonizing, and populating or depopulating of distant places occurs because of land (Said 1994, 78). Dispossession, however, is more than the dispossession of land as a means of production; land is central as an "ontological framework for understanding relationships" (Coulthard 2010, 80).

Settler colonialism concerns itself with managing spaces and bodies in the service of the economy. According to Wolfe (2006), Indigenous peoples were displaced, driven away, or fenced in, their ancestry was regulated, and their children were abducted and resocialized in residential schools in an attempt to reduce their number. The term "settler," which colonizing populations have typically used to define themselves, is problematic since it conceals their role as colonizers. However, settler colonies by definition involve the displacement, eradication, or absorption of Indigenous populations by a new regime. Exploring how specific colonial formations have shaped historical geographies helps to identify Indigenous peoples' responses and their practices of articulation. British Columbia is a province where treaties were not signed, except in a small area. Crown claims of ownership have historically relied on the assertion of a lack of prior use and occupation and on constructions of nature that have persisted through socio-economic activities such as forestry and fishing (Rossiter 2007).

Historically, the northwest coast of North America was home to several highly structured Indigenous societies with distinctive politics, economies, and social organization based on rank, status, and lineage. Among the coastal peoples were the Nisga'a, who call themselves "the people of the Lisim," or the people of the Nass River, and live in the valley known as Ts'ak'hl Nisga'a. Prior to the arrival of European settlers, coastal peoples were territorially dispersed and hierarchically organized into clans and ranks according to their specific ancestors. Although geographically dispersed, such communities were linked by marriage and elaborate networks of local and extended lineages that wove complex identities embodying multiple statuses and asymmetries (Saunders 1997, 139). The Nisga'a were characterized by their highly complex social and economic organization based upon four clans symbolized by the eagle, wolf, killer whale, and raven. As part of its political organization, Nisga'a society had clearly defined and inherited positions of political leadership.

The Nisga'a, like other coastal Indigenous peoples, developed elaborate resource-management systems deeply embedded in their social organization and knowledge systems. These systems governed access, rights and obligations, allocation of costs and benefits, and harvesting. These systems were also intricately connected to the governance, spirituality, and social relations of the people. Under each *wilp* (house), specific matrilineal branches of extended families collectively owned well-defined territories, including marine and riparian resources (Roth 2002, 146). The house chiefs had the rights, privileges, and responsibilities of a chieftainship, as conferred by their chiefly names. The certainty of inheritance meant that future leaders were prepared from childhood, which contributed to the strength of the clan. Potlatches and feasts, as repositories of legal authority, provided the forum where hereditary status and the property and resources associated with it were validated and confirmed.

The Nisga'a's system of governance and their sense of place and being in the world gradually came into conflict with colonial knowledge, economic systems, and resource management. In sites where coastal men and women gathered to fish and trade oolichan, also known as candlefish, a profitable fur trade led by the Hudson's Bay Company flourished from 1785 to 1825. Some scholars suggest that initially women's and men's labour and participation in the fur trade were equally relevant. Indigenous women's involvement started to diminish as traders started to favour men in the fur trade. High-ranking males gained economic advantages, and a new rationality of social and political prerogatives crystallized around new concepts of stewardship over lineage resources and male authority (Littlefield 1987; Fiske 1991). According to Rossiter (2007, 775), although Indigenous lands were part of colonial calculations during the fur trade, many Indigenous peoples remained in control of their territory.

By the early nineteenth century, however, the economy had shifted from fur trade to land (Harris 2004, 169). As white settlers advanced within Indigenous territory, land conflicts arose around competing claims of sovereignty, authority, and the right to control resources. Harris (2002, xxvii) notes that the making of "Native space" involved the physical and material displacement of Indigenous inhabitants from their territories. In this separation, land and resources were redefined by the rights and values of the colonial, capitalist economy. In British Columbia the advancement of white farmers, miners, loggers, fishermen, and prospectors driving the Gold Rush put immense pressure on Indigenous lands. To deal with this situation, the British created the new colony of British Columbia on the mainland, which was administered by James Douglas, the governor appointed by the Colonial Office.

To attract settlers to the island and the interior lands, the British government instructed the governor to implement the same policy used in other parts of the Dominion of Canada: the signing of treaties to extinguish Indigenous land title. Douglas, however, signed treaties in only a very small portion of British Columbia. In the remaining area, he created small reserves without properly extinguishing Indigenous land title. A review of documents related to the land question shows that whereas reserves in other parts of the dominion had been created on the basis of eighty acres per Indigenous family, the provincial government decided to create reserves that fitted the "local situation and needs," which dictated that twenty-five acres per family were plenty (Government of British Columbia 1877). Within a few years, the Nisga'a's lands had been surveyed, and the Nisga'a ended up in small reserves up and down the river. Why was the Indigenous policy implemented in British Columbia different from the one applied in other parts of the Confederation?

Scholars debating the reasons for this difference have suggested that it was due to a combination of racism, colonial pragmatism, and high costs. By establishing small reserves as the only legitimate Indigenous space, government officials effectively cleared the majority of the province's land for settler capitalists (Grek Martin 2009, 5). The Gold Rush marked the beginning of a resource economy in which resources were no longer provided by Indigenous peoples. The industrial economy required both land and labour. This meant separating Indigenous lands from the communities they were attached to, which forced people to find new ways to survive. Private property facilitated colonial capitalism by creating a legal and imaginary landscape in which "civilized" white settlers were accorded a higher status than the Indigenous "savage" living on lawless frontiers. Rossiter (2007, 778) observes that forests containing valuable resources were among the first target of state regulation and that the creation of the Crown timber business was envisioned as the means to transform British Columbia into a successful phenomenon.

Although coastal Indigenous peoples had used the land and fished according to their own legal frameworks, the dominion government constructed forests and fisheries as open-access spaces that needed to be regulated through a bundle of rights regarding use and exclusion that openly privileged European settlers. Both the fishery and forestry industries were developed on top of Indigenous sites and relied on Indigenous labour. In her detailed historical account of fishing activities among coastal and inland Indigenous peoples, Newell (1993) demonstrates that the government's regulation strategies were designed to generate cheap labour for the canneries and to prevent Indigenous peoples from competing with white settlers in the fishing industry. Newell also shows that the government's regulations were supported by the use of intimidating practices such as raids against fishing camps and the destruction of traps.

Since salmon was an extremely important resource for coastal peoples, imposed regulations represented an attack on Indigenous economic self-sufficiency and social reproduction, forcing Indigenous communities to step into the wage economy in a seasonal manner. By the 1840s Indigenous workers were consistently engaged in fishing and logging.

The Nisga'a as well as other coastal peoples entered the wage labour economy in customary ways: seasonally and in family units. Clan chiefs and house leaders became middlemen in charge of recruiting labour among their own people. The men went to the fishing grounds, and the women worked in the canneries during the fishing season, the time when coastal people harvest food. Nisga'a women provided cheap labour because of their association with male producers and the persistence of their nonmonetary exchange of resources such as oolichan. Indigenous women's experiences as labourers reflected the transformation of Indigenous economies and social structures and the unevenness of the gendered division of labour (Muszynski 1996; Butler and Menzies 2000).

By participating in the wage economy on their own terms, Indigenous communities were able to maintain their social organization and kinship obligations. In doing so, communities adapted to the realities of their changing environment but controlled the pace and nature of their adaptation (Alfred 2009). The result of Nisga'a engagement with labour was a mixed economy in which men and women deployed labour power while maintaining their subsistence activities. In the process, the Nisga'a revitalized Indigenous concepts and cultural roots to recreate spaces of identity and to frame their political claims. They reclaimed traditional management, ownership, and communal resource allocation to resist colonial penetration and intervention.

The dispossession of Indigenous lands and resources was coupled with other colonial strategies aimed at dismantling Indigenous peoples' abilities to resist the imperative of progress. In partnership with Christian churches, the federal government intervened in many other aspects of "Indian" affairs, including the education of children, who were taken away from their families at an early age and placed in residential schools. The management of Indigenous populations also included banning the potlatch, matrilineal inheritance, customary marriage ceremonies, and the use of personal Nisga'a names (Tennant 1990).

The ban on the potlatch disrupted Indigenous peoples' ability to openly govern resource allocation and fuelled Indigenous discontent and rivalry among coastal peoples, who used to fish along the lower Nass River. At the same time, the ban provided a solid ground for the syncretism of Christianity and Nisga'a traditions. The history of missions in the Nass Valley started in 1860 when the Anglican missionary William Duncan arrived at the Nisga'a villages, after having founded Metlakatla, one of the most controversial social experiments of its time. Metlakatla and other subsequent mission "colonies," such as Gingolx and Aiyansh, were modelled on rural English communities with the intention of displacing the Indigenous social order and inculcating Indigenous peoples with Christian values (Usher 1974; Murray 1985). These mission communities were supposed to influence surrounding Indigenous pagan villages. However, the missionaries were not able to succeed as much as they had hoped in this area because of Indigenous resistance.

Even though the church formally applied the law, missionaries allowed the celebration of revival meetings, which mimicked the feast system that the Nisga'a employed to transfer clan names and ownership rights and that was connected with funerals and the erection of tombstones or with settlement feasts. As Tennant (1990, 78) argues, these revival meetings were, in fact, concealed potlatches at which the host made "payments" to those who had contributed to the funeral, basically following the potlatch practice of distributing wealth. Nisga'a traditionalists insisted on potlatching and participating in secret societies, maintaining a strong sense of their identity and traditions in opposition to the missionaries' objectives (Harkin 1993, 2). The missionaries soon understood the importance of the chiefs to the Nisga'a and the futility of working against them. Over time, missionaries undertook efforts to rewrite the liturgy in the Nisga'a language, endorsing the practices established by the Nisga'a themselves (Barker 1998, 439).

Eventually, the Nisga'a and the Anglican Church developed a relationship in which the one legitimized the other. The Nisga'a leaders helped the church to diminish resistance among villagers; in turn, the church recognized the authority of male chiefs. The relationship between the two slowly contributed to forging the syncretic modern yet traditional face of the Nisga'a nation.

Missionaries provided leaders with a new and critical resource: literacy. Missionaries invented the Nisga'a orthography to disseminate the word of the Gospels and the use of English through a newspaper, which the Nisga'a later used to promote the land question. Moreover, literacy helped the

Nisga'a to access new information and legal tools such as the Royal Proclamation of 1763 in order to advance their claims and appeal to both the
federal and BC governments. A Nisga'a delegation went to Victoria, and
representatives from the Tsimshian (a coastal people living adjacent to
the Nisga'a and Gitksan) went to Ottawa to raise their concerns. For years,
the Nisga'a refused to allow Indian Agents to be stationed in their territory,
and by 1886 they were actively holding community meetings to discuss the
land question and to organize joint actions with other Indigenous peoples
(Fisher 1977, 205).

By the turn of the twentieth century, things had changed. A younger
generation, whose members had attended residential schools and were active in the fishing industry, had displaced the older chiefs in the Nisga'a land
movement. Scholars have explored the importance of labour relations in
Indigenous people's lives. Parnaby's (2008) work on the Squamish long-
shoremen in the early twentieth century demonstrates that their daily labour
experiences and the realities of their lives in the colonial and capitalist
environment shaped their political activism. Before unions were formed,
Indigenous fishers consistently bound together with non-Indigenous fishermen to reach better deals (Drucker 1963; Jamieson 1968). Similarly, Jamieson
(1968, 223) observes that besides purely economic considerations, unionism has been one of the few contexts in which Indigenous peoples in British
Columbia have had the opportunity to participate on an equal basis and to
share losses and gains. Furthermore, Jamieson argues that this participation
did not diminish the centrality of Indigenous identity. Rather, unionism supported and stimulated Indigenous organizations. Many of the Indigenous
leaders politically active in the fishing industry were also heavily involved in
the struggle for land and resource rights.

The first BC Indigenous organization was the Nisga'a Land Committee,
created in 1907 and made up of chiefs who had both high-ranking names
and religious positions within the local churches and who worked in the
fishing industry. Whereas the initial concern of coastal people was the acreage allotted to families, the Nisga'a movement slowly started to focus on
land title (LaViolette 1973, 118-19). In doing so, this movement articulated
Nisga'a identities in ways that simultaneously resisted and conformed to the
norms of the dominant society (Raibmon 2006). This simultaneous process
of resisting and conforming became a strategy of survival in dealing with the
settler society. The Nisga'a Land Committee articulated a nationalist discourse and used Euro-Canadian legal tools to claim territorial rights. For
example, this committee used the Royal Proclamation of 1763 to legitimize

Nisga'a land title, as shown in the following statement protesting the impact of white settlers in the Nass region:

> we, the Indian peoples of the above mentioned valley, being lawful and original inhabitants and possessors of all the land contained there from time immemorial and being assured in our possession of the same by the proclamation of His Majesty, King George III, under date of 7th October, 1763 ... Up to the present time, our lands have not been ceded by us to the Crown, nor in any alienated form from us by any agreement or settlement between the representatives of the Crown and ourselves. (Indian Land Committee 1910)

Unlike the language used by previous leaders, who spoke of acreage allotment, the Land Committee's language substantially focused on kinship, connection to the territory, and resources, and it alluded to Euro-Canadian tools to justify Nisga'a claims. Despite this organization's activities, the provincial government continued to ignore Indigenous claims.

Besides creating smaller reserves, the BC government also left the remaining portion of the northwest coast, including the Nass Valley, completely open to white pre-emption. This situation prompted the Nisga'a to contact other coastal peoples in order to discuss a broad political response to the province's policy. Several coastal peoples met in Victoria in December 1909 and agreed to create a pan-Indian organization, the Indian Rights Association of British Columbia. Yet this movement failed in its efforts to maintain a steady collective response.

In the end, the Nisga'a Land Committee decided to act alone and ignore both the federal and provincial governments by appealing directly to the imperial government. This appeal represented the first formal international intervention by Indigenous peoples (Wilmer 1993). In the Nisga'a petition of 1913, the committee reiterated its concerns regarding three issues: the recognition of Indigenous title as stated in the Royal Proclamation, the signing of treaties, and self-government. In addition, the petition contained a declaration of Nisga'a political sovereignty and, at the same time, affirmed that British sovereignty had been accepted on the understanding that Nisga'a land would be respected according to the Royal Proclamation (Nisga'a Tribal Council 1980, 168). The British government avoided dealing with the Nisga'a petition and returned it to Canada. In response, the Canadian government modified the Indian Act in 1927 to make it illegal to press Indigenous land claims and to hire lawyers for such purposes. This modification to the Indian

Act contributed to the dismantling of much of the Indigenous movement of the time. Basically, Indigenous cultural and political activities had to remain underground. Community churches and the fishing industry provided space for the Nisga'a to continue to discuss and seek solutions to their dispossession (Barker 1998, 444).

By the 1950s the forestry and fishery industries had undergone major transformations that had a negative impact on Indigenous peoples. In the forestry industry, hand-logging had been replaced by industrial logging and sawmilling, which required a smaller labour force. Hand-logging had combined well with Indigenous subsistence practices. In their analysis of Tsimshian women's participation in forestry, Butler and Menzies (2000) argue that after the Second World War, Indigenous families found it increasingly difficult to maintain their local economies and wage labour; large companies controlled Indigenous lands, undermining livelihoods and creating fewer jobs. The Nisga'a saw the rapid and intensive extraction of timber from their territories.

The fisheries also experienced major changes. Having to adjust to the reduction in salmon, canning companies started to amalgamate and centralize their operations, which was possible with the introduction of refrigerators. Indigenous men and, particularly, women were among the most affected by the job loss, with women becoming even more dependent upon their husband's and father's incomes. The introduction of new harvesting technologies and government regulations had made it more difficult for Indigenous fishermen operating small boats to compete with larger vessels. Indigenous fishermen often complained that government regulations and the Indian Act prevented them from participating in the fishing industry and from accessing credits to meet such regulations (Jamieson 1968; Newell 1993).

Representing Nass fishermen was Frank Calder, the adopted son of one of the founders of the Nisga'a Land Committee. James Gosnell, a skilled gillnetter and later the president of the Nisga'a nation, also participated in the discussions over the regulations that negatively affected Indigenous communities. Unlike other organizations that linked Indigenous identity with access to fisheries for traditional purposes, Calder conveyed the idea that fishing, whether for domestic or industrial purposes, was crucial to cultural and economic survival (Wright 2008). When Calder became a member of the provincial legislature in 1949, he used it as a platform to address Nisga'a concerns.

Under Calder's leadership, the Nisga'a Tribal Council (NTC) was created in 1955 to continue the work of the Land Committee. Frank Calder brought the land struggle to a new stage. His moral status among the Nisga'a allowed him to unite the four clans (Raven, Wolf, Eagle, and Killer Whale) and the four villages (Gingolx, Aiyansh, Gitwinksihlkw, and Laxgalts'ap). Unlike the Land Committee, the NTC was founded as an organization representing the Nisga'a people, not only the chiefs. This difference meant that every member of the Nisga'a villages had a vote in the council assemblies. Bringing the Nisga'a together was not an easy task. When asked to expand on this difficulty, a Nisga'a research participant explained, "At the beginning, the Nisga'a living [here] in the Nass [Valley] did not want to include those living in Prince Rupert and Terrace. They did not want to recognize those people's rights. However, those living here gradually understood that it was important to take them into account, because that would make us stronger" (New Aiyansh, Nass Valley, July 2004).

The transformation of the Nisga'a chiefs' Tribal Council into a "popular" nationalist movement had important implications. First, this transformation created a distinct constituency of people. Second, the introduction of a popular vote was a major political change to the governance structure of this people. Third, since colonial policing and land dispossession had produced skepticism about the Land Committee's authority among the Nisga'a, the transformation of the NTC into a "popular" movement helped it to transcend internal divisions by diminishing the antagonism among the villages. Importantly, these changes shifted the Nisga'a movement away from the system of landholding *wilps* and toward the "common bowl" approach, in which authority over the territory rested with the NTC as opposed to the *wilps*. Fourth, the creation of the NTC initiated a new era of tribalism in British Columbia, which saw the tribal nation, not the community, as the entity of political action. Tennant (1990, 123) argues that as an organization created to pursue land claims, the NTC sought to secure both customary and industrial access to fisheries, showing the importance of labour to Nisga'a organizing.

Like its predecessor, the NTC tried to establish a province-wide Indigenous movement in order to revive the land question and build a common front for pursuing a legal strategy. However, most Indigenous organizations were reluctant to follow this approach. Moreover, this proposal was viewed with suspicion because of Calder's partisan position (Tennant 1990, 136). Indigenous organizations such as the National Indian Brotherhood were exploring other means, including transnational alliances. In the 1950s the brotherhood sent three representatives to New York to address the United Nations. Like the other previous Indigenous delegations, they were advised to work within the Canadian legal and political framework.

The NTC sued the provincial government in 1967, and the Calder case came to trial almost two years later, with the Nisga'a represented by Thomas Berger (*Calder et al. v. Attorney General of British Columbia* [1969]). At that point, the provincial government managed to convince the judges that Aboriginal title had not existed at the time of "discovery" and settlement in British Columbia and that, even if it had existed, it had been extinguished by colonial legislation passed in Victoria prior to Confederation. In using these arguments, the BC government was reclaiming the concept of terra nullius, which had underpinned the development of a resource economy in this province.

To counteract the provincial arguments and the court's decision, the Nisga'a quickly filed an appeal in 1970, defining Indigenous land title as coming from the immemorial occupation of a given territory, not from a government statute. Accordingly, a government had to extinguish Aboriginal rights in order to get clear title to Aboriginal lands (Nisga'a Tribal Council 1980). However, the BC court once again rejected the Nisga'a claim by emphasizing the supremacy of colonial and provincial laws over "Indian rights." The next step for the Nisga'a was to continue the fight in the Supreme Court of Canada. The Nisga'a's failure in the BC court led to further dissension with other First Nations peoples, who feared that the Nisga'a appeal to the Supreme Court of Canada would forever close the door to all Indigenous claims. The National Indian Broterhood, for example, called for a pause in the NTC's action. The Nisga'a organization refused, and in 1971 the Calder case was heard by the federal judges.

In a climate of Indigenous transnational activity and Indigenous domestic unrest, the federal judges rendered their verdict on the Calder case. Surprisingly, the judges recognized the existence of Aboriginal title before the assertion of British sovereignty. However, they disagreed on whether this title continued to exist. Three judges ruled in favour of the claim and four against it by arguing the Nisga'a had brought the suit before the court improperly (Godlewska and Webber 2007, 7-8.) In the end, the last resort had failed to produce a clear resolution of the question of Aboriginal title; therefore, the ball was once again in the hands of politicians.

Prior to the ruling in the Calder case, the federal government's Aboriginal policy was not clearly defined. In 1969 the government of Prime Minister Pierre Elliott Trudeau introduced the Statement of the Government of

Canada on Indian Policy, or the White Paper, to abolish the Indian Act and eventually to eliminate all Aboriginal "privileges" while promoting equality for Aboriginal peoples. Although some Indigenous organizations such as the National Indian Brotherhood had adopted a discourse of equality, most Indigenous peoples rejected this proposal. To most Indigenous peoples, the word "equality" suggested the elimination of Indigenous rights. Indigenous activism stopped the White Paper (Sanders 1995).

The NTC was the only organization that agreed in principle with the government on the White Paper. Only years later did the NTC clarify its position. According to this organization, the Nisga'a supported the notion of "true equality" included in the White Paper, which presupposed that Indigenous peoples had the right to full and equal participation in the cultural, social, economic, and political life of Canada. Nonetheless, to the NTC, such support did not mean the acceptance of the further steps suggested by the White Paper because Aboriginal peoples should be regarded as "citizens plus" (Nisga'a Tribal Council 1980, 17). Clearly, the Nisga'a position on the White Paper had deepened the dissension with other Indigenous organizations.

The Nisga'a were trapped in the middle of a jurisdictional wrangle. Successive BC governments refused to negotiate with the Nisga'a, arguing that land claims were a federal responsibility and forcing the NTC to explore other political arenas. In 1972 Calder ran for a seat in the New Democratic Party (NDP) and won the provincial election. Calder became a minister without portfolio with special responsibilities for Indian affairs. However, he was not able to influence the province's traditional stance on Indigenous claims. The NTC's support of the White Paper had proven to have political consequences for the Nisga'a. Neither Indigenous leaders nor the NDP had forgotten this support for the federal Liberals. Indigenous leaders believed that neither Calder nor the NTC was really committed to advancing Indigenous claims. To the NDP, on the other hand, Calder was not loyal enough to the party because he continued to have strong ties with the federal Liberals. In fact, this linkage drove Calder to lobby Ottawa directly to begin negotiations on the Nisga'a claim (Raunet 1984, 163).

The NTC focused on looking for new political avenues to force the provincial government to negotiate. At their 18th Tribal Convention in Greenville in 1979, Calder announced he could no longer run for his party, the NDP, and that instead he would join the Social Credit Party. In addition, the NTC demanded that both the provincial and federal governments negotiate without extinguishing Nisga'a title in clear reference to the land claims agreements negotiated with the Cree of Quebec (Nisga'a Tribal Council 1980, 13). Although both the federal and provincial governments agreed to negotiate land claims and self-government with the Nisga'a, the tripartite negotiation evolved into a slow process revisiting old positions, rhetoric, and a broad exploration of issues such as fishing, hunting, and forestry, with no visible progress until two events impacted the treaty-making process: the Constitution Act of 1982 and the ruling of the Supreme Court in the Sparrow case (Exell 1990), which held Aboriginal fishing rights to be constitutionally protected.

In the context of an economic crisis affecting the softwood lumber industry, the provincial government announced it would abandon its longstanding policy of refusing to participate in the negotiation of Indigenous claims and would promote, instead, a "certainty policy" as a way to achieve the stability necessary to encourage long-term investment in the province. The negotiation of land claims was seen as necessary to satisfy corporate demands upon lands and resources in British Columbia (Haythornthwaite 2000). In December 1991 the NTC met with the provincial government to initiate a new process aimed at solving the longstanding Nisga'a land claims. After seven years of formal negotiations, in 1998 the Nisga'a Final Agreement was signed within the context of a renewed partnership between the Canadian government, Aboriginal peoples, and the provinces. The signing of the Final Agreement was a historic moment representing the end of a very long journey. In referring to this event, Chief Joseph Gosnell, the then president of the NTC, stated that "the canoe had arrived" (*Nisga'a Final Agreement 2001/2002 Annual Report* 2002).

### Place and the Arrival of the Canoe

Place is embedded in a complex relation of memory and power. Indigenous collective articulations linking place and memory are aimed not only at building new relationships that break away from the colonial but also at re-establishing self-determined, ancient jurisdictions in place(s). Place is premised on daily practices, social interactions, and relationships. It is through these interactions and relationships that people think of themselves as belonging in place and fulfilling their obligations. Place is produced through cultural symbols that have and convey meaning (Greider and Garkovich 1994). Interactions between individuals result in social understandings of place, and the meanings of a particular place are conveyed and created through discourses, practices, and ways of acting in the world. Who we are, how we fulfil our obligations, and what we value shape and are shaped by these interactions.

On the other hand, the articulation of indigeneity develops on different scales, involves power relations, and raises questions about the processes that are appropriating and transforming global discourses in place. As previously noted, the articulated nature of indigeneity evokes a sense of the political. If land claims are based on specific articulations of indigeneity, does it matter how land studies are done and whose knowledge is included? I argue that although the common bowl facilitated the negotiation of the agreement, different meanings of belonging, myths of origin, borders, and gender roles have been articulated and contested in place. Two aspects with several implications are particularly relevant to this discussion: (1) the political and legal challenge to the Nisga'a agreement by the house chiefs of Gitanyow and (2) the internal contestation of the Nisga'a agreement.

For the Nisga'a to claim their territory, they had to demonstrate that they had used and occupied a fixed territory. This test of indigeneity is exclusive, and its success depends on Indigenous peoples' ability to fit preconceived indigeneity criteria that are often far from their own laws and stories. The Ayuukhl Nisga'a (Nisga'a code of laws) tells the story of how the Nisga'a have lived, used, and occupied the Nass River region and its watershed since time immemorial. The Nass River watershed is a major river system flowing from the southwest through the Coast Range Mountains along the northwest coast. The river, which originates at Nass Lake, is 380 kilometres long, and the watershed encompasses 21,567 square kilometres (Rose 2001, 38). According to the Nisga'a, the Nass Valley, from "mountaintop to mountaintop," is their territory.

However, the Nisga'a claim to this territory was legally challenged by the Gitanyow community, whose members had a different understanding of borders. According to this people, their traditional use and occupancy of the disputed territory is described in the *Adaawk* (laws and songs), which tells their history. According to the Gitanyow, more than 80 percent of their traditional territory sits within the Nisga'a area of wildlife co-management, suggesting that the Nisga'a inflated their claim at their neighbours' expense (Hume 2000, 59). Furthermore, the Gitanyow's legal argument, documented in the book *Tribal Boundaries in the Nass Watershed* (Sterritt et al. 1998), is that Canada and British Columbia had no right to hand over control of areas that this people had traditionally used and occupied since time immemorial. According to Sterritt and colleagues (1998), the underlying objective of the Gitanyow is to defend the 80 percent of the lands that the NTC surrendered to the Crown through the Nisga'a agreement. When asked to reflect on this overlapping conflict and issues of borders, a Nisga'a research participant stated, "Traditionally, clans and tribes used to share; now the Gitksan, the Gitanyow, and the Nisga'a, we are all competing for the resources that once we all shared" (New Aiyansh, Nass Valley, July 2004). In my view, this statement reveals some of the complexities of representing Indigenous knowledge and land-use patterns in land claims processes. Representations of land-use patterns that depict territorial boundaries as rigid and unchanged since the point of contact can be easily misinterpreted because, in fact, boundaries might reflect migrations and shifts that occurred at various points after contact (Stocks 2003).

Competing claims first emerged when the Nisga'a advanced their petition in 1913, in which they claimed as theirs a portion of the Gitanyow's land. Initially, the Gitanyow community had supported the Nisga'a petition, but when its members learned of the extension of the Nisga'a's territorial claim, they withdrew their support. At the core of these competing territorial claims was a series of migrations that resulted in a large group of Gitksan, including chiefs, moving into Nisga'a villages.

Trading patterns and marriage alliances had always ensured a movement of people between the Nisga'a and the Gitksan, but the relocation pattern changed drastically in the late nineteenth century. The development of missionary settlements and schools near the Nass River – particularly in Gingolx, Greenville, and Aiyansh, where missionaries actively encouraged the creation of settlements to facilitate conversion – produced family movements, the separation of villages, and even competition among the nobility. In addition, the establishment of canneries at the mouth of the Nass River attracted a number of Gitksan who were seeking economic opportunities and ended up living in Nisga'a villages. In fact, when the Nisga'a Land Committee was founded, it included several Gitanyow chiefs, who were also fighting for their land (Patterson 1992).

The Nisga'a and the Gitanyow have had different views regarding the latter chiefs' territorial possessions. According to Sterritt and colleagues (1998, 146), the Nisga'a assumed they had "absorbed" the Gitanyow chiefs and their territories. The Gitanyow, in contrast, believed that the adopting nation could not claim the territorial possessions of the adopted. This people protested the extension of the land claims, so the Nisga'a removed the Gitanyow territory from their claims. Nonetheless, in later assertions of ownership, the Nisga'a again included the Gitanyow territory.

Sterritt and colleagues document how the Nisga'a modified their boundaries in different instances. In the Calder case, the authors note, the Nisga'a claimed an area of 4,303 square kilometres. Later in 1979, arguing that

Gitanyow descendants were living in the Nass Valley, the NTC included a map in a public document that extended Nisga'a territory 120 kilometres farther into the Gitanyow territory. In an ownership statement in 1995, Sterritt and colleagues continue, the Nisga'a further extended their territory into the Tahltan people's territory (Sterritt et al. 1998, 79). The NTC's changing representation of the Nisga'a territory may have sent a signal to the government that the Nisga'a were willing to accept a more conciliatory settlement than were the Gitanyow. The NDP government of that time built its political future on the success of the Nisga'a agreement, so this government ignored evidence showing the complexity of the occupation of the Nass Valley (Roth 2002, 153).

Contestations over borders extended to Nisga'a communities as well. The adoption of the common bowl transferred authority over the land from the *wilps* to the NTC. In the lower Nass Valley, many Gingolx *wilps'* territories were not included in the 8 percent of the lands retained by the NTC. Negotiators, based mainly in New Aiyansh, made sure most key house territories in the core settlement lands were preserved. Roth (2002, 151) notes that by adopting the common bowl philosophy, the NTC effectively moved negotiations away from the Nisga'a legal order, ignoring the history and knowledge of Gingolx house-title holders. Two Gingolx lineage heads, Frank Barton and James Robinson, legally challenged the Nisga'a agreement, citing irregularities in the internal Nisga'a referendum on the agreement (Hume 2000). However, the case was dismissed in 2005 on technical grounds. The court agreed to reopen the case after Robinson, also known as Chief Mountain, argued that his and other Nisga'a ancestral lands had been surrendered by the negotiators, who were never elected to have authority to surrender lands. According to Robinson, as a result of this political position, members of his *wilp* had been discriminated against (*Chief Mountain v. British Columbia (Attorney General)* (2011)). In contravention of Nisga'a customary law, the Nisga'a Final Agreement transferred the ancestral lands belonging to the *wilps* to the new centralized Nisga'a government.

### Strong Matriarchs, Forgotten Landowners?

This section discusses how gender becomes salient and is reproduced through land claims. Although land claims suggest that the goal is to protect the traditional way of life of Indigenous peoples and to provide them with new opportunities for economic development, Indigenous peoples are forced to accept new relationships to land and resources. These relationships are often based on Western notions of knowledge and property and have a profound impact on Indigenous peoples, particularly women (Natcher 2001; Bryan 2009).

When the Supreme Court of Canada agreed to reopen the Chief Mountain case, Nisga'a matriarch Mercy Thomas testified in court (Canadian Constitution Foundation 2007). She argued that at stake in this case were the Nisga'a's proprietorship rights, which are passed down according to their matriarchal system. In the past, Nisga'a men and women had clearly differentiated roles in their people's complex social organization and in the production cycle. Scholars have documented how coastal women controlled critical resources that secured their economic and social autonomy. Through this process, women developed an extensive knowledge of the land and of the production cycle (Fiske 1991, 510). Gender-demarcated participation in and control over the production cycle were particularly significant to the rationalization of social status, which was gained through ceremonial wealth distribution and which legitimized authority, chiefly positions, ownership, and names. The more wealth a chief was able to distribute, the more prestige and authority his *wilp* had. To accumulate wealth, chiefs not only had to exploit their resources but also had to trade them with their neighbours. In the past, each house established its own trade partnerships and alliances, which included social and political obligations to other neighbouring villages (Littlefield 1987, 180). To gain prestige, men and women had to have access to the "means of prestige and status," namely those ecological spaces and resources that enabled them to perform their duties.

With the adoption of the common bowl approach, the role of women in this governance process and the passing-down of the ownership of land and resources were erased. Although this was not the point made by Mercy Thomas, it could be argued that Western notions of property, which were originally based on concepts of patrilineal descent and lineage, altered even more profoundly the relationships to land and resources of those Indigenous communities that instead recognized matrilineal descent and lineage (Daly 2005). Thus many Indigenous women felt the effect of the translation of Indigenous understandings of land into the Western legal language of property even more profoundly than did the men in their communities.

However, the Nisga'a government discredited both Robinson and Thomas for the support they were getting from ultra-conservative think-tanks. At the time of the field research for my doctoral dissertation, some interview participants lamented these conflicts and saw them as outcomes of a pragmatic land claim. Female participants were also proud of how at least Nisga'a citizenship had recentred the matriarchal system. The Nisga'a continue to define themselves as comprising a matriarchal society, where chiefs and matriarchs share power. A male participant noted that "women are more important than men [in Nisga'a society]. All that I have, I got from my mother; the language, traditions, culture, and my Nisga'a name" (New Aiyansh, Nass Valley, July 2004). Reducing a matriarchal system to a notion of citizenship that separates the nation from its material resources, however, is problematic and perpetuates nationalist ideologies that represent women exclusively as reproducers of the nation.

Citizenship also comes from the mother's side, as enrolment in the Nisga'a nation and enjoyment of rights depend on ancestry. A person may be enrolled if she can demonstrate that her mother was Nisga'a and belonged to any of the four clans as far back as five generations. The Nisga'a's insistence on calling themselves "citizens of the Nisga'a nation" challenged the assumption of many non-Indigenous Canadians (Blackburn 2009, 70). The ensuing public debate was fuelled by perceptions that the agreement would form a "race-based" government that would grant exceptional prerogatives to members of the Nisga'a nation. Those who maintained this position accused the Nisga'a of adopting a system based on blood and the particularities of birth, which worked against democratic principles. The Nisga'a defended the connection of citizenship to ancestry as being culturally appropriate. Nisga'a women with whom I talked noted that the system of Nisga'a ancestry counters some of the injustices that have resulted from the government's regulation of the birthrights of First Nations women.

Although some scholars take this notion of Nisga'a citizenship to signify a radical change, others argue otherwise. Palmater (2011), for instance, argues that even though the eligibility provisions of the Nisga'a Final Agreement allow enrolment in the nation by the descendants of those with Nisga'a ancestry and by the descendants of mothers who were born into a clan, it is not clear how far this inclusion goes. Specifically, Palmater is concerned with whether these criteria for enrolment include all descendants from future generations or just the first generation of descendants. She makes the argument that since the Nisga'a included the 1982 Charter of Rights and Freedoms in their agreement, a possible outcome is that the distinctions made between members based on sex may be considered discriminatory under Section 28 of the Charter (Palmater 2011, 172-73). Thus, although the notion of Nisga'a citizenship based on female ancestry may rectify some past injustices, it extends neither to land rights nor to all future Nisga'a descendants.

Furthermore, when I asked research participants what role Nisga'a women have played in politics and the land claims process, a female respondent stated, "We [women] supported our husbands, brothers and our negotiators. We took care of the household, we took care of their children, we helped them look good" (New Aiyansh, Nass Valley, July 2004). The linking of specific understandings of gender to tradition relegates women to the status of reproducers of the nation, whereas men become the leaders of the nation.

Nisga'a women have not only been marginalized from the territorial claims process but also prevented from putting forward their knowledge and stories about the central role they have played in their societies. Being "Janus-faced," Nisga'a nationalism portrays the nation both as a modern, male, business-centred, equal participant in Canadian society and as a traditional, female-centred locus of the symbolic past.

In agreement with Blackburn (2007), I argue that Nisga'a citizenship juxtaposes tradition with individualistic, market-oriented entrepreneurialism. Although tradition continues to be reproduced in certain spheres, economic development is the process by which the Nisga'a nation seeks to improve its socio-economic condition and to support self-government. As noted in Chapter 1, this is the notion of Indigenous citizenship promoted by the United Nations Declaration on the Rights of Indigenous Peoples. The declaration states that "Indigenous peoples have the right to maintain and strengthen their distinct political, legal, economic, social and cultural institutions, while retaining their right to participate fully, if they so choose, in the political, economic, social and cultural life of the State" (United Nations 2007, Article 5).

From this perspective, economic development and indigeneity are not seen as being antithetical but rather as two complex yet complementary worlds. As the title of the documentary *Nisga'a Dancing in Both Worlds* suggests, walking in both worlds involves embracing specific articulations of indigeneity and self-sufficiency that stand against notions of the collective often associated with Indigenous peoples. The necessity of walking both worlds highlights the contradictory character of indigeneity articulation as it intersects with neoliberalism. As a form of governance, neoliberalism simultaneously drives Indigenous peoples to fit certain criteria for recognition and to fail to maintain such difference.

## Property, Self-Sufficiency, and Conservation

When the provincial government announced that it would start negotiating land claims and formulated its "certainty policy," the province was embedded in an economic crisis affecting the softwood lumber industry and was confronting a marked decline in natural resources. A variety of environmental nongovernment organizations protested industrial resource extraction and clashed with Indigenous peoples (Rossiter and Wood 2005). The negotiation of land claims in British Columbia was seen as necessary to satisfy corporate demands upon lands and resources and to address environmental concerns. Land claims involved the reorganization of Indigenous societies along the lines of decentralization, the reduction of the state, the affirmation of basic human rights, environmentalism, and development. Land claims are good examples of how neoliberalism brings together global discourses on difference, rights, and the environment that have important implications for Indigenous places and senses of place. As Swyngedouw and Heynen (2003, 898) have noted, these processes unfold in the sphere of power, where actors defend and create their environments in contexts of gender, ethnic, and class conflicts.

This section analyzes the opportunities and constraints created by the Nisga'a Final Agreement. I argue that neoliberalism is driven not only by governments aiming to reproduce a particular type of environment and development but also by Indigenous leaders, causing neoliberalism to materialize differently in specific places. In British Columbia, neoliberalism has involved policies granting new rights to corporate actors and policies encouraging place-based actors to achieve independence from corporate resource extraction and instead to mobilize local entrepreneurialism as a way of directly participating in the economy (Young 2008, 1). Moreover, the extension of corporate rights and the reordering of Indigenous spaces create power imbalances because the economic strategy promoted by the provincial government is the creation of a diversified, value-added forest sector made up of small-forest right holders. Specifically, value-added wood products, nontimber forest products, and environmental services are conceived of as the market opportunities for Indigenous peoples in British Columbia (Ambus et al. 2007, 89). A critical reading of the Nisga'a Final Agreement offers some important insights into how land claims as a state practice shape the spatial and social reconfiguration of landscape and community.

In May 2000 the Nisga'a Final Agreement came into effect (Department of Justice Canada 2000). The first of its most relevant provisions is that the Nisga'a lands consist of 1,930 square kilometres in fee simple, about 8 percent of what the Nisga'a claim as their traditional territory. Ownership of some of the lands includes resources such as oil, minerals, gas, and forests. Second, the Nisga'a received a harvest allocation of 13 percent of the total allowable catch of sockeye and 15 percent of pink salmon for twenty-five years. Nonsalmon species such as oolichan used by the Nisga'a for domestic purposes are considered an Aboriginal entitlement. Third, the Nisga'a own the forests on Nisga'a land. Four, the Nisga'a government can grant or withhold Nisga'a citizenship. Five, the Nisga'a can participate in most land-use decisions involving Nisga'a lands, but this participation is limited to a consultative status outside of these areas. Six, the Nisga'a government shares power with Canada and British Columbia. Seven, the Canadian Charter of Rights and Freedoms applies to the Nisga'a government and its institutions. Eight, a Nisga'a court will make and apply Nisga'a laws. Nonetheless, the rulings of this court can be appealed through the provincial appellate system. Nine, the Nisga'a government will be able to tax Nisga'a residents in order to maintain self-government.

Although historic, the signing of this treaty generated criticism on several fronts, revealing the complexity of this land claim. The debate on the BC treaty-making process has been framed by two main positions. The first is a liberal viewpoint advocating the buying of social peace by adopting the Nisga'a's agreement style, which involves some money, municipal-style powers, and limited resource rights. The second is the conservative position arguing that First Nations already enjoy too many privileges (Haythornthwaite 2000). Parties such as the commercial fishery and forestry lobbies often reject the negotiation of land claims.

Nisga'a leaders also faced criticism from other First Nations leaders who opposed the agreement and argued that the Nisga'a's "treaty style" had surrendered Indigenous sovereignty for a pragmatic self-government deal. According to this view, land title, which was central to the Nisga'a struggle, was after all undermined by this agreement. Under fee simple, Nisga'a lands have been defined by the legal system of the dominant society. Even though the agreement does not include the term "extinguishment," it provides "certainty" with respect to Nisga'a land rights and self-government obligations, reassuring both the province and private investors that the Nisga'a's rights can never be renegotiated (Rynard 2000, 223).

The Nisga'a government can be considered a "municipality plus" or a "third order of government." It is composed of the Nisga'a central government, which is responsible for intergovernmental relations and consists of executive and legislative branches, a Council of Elders, and four Nisga'a village governments. The Council of Elders, made up of chiefs, matriarchs, and respected elders, is an appointed body that provides guidance on matters related to the traditional values of this people.

The agreement stipulates that the Nisga'a will participate in Canadian social benefits and that they will contribute to the cost of these benefits on the same basis as their Canadian counterparts. As part of the agreement, Canada, British Columbia, and the Nisga'a government committed themselves to providing services and delivering programs to Nisga'a citizens at a level that is reasonably comparable to other regions of British Columbia. In this agreement, Nisga'a citizens themselves contribute to the cost of self-governing through the payment of taxes.

Because the agreement's provisions were designed to ensure the Nisga'a contribute to their own governance in an amount equal to the tax revenue raised by other governments, the Nisga'a government assumes the consequences resulting from any operating costs and inefficiencies, including translating the complex agreement into government structures and institutions. The Nisga'a agreement brings a new degree of certainty that is extremely appealing to both the provincial and federal governments, as it transfers government responsibilities to the Nisga'a themselves but maintains government control.

Under the land claims approach pursued, Indigenous rights have been effectively liberalized so that Indigenous communities can use their land as collateral to participate in the market economy. In this environment, government programs and services have also been reduced, and more responsibilities have been delegated to local governments. Mortgaging the land and selling fish and timber were conceived of as ways for the Nisga'a to enter the market, but neoliberalism has also brought other opportunities. In 2008, when the Nisga'a government was considering the introduction of private property in the four Nisga'a villages, its website made the following statement concerning fee simple lands:

> The provincial land title system is a fundamental part of real property rights in British Columbia. It provides the means for owners and purchasers of land, and holders of interests in land such as mortgages or rights-of-way, to have certainty about their interests. If an interest in land is registered in the provincial system, that interest is guaranteed by the provincial assurance fund. While the Treaty provides the Nisga'a Nation with the authority to establish a Nisga'a land registry or land title system, it may be that to achieve the full economic benefit of a particular parcel of land it will be advantageous to have title to that parcel registered in the provincial system. (Nisga'a Lisims Government 1998)

In the media the Nisga'a's move toward private property has been portrayed as revolutionary. In 2003, when this research was conducted, some Nisga'a talked of shifting to private property and argued that it would encourage local entrepreneurs. Some research participants expressed concerns that the Nisga'a had to do all of their business in Terrace, a city on the Skeena River, instead of generating local business and intercommunity trading. Some thought private property would help to fix the situation. For example, the chair of the Nisga'a government, Kevin MacKay, noted, "This is very significant for the Nisga'a as a step toward true self-government" (cited in Findlay 2010).

Inspired by the ideas of Peruvian economist Hernando de Soto, Nisga'a leaders have turned to private property in order to end poverty, an argument that resonates with other First Nations leaders. In the Nass Valley the unemployment rate is 60 percent, and the Nisga'a government is steadily reducing its capital base as a result of assuming more responsibilities. The government's net financial assets have plummeted from $263 million to roughly $154 million (Findlay 2010).

In the media less has been said about the role of the government in pushing this approach forward so that the land owned by Indigenous nations can be used to finance the delivery of the services defined under self-government agreements, to fight poverty, to address gender bias matrimonial property concerns, and to build community capacity (Conservative Party of Canada 2006). The current Conservative Aboriginal policy focuses on strategies and programs to alleviate Aboriginal poverty that are grounded in "common sense," the acceptance of everyone's responsibility, the discourse of rights, and the protection of vulnerable groups (Harper 2006).

"Common sense" foregrounds individualization. Under neoliberalism, individuals are responsible for their betterment. According to Brodie (2010, 1589-90), individualization downloads responsibilities for systemic changes, including economic crises and social challenges, to individuals and families. This approach treats all people the same and demands that they find the causes of and solutions to their own circumstances whatever they are. Moreover, this approach assumes that identifiable barriers such as discrimination and racism have been long removed. Private property is seen as a mechanism for Nisga'a individuals to pursue credit for small businesses. However, other economic projects involving natural resources have been centred instead on conservation.

In the 1990s the Canadian government initiated a process of decentralization by implementing a co-management approach that incorporates conservation and local ecological knowledge into resource management. Proponents of co-management have argued that this approach empowers Aboriginal peoples and hunters who hold this knowledge. Co-management, however, has been reduced to a series of technical problems resulting from the integration of knowledge (Nadasdy 2005, 323). In practice, this has meant that under co-management Indigenous peoples are given some voice and granted an allowable quota of resources, which must be well managed "for the benefit of present and future generations" (*Nisga'a Final Agreement: Implementation Report 2006-08* 2008, 9). Specifically, the federal Department of Fisheries and Oceans imposed the use of selected fishing gear, including fish wheels and floating and mobile fishing traps, to improve the salmon fleet's fishing ability. Indigenous rights, despite acknowledging ownership, are subject to government control.

For over a decade, the Nisga'a have steadily built a reputation of sustainability. Between 2000 and 2005 the Nisga'a salmon harvest varied but was dramatically reduced in 2006 and 2007. Although the Nisga'a are entitled to receive 13 percent of the total allowable catch of sockeye and 15 percent of pink salmon, depressed prices and lower than average returns have challenged the Nisga'a to think of other options. The number of commercial licences have declined and conservation concerns have influenced the use of fishing methods that maintain desired stock levels when fishing. These methods are focused on conserving specific salmon runs. A reduced salmon harvest earned the Nisga'a top marks from the Sierra Club of Canada in 2006 for their management practices (*Nisga'a Final Agreement Implementation Report: 2006-08* 2008).

With regard to forestry, even though the Nisga'a's annual allowable cut is 135,000 cubic metres, they face additional challenges resulting from the high cost of transportation and limited infrastructure. Importantly, the Nisga'a's ability to export timber harvested from their lands over the past years has been limited by the provisions of the agreement, which states that the Nisga'a cannot build any lumber facilities on their land until the end of a ten-year transition period. After this period, the Nisga'a may apply for a permit to export lumber, and this permit will be regulated by the province's laws and policies (Department of Justice Canada 2000, Chapter 5).

This situation means that the amount of logging taking place on the Nisga'a's lands is below the allowable quota because their participation in the market economy is limited in comparison to that of non-Indigenous peoples. The Nisga'a also have harvest rights to nontimber products, including pine mushrooms – a delicacy in Asia – and medicinal herbs, which have

been an important element in the livelihoods of this people. The commodification of pine mushrooms has displaced the value of Nisga'a livelihoods in
favour of exchange value.

Neoliberal conservation extends to forests and tree planting. The Nisga'a
government amended the Nisga'a Forest Act to enable ecosystem restoration and carbon-sequestration projects on Nisga'a lands (Bull 2010). The
legislation grants the Nisga'a government authority to enter contracts
where the Nisga'a nation grants an ecosystem-restoration contractor the
exclusive right to deal with carbon credits generated from planting trees.
According to a Nisga'a government press release, "The purpose of the new
legislation is twofold. First, and foremost, it will encourage the restoration
of the areas of Nisga'a Lands that were devastated by logging that took place
in the 1960s and 1970s. Second, it will enable economic benefits to be derived from the carbon that will be stored in the trees that will be planted in
those restored areas, by taking advantage of emerging forest carbon sequestration markets" (Bull 2010).

The emergence of carbon markets creates opportunities that align with
"traditional lifestyles" and resource-management practices. As a commodity, it is claimed that carbon credits benefit both the economy and the environment. In this approach, economic opportunities open for Indigenous
peoples involve receiving payment for providing ecosystem services such
as carbon sequestration, biodiversity and watershed protection, and landscape beauty. These services can be bought by corporations, donors, governments, and tourists, and the premise is that the natural environment
can be better protected by valuing and managing environmental services as
commodities. The Nisga'a will "produce" carbon credits through the trees
planted on their lands.

The commodification of environmental services resonates with neoliberalism, which contends that the market allocates scarce resources more
efficiently (Wunder 2005). Moreover, although environmental services are
increasingly valued in the global economy, the exchange value of environmental projects is undermined by a dominant state logic, which continues
to privilege the extraction of conventional natural resources such as minerals, oil, and gas (Baldwin 2009, 239). This means that the historically contingent, unequal distribution of economic power and property rights in the
market is reinstated.

The Nisga'a articulation of indigeneity draws on notions of entrepreneurialism, the self, and the environment. This articulation allows the Nisga'a to
ground themselves in environmentalism and to increase the flow of capital

into their communities. Although apparently contradictory, these articulations facilitate different capital circulation and commodification of nature.
As in the case of the Inuit, engagement with the economy is seen by many
Nisga'a as empowering and allowing the individual to satisfy needs and
aspirations. As in the case of the Inuit, the signing of an agreement does not
mean the federal government will fulfil its obligations. The twenty modern
agreements that the Government of Canada has signed have not been fully
implemented. Although the government's Comprehensive Land Claims
Policy of 1986 states that land claims agreements are more than just "real
estate transactions" (quoted in Land Claims Agreements Coalition 2008),
the government has tended to block their implementation by finding ongoing disagreements about the specific meanings of land claims.

The Land Claims Agreements Coalition (LCAC), which includes James
Bay and northern Quebec (1975), Nunavut (1993), the Nisga'a nation (2000),
and the Labrador Inuit (2005), among others (Land Claims Agreements
Coalition 2011), has challenged the Government of Canada to develop a new
national policy that mandates implementation of the land claims agreements. Although each agreement is unique, all modern agreements include
promises of employment, education, cultural protection, training, and
opportunities for socio-economic development. The LCAC (2008) claims
that the government has failed universally to fully implement the intent and
the broad socio-economic objectives of all modern agreements. Similarly, the
Standing Senate Committee on Aboriginal Peoples of the Parliament of
Canada (2008, vii) has reported that by not providing the necessary funds
promised to promote political, social, economic, and cultural development,
the federal government has been responsible for "the diminishment of the
benefits and rights promised to Aboriginal peoples under these agreements."
The government has refused to design a national policy on land claims implementation, leading to major lawsuits against the Government of Canada.

Modern agreements have been used as a means to ensure that Indigenous
peoples maintain the state's political and economic project. The government's unwillingness to fulfil its promises and obligations perpetuates a relation of domination in which the settler continues to neutralize, undermine,
subsume, and co-opt Indigenous "Others." Both the Nisga'a and the Inuit
have struggled to preserve some Indigenous rights and powers within the
capitalist system.

By "walking in two worlds," the Nisga'a aim to take control of their
lives and to participate in the economy. By engaging with – and, at times,
resisting – colonialism and the economy, the Nisga'a have forged alliances

and relationships based on their political agenda and changing context. As subjects that engage with neoliberalism, the Nisga'a have made important compromises. Without the fulfilment of land claims agreements, Indigenous peoples have little room to truly strengthen their participation in the market economy even when they choose to do so.

## Conclusion

According to Lakota philosopher Vine Deloria Jr. (1992), the difference between Indigenous and Western ontologies is the importance of land to modes of being, thought, and ethics. Land is place, a way of being in and relating to the world. At the same time, place is not a given but a contested terrain that shapes people's experiences and everyday practices. Intelligible understandings of indigeneity reduce place to cultural practices that have the effect of undermining Indigenous peoples' diverse experiences and relationships. The contested issues surrounding the Nisga'a agreement call attention to the implications of the test of indigeneity, particularly the notion of rights and property as frameworks for organizing Indigenous human and nonhuman relations.

This chapter has shown that labour and indigeneity constitute two axes of articulation through which the Nisga'a have attempted to survive as a distinctive people. Contrary to those arguments noting that Indigenous peoples' economic dependency is due to their lack of participation in capitalism, this chapter has shown that Nisga'a participation in the wage economy is not new and has been crucial to their survival as a culturally distinct people. Through the Final Agreement, the Nisga'a are engaging with neoliberalism and, in doing so, have articulated a vision of indigeneity that is both entrepreneurial and conservationist. I argued earlier that articulations of indigeneity are diverse and dynamic rather than homogeneous. Certain articulations may indicate a gradual and inevitable assimilation into the settler society, whereas others may be more socially transformative. The intersection of the rights framework with development, knowledge, and colonialism has so far limited the Nisga'a's ability to exercise self-government and to benefit from economic development on their lands.

# 5

## The Zapatista Movement

Place-Driven Recognition?

> The universal need for a more just and inclusive world, in
> opposition to the commodified and exclusionary world
> of neoliberalism, is the great event of our century; it
> opens the possibility of joining together local, national,
> sectoral and class struggles, in one single struggle for the
> formation of a Planetary Community, the self-realization of
> civil society and the construction of a world "where many
> worlds fit." (EZLN, quoted in Stahler-Sholk 2000, 7)

For over a decade, the Zapatista movement in Chiapas, Mexico, has captured people's political imagination. To many, the Zapatistas are an example
of Indigenous resistance to neoliberalism and of the creative use of the por-
ousness of a globalized world. When the Zapatistas first launched an armed
uprising on 1 January 1994, the date that the North American Free Trade
Agreement (NAFTA) went into effect, they appeared to be another guerrilla
group. However, compared to previous social and guerrilla movements, the
Zapatista movement defies easy classification since it links Indigenous
rights to calls for an insurrection by civil society, the democratization of
Mexico, and a global struggle against neoliberalism.

The extensive literature on the Zapatista movement has offered explanations for the dilemmas this movement has faced and for the changing

strategies it has followed. This chapter explores how the Zapatistas' construction of place and articulation of indigeneity in response to the larger, abstract phenomena of neoliberalism and environmentalism have made certain political visions (im)possible. Two questions guide this chapter. First, how can a de facto model of autonomy challenge neoliberalism and alter existing colonial, social, economic, environmental, and gender hierarchies? Second, how might a place-based model of autonomy provide alternative ways of conceptualizing gender, indigeneity, rights, and responsibilities? I argue that indigeneity, the rights discourse, and environmentalism have comprised a critical platform for neoliberal interventions in Chiapas. The commensurability of indigeneity with hegemonic understandings of rights, environmentalism, and neoliberalism is essential to the effectiveness of being recognized as Indigenous.

In asserting that the world they want is one "where many worlds fit," the Zapatistas have articulated a meaning of indigeneity and cultural difference that is outside of this neoliberal grid. Rather than adopting the "neoliberal multiculturalism" offered by the Mexican state, the Zapatistas have sought to formulate a model of indigeneity that is not state-driven, that selectively engages with the rights discourse, and that is aimed at controlling place. In this process, different communities of Mayan descent are articulating indigeneity in opposition to "authentic Indians," women's demands, Mestizo society, and civil society.

First, I discuss colonialism in Chiapas and argue that to understand the Zapatistas' uprising and their articulation of indigeneity, it is useful to think of Chiapas as a frontier. Second, I explore how environmentalism has been a crucial site of neoliberal intervention in Chiapas and has been implicated in the distinction between "authentic" and "inauthentic Indians." Third, I discuss how Zapatista women have shaped and been shaped by the Zapatistas' articulation of indigeneity. Fourth, I analyze how the Zapatistas have moved away from static and state-centred definitions of power, governance, and indigeneity.

## Land and Labour in Colonial Chiapas

Chapter 1 distinguished between settler colonialism and extractive colonialism. I noted that settler colonialism is driven by land and that extractive colonialism is driven by labour and a determination to exploit and sustain the *permanent* subordination of the colonized. As a form of discipline and a set of practices, labour involves not only modes of work but also the everyday practices of people's experiences, negotiation, appropriation, suffering, and living in a given labour regime. Although colonizers used labour to extract wealth, Indigenous peoples maintained some degree of social agency to exercise circumscribed autonomy, resist, and reconstruct their identities. Although land and labour are at the core of the analytical distinction between the two different modes of colonial governance, the specific modalities of either type of colonialism vary across time and space and can involve both land and labour at particular times.

The term "frontier," which has often been associated with settler colonialism, refers to a geo-political space that is at the margins of colonial administration and characterized by violence, cultural encounters, racial diversity, resistance, and negotiation (Adelman and Aron 1999; Evans 2009). The term "frontier" has also been used to define Chiapas, its colonial structural configuration, its mountainous terrain and unknown forests, and its distance from centres of colonial administration. During the colonial period, Chiapas fell under the authority of the Audiencia de los Confines (Tribunal of the Frontiers), the colonial court that dealt with the most remote territories. This section of the chapter analyzes how the colonial frontier is implicated in the perpetuation of injustice in Chiapas. I suggest that it is crucial that we explore the frontier as a "legal space of violence" (Evans 2009).

Chiapas is home to the Mayan people, one of the most well known of the Indigenous civilizations that inhabited a larger region encompassing modern southern Mexico, Guatemala, Belize, Honduras, and El Salvador. Although the Mayan civilization reached its splendour during the classic period (AD 300-900), archaeological and ethnohistorical research has shown that descendants of the Mayan civilization constituted scattered stratified communities, whose identity centred on the community rather than on larger political entities. These communities formed alliances with each other and participated in a complex economic system based on the trading of valuable goods, including cacao beans, a highly valuable commodity among noble Mayas (McKillop 2006). Trade networks between Mayan city-states were the primary mechanism for economic growth and prosperity.

The Spanish colonization of Chiapas exploited these networks and reorganized Indigenous communities through notoriously violent techniques and the dissemination of diseases that decimated the Indigenous population. Communities were organized into small *cabildos* (municipalities) with the purpose of making labour accessible for the *encomienda* system. Communities had to render cacao beans and labour to Spanish *encomenderos* and to work for their social reproduction. When communities could not pay their tribute, the Spaniards punished Indigenous males. The *encomienda* gradually evolved into the *repartimiento* system of forced labour and consumption and was adapted to the local circumstances.

Lacking precious metals and valued coasts and being far from centralized colonial surveillance, Chiapas developed a colonial economy that was heavily dependent upon agriculture and the production of valuable commodities such as cacao and cochineal for the European markets. Taking advantage of Indigenous trading networks, the colonizers slowly developed an extensive economic system of forced consumption to create an artificial local market. The *repartimiento* system saddled Indigenous labourers with permanent debt by forcing them to sell their harvests of beans, corn, and other produce at a deflated price so that they could buy cochineal or cacao from growers elsewhere. Once they had transported these commodities, Spanish officials forced them to accept whatever price was offered and then to buy back at much higher prices the produce they had initially sold to get cash (Larson and Wasserstrom 1983, 63).

Mayan communities often revolted against what they considered the limits of acceptable exploitation and Spanish interference in their community affairs. Although communities constantly petitioned for relief in times of scarcity and famine, Spanish officials continued with the model of "forced consumption," pushing the Maya to increase their debt (Larson and Wasserstrom 1983, 63). Indigenous uprisings in Chiapas were notable not only because of the number but also because of the brutality with which they were suppressed. The Tzetzal revolt of 1712 in Cancuc was the longest and bloodiest uprising. It was grounded in an alternative Indigenous interpretation of the Gospels and for decades challenged the continuity of the colonial project. Although these rebellions were often portrayed as incidents in a "caste war" against the Spanish and Creole population, they were attempts at reinstating a lost social order and defending Indigenous lands and resources (Rus 1983).

Rather than correcting the abuses, royal authorities increased tribute collection. In an effort to improve commercial production, central Chiapas was divided into two separate jurisdictions to increase both forced sales and public whippings. As the Indigenous population decreased, so did consumption and the labour force. To face the economic crisis, the Spaniards started to produce cattle and sugar on Indigenous lands. Religious orders were particularly successful with these activities, having access to cash from donors and Indigenous *cofradías* (brotherhoods). Soon religious orders accumulated enough wealth and land to be in a position to lend money to *hacendados* (large landholders) interested in starting cattle and agricultural enterprises. The religious orders became corporations that took more and more land from Indigenous communities, reorganizing the commercial networks and exploiting Indigenous labour (Larson and Wasserstrom 1983, 66). By the end of the eighteenth century, a number of Spanish and Creole ranchers had made their way to Chiapas, putting more pressure on Indigenous lands, which were defined as "waste lands," and resistance to forced labour was framed as sinful (Sluyter 2002). Unlike the Nisga'a, the Maya were dispossessed of both their means of production and the means to commodify their labour.

In 1824 Chiapas decided to join independent Mexico. The post-independence liberal regime accelerated commercial growth and increased the fragmentation and sale of Indigenous communal lands, contributing to the formation of impoverished, rebellious, landless communities. Wealthy Ladinos and foreign families succeeded in accumulating large chunks of land and developing coffee *fincas* (estates), which became the "postcolonial" version of the *repartimiento*. The *finca* froze colonial servitude, social relations, racialized hierarchies, and attitudes in time. As Washbrook (2007, 800) has suggested, this economic model of debt bondage inherited from colonial Chiapas was a means to discipline labour through a double dispossession. Thus debt bondage was not about opening up a free labour market but about closing it.

Indigenous peoples who signed up for peonage were forced to shop at the *finca*'s commercial establishment, buying overpriced goods and accumulating large debts that prevented them from leaving the estate. Through these commercial establishments, estate owners exerted control over other aspects of Indigenous social life, including the moral economy of reciprocity and the status, prestige, and authority associated with the distribution of goods and gift giving. By controlling key products associated with Indigenous religious rituals and celebrations such as bread, alcohol, and candles, *finqueros* also controlled which individuals were allowed to fulfil their obligations within the community.

Although more research is needed to understand the magnitude of social and political transformations in Indigenous societies, it has been shown that debt bondage reshaped communal work practices and migration patterns and introduced a new gendered division of labour, shifting communal affairs toward a more male-dominated model. As out-migrations from Indigenous communities lengthened, women and children started to accompany men to *fincas*. In some cases, Mayan women, particularly *molenderas* (corn grinders and tortilla makers), found ways of making some earnings and empowering themselves within the system of domination (Carey 2006). In most cases, however, female domestic dependency increased since men controlled the movement of women and their access to the wage economy (Nash 1993; Komisaruk 2009).

When agricultural Indigenous lands were privatized, Indigenous forests such as the Lacandon Forest became integrated into an international market for hardwood. The late 1890s witnessed a boom economy in which European, American, and Mexican investors established logging camps and plantations in the tropical regions of Chiapas to extract precious hardwood such as mahogany and cedar and to grow sugar, coffee, and cacao (Benjamin 1996, 39). This boom did not benefit Indigenous communities. Rather, Indigenous labour continued to be essential to economic development in Chiapas. As in the colonial period, Indigenous revolts were concomitant with the exploitation of labour and merged with the Mexican Revolution in 1910.

Although this movement and particularly Article 27 of the Mexican Constitution of 1917 opened the space for redistributing land in the 1930s, it did not challenge large landholdings. Having to deal with land claims, the federal government declared the Lacandon Forest to be the last agricultural frontier. New communities were founded deeper inside the forest by dispossessed Indigenous peoples, including the Tzotzil and the Tzetzal, who were newly free from serfdom (Leyva and Ascencio 1996). In the early 1970s the scientific community began to notice the destruction of the forest by waves of colonization and logging and to mobilize in order to protect the Lacandon people. Represented as the original inhabitants of the Lacandon Forest, the Lacandon were depicted as the most "primitive" people in Mexico, the very essence of indigeneity.

In 1972, in response to environmentalists' criticisms, Mexican president Luis Echeverría recognized the historical land rights of the Lacandon people and tried to stop new migration waves into the forest. The size of the Lacandon territory was determined by what was considered their "traditional" way of life as "hunter-gatherers." However, some of this territory was occupied by dispossessed Indigenous peasants, who had been encouraged by the Lázaro Cárdenas government (1934-40) to settle in the forest. The federal government's decision to set aside 380,000 hectares at the core of the forest for the UNESCO-sponsored Montes Azules Biosphere Reserve and to declare all Indigenous settlements illegal contributed to the eruption of an ongoing conflict. Communities' defiance of the Montes Azules eviction notice was not well received by environmentalists, who were pressuring the government to preserve the biosphere for the sake of both the forest itself and the Lacandon people who resided there. In this context, whereas the Lacandon were represented as "noble savages" and the "last living Mayas," who existed in harmony with nature, landless Mayas who had settled in the forest became squatters. By supporting the claims of the Lacandon people over other Indigenous peoples, the Mexican government attempted to pursue its own interests and rectify past decisions.

In this regard, García de León (2002, 43) has observed that the land issue in Chiapas is intertwined with racism, the continuity of a colonial ideology, and the existence of precapitalist relations of production that have persisted because the nation-state itself has conveniently perpetuated them. Colonization forced Indigenous peoples off of their lands to become servants and sharecroppers, the current economic elite continue to maintain control over huge tracts of land, and internal refugees fight over fewer productive lands.

In the practice of statecraft in Chiapas, the Mexican state reproduced the colonial frontier, where weak political institutions and indirect surveillance worked to favour Ladino politics and interests. In the 1930s, to integrate communities, the federal government co-opted young, Indigenous professionals who understood the logic of the electoral system and the dominant party and who were willing to create state-driven political organizations. The introduction of this new logic in the Chiapas Highlands created deep conflicts between the old and new generations of leaders over what constituted "authentic Indigenous governance." Slowly, the members of a young leadership became the brokers between the Ladino elite, the Partido Revolucionario Institucional, and their communities. Traditional governance structures, grounded in Indigenous civic-religious worldviews, were subordinated to the constitutional municipality. To gain legitimacy, the new Indigenous elite adopted some Indigenous traditional practices and integrated them into the political structure of the constitutional municipality. Indigenous people who opposed the Ladino ruling class often faced repression.

The arrival of the Protestant Church in the 1950s and later the Catholic Church in the 1960s, particularly the latter's liberation theology, created further contradictions within Indigenous communities. On the one hand, the Protestant Church introduced notions of individualism and freedom that stood against Indigenous collective responsibilities. On the other, the Catholic Church's liberation theology legitimized collective practices, encouraged resistance, and fostered the development of women's spaces. In an interview, a sister associated with the Diocesan Coordination of Women explained this process:

> As members of the Catholic Church, we started to pay attention to women's conditions of life in the 1970s, but it was not until 1976 that we started to work specifically with Indigenous women. We have always emphasized women and men's equality before God's eyes and the dignity of Indigenous women. These women have grown up. This has been a very slow transformation, but nobody can stop it. (San Cristóbal de las Casas, January 2003; my translation)

This statement illustrates the consolidated position and influence of the Catholic Diocese of San Cristóbal among Indigenous communities. The diocese became a vital instrument for these communities to express their concerns in areas such as economic exploitation, human rights violations, and Indigenous culture (Flores Vera 2000, 104-5). The alliance created between independent Indigenous organizations and the church during the 1970s and 1980s was important to questioning the Partido Revolucionario Institucional's imposition of municipal authorities and to documenting human rights violations. When I asked a *miliciano* (militiaman) why he had joined the Zapatistas, he explained,

> It was fear. Can you imagine what it is like to live in constant fear and unprotected by your own government? We could not do anything, we could not speak up, we could not complain. If we did, we were forced to leave and abandon our houses and lands. I joined the organization [the EZLN] when I was young and my son was little. We used to knock door by door and ask people to join us. We used to say, "Look at how you live, look at your house, your food. Not everybody lives like that. Have you seen the houses in Jovel [San Cristóbal de las Casas]? This is what the government does to us." People used to say, "Yes, that is true." (San Andrés Larraínzar, January 2003; my translation)

Land dispossession, a highly repressive state, and the actions of paramilitary groups motivated others to join the Ejército Zapatista de Liberación Nacional (EZLN) (Zapatista Army of National Liberation), extending its presence to the Lacandon Forest, the coast, and the Chiapas Highlands. By the mid-1980s, nongovernmental organizations (NGOs) had started to reach rural areas, where they supported economic consciousness-raising projects, and liberation theology continued to support Indigenous communities. All of these different political actors accompanied and documented human rights violations against Indigenous communities and provided technical assistance to Indigenous organizations. While improving governance and promoting new configurations of power beyond the Mexican state, the increased presence of these international organizations facilitated the dissemination of the rights discourse. However, as several scholars have shown, Indigenous peoples and communities did not passively accept this discourse. Rather, through local knowledge and experience, Indigenous peoples reconstituted the notion of rights (Speed 2008; Merry 2006a).

When the government of Carlos Salinas de Gortari came to power in 1988, neoliberal governance reconfigured relations between the state, market, and civil society and specifically targeted Indigenous lands. The new Indigenous policy, which was aimed at remaking cultural difference and liberalizing Indigenous peoples' control over their land, had an enormous impact in Chiapas, where colonialism had dispossessed many Indigenous communities and where only 47 percent of the surface area had been redistributed to Mayan communities in the form of *ejidos* (land plots) by the government. From dispossessed communities' perspectives, the agrarian counter-reforms of 1992 constituted a landmark because they cancelled the promise of land distribution. From the World Bank's perspective, it was lamentable that Indigenous youth in Chiapas, who constituted 55 percent of the population, had the aspiration to reproduce themselves as "peasants," leading to strong pressure for land and to political explosiveness (World Bank 1994).

This was the context of the Zapatista uprising on 1 January 1994. As the armed conflict developed and as the violence of military and paramilitary groups increased, Montes Azules became a refuge for Indigenous people from the Chiapas Highlands looking to escape violence. Massive national and international protests forced the government to negotiate with the EZLN. For almost two years, government and Zapatista representatives participated in the National Dialogue on Indigenous Rights and Culture, concluding with the San Andrés Accords on Indigenous Rights and Culture, signed in February 1996. These accords were later translated into a bill by the Comisión de Concordia y Pacificación (COCOPA) (Commission for Agreement and Peace). In November 1996 the COCOPA presented its bill to the Zapatistas and to the federal government. Despite strong support for the Zapatistas and the legitimacy that Indigenous claims enjoyed in some sectors of the Mexican population, the COCOPA bill was not passed.

Instead, the government pushed for the approval of a very different Indigenous law, which completely changed the spirit of the San Andrés Accords. Like previous neoliberal reforms, the spurious Indigenous law passed in 2001 draws on the distinction between cultural rights and political-economic empowerment. Although this law concedes limited self-government based on the recognition of Indigenous "*customary* law," territorial rights are not included as part of the "cultural rights" package granted to Indigenous peoples.

**Neoliberalism, Conservation, and the "Noble Savage"**

Neoliberalism has manifested not only in deregulation but also in re-regulation. The creation of new commodities and the production of difference occur through new governance techniques and strategies. Environmental conservation, which was traditionally conceived as a bulwark against the voracity of capitalism, is now implicated in the reproduction of capitalism (Igoe and Brockington 2007, 433). Scholars have documented how the Latin American region has been reconfigured through the logic of green capitalism (McAfee 1999; Sullivan 2008-09; Valdivia 2005; Kilbane Gockel and Gray 2011). Although the commodification of ecosystems started in the 1970s, it was not until the 1980s that a model of "debt-for-nature" involving NGOs, debt-holding governments, and international financial institutions started to be implemented in the global South. The purpose of this model was to swap a portion of a given country's national debt for the conservation of "natural" tracts of land, thereby forcing "inept," "inefficient" states to set aside natural protected areas. Since then, state-sponsored protected areas have proliferated, as have the market-driven conservation ventures of transnational environmental NGOs. Adding to this literature, this section discusses whether specific understandings of indigeneity have merged with neoliberalism and conservation in Chiapas. I argue that environmentalism has been a critical framework for the articulation of essentialized indigeneity in Chiapas and for the distinction between "authentic" and "inauthentic Indians." This distinction functions to disqualify the claims of dispossessed Indigenous communities.

In Mexico, NAFTA has been the most obvious expression of neoliberalism. At the time this agreement was being negotiated, Conservation International (CI) bought the right to establish a genetic research station at the heart of the Montes Azules Biosphere Reserve through a debt-for-nature swap. Both the Mexican government and CI launched a campaign against some Indigenous communities, which were accused of destroying the Lacandon Forest, and emphasized the need to protect the reserve and create ecologically friendly business ventures for some of its Indigenous inhabitants (Tokar 2005). Through environmental ideologies, CI represented the Lacandon people as the last "primitive" people living in harmony with nature. Propagated by the government, anthropologists, and tourists alike, these representations of the Lacandon provided justification for pursuing CI's conservation efforts and for relocating other Indigenous communities, which were constructed in opposition to the "authentic Indian."

The distinction between "authentic Indians" (Lacandons) and "inauthentic" dispossessed Mayan communities grounded indigeneity in an ahistorical understanding of land and colonialism, providing a tool for defining who deserved protection and rights and who did not. At the heart of this distinction was a struggle over new natural commodities (Harvey 2001). This understanding has some important implications. First, "real Indians" not only maintain a close connection to the land but also "care" about it; they do not work the land. This distinction has been used to disqualify landless Indigenous peoples' claims. Second, because nature is the object of neoliberal environmental governance, Indigenous peoples' relation to land is constituted in terms of their vulnerability to both state-led development and "destructive peasants." In the context of Chiapas, indigeneity claims subject Indigenous peoples to a double bind: for people to claim land, they must be Indigenous, yet to be recognized as Indigenous, they must live in nature according to the imagery of the idealized "Indian," which is far from most Indigenous experiences in the region of Middle America.

Despite criticism of CI's conservation efforts, in 1996, after the Zapatista uprising and the eruption of the economic crisis that severely affected Mexico, this approach was formalized. The Mesoamerican Biological Corridor (MBC) emerged as an example of transnational co-operation on security, trade, and environmental protection that promised to transform Central America, a region torn by war and poverty. The MBC is a comprehensive effort by participating countries to connect the natural habitats of Mexico, Central America, and Colombia (World Bank 2011).

Whether donors and international financial institutions are interested in carbon trade, bioprospecting, environmental services, or hydroelectric power, the livelihoods of Indigenous and rural communities are being reoriented to assist with green capitalism (Finley-Brook 2007, 109). Because the world has changed, the threats to the MBC highlight narco-terrorism, terrorism, Islamic radicalism, natural disasters, and mass migration, all of which require a new approach that openly justifies the institutionalization of violence. From this point of view, it can be argued that framing certain spaces as "frontiers" creates a blank slate on which governments, environmentalists, academics, and financial institutions all shape a space's image and social relations (Haenn 2002, 1).

In Chiapas, government institutions such as the Ministry of Tourism, the Ministry of Communications and Transport, the Ministry of National Defence, and the World Bank have co-ordinated actions that seek to redraw community borders, build infrastructure, certify *ejidos* and communal lands, promote agricultural programs, and increase accountability. The strategy of remapping space is closely related to the restructuring of Indigenous peoples' local economy and to the concentration of dispersed communities in order to create regional markets and ecotourism (World Bank 2003, 25).

Whereas Indigenous communities located on the MBC's borders are targeted because of the knowledge their members possess of their habitats and because they are considered the "strongest allies in the conservation process" (World Bank 2000, 12), peasant Indigenous communities are either excluded or constructed "as ignorant and environmentally destructive fire setters" (Mathews 2009, 76). Thus spatial reorganization "according to communities' levels of social organization" (World Bank 2000, 12) has continued to distinguish between authentic Indigenous and inauthentic peasant Indigenous communities and to isolate Zapatista sympathizers. Moreover, this distinction has been legalized. When Article 27 was reformed, peasants' lands were liberalized. In contrast, communal forested lands were re-regulated. Indigenous forest dwellers can keep communal ownership only if they are ruled by Indigenous legal systems (Haenn 2006; Agrawal 2007). Failure to maintain Indigenous normative systems means that the state becomes the owner of Indigenous communal lands. In practice, this means that Indigenous forest dwellers are given no room for their legal systems to evolve.

Besides land-tenure reforms, the policy implemented in Chiapas has focused on co-opting prominent Indigenous leaders and intellectuals into government agencies to derail the creation of autonomous municipalities within the Zapatista region and has emphasized providing selective financial support to communities (Otero 2004, 223). I argue that the formula involving environmentalism, security, rights, and indigeneity is not intended to solve the inequalities that exist in Chiapas or to reverse biodiversity loss. Rather, this formula reflects the contested and violent character of neoliberal multiscalar governance and its utilitarian approach of recognizing difference as long as it is aligned with market-driven conservation.

These neoliberal interventions, the legacy of colonial dispossession, the government's rejection of the COCOPA bill, and a highly exclusive articulation of indigeneity contributed to the Zapatista movement's radicalization and the consolidation of the Zapatista *caracoles* (administrative centres). Unlike the state's neoliberal model of cultural recognition and essentialized indigeneity, the Zapatista project has pushed for an alternative articulation of indigeneity that is inclusive, place-centred, and outside of the state's power, as shown in the last section of this chapter.

**Indigenous Laws, Rights, and Gender**
As seen in the previous section, Indigenous peoples' demands for recognition of their legal orders as a key component of maintaining their collective lands have to do with changes made to Article 27 of the Mexican Constitution. Whereas conservationists and governments favour an essentialized definition of indigeneity that excludes most Indigenous peoples in Mesoamerica, many Indigenous peoples have insisted that the source of their collective identity is their legal systems. This claim, however, has been highly contentious and contradictory. So-called customary law refers to the principles and norms that are generally accepted by a particular community and supported by sanctions. The general acceptance of a rule of conduct by a specific Indigenous community is what gives this legal system its binding and enforceable character. Because of its nonwritten, fluid, and adaptive character, Indigenous law has been the target of "modernist" claims, which have reproduced the distinction between authentic and inauthentic "Indians" and between collective and individual rights.

For some, Indigenous normative systems have been so "contaminated" by non-Indigenous legal systems that they can no longer be considered "authentic." Moreover, Indigenous law also "measures" Indigenous peoples' treatment of Indigenous women. The recognition of Indigenous legal orders has been constructed as being against human rights, specifically Indigenous women's rights. Thus, when the EZLN demanded both the right of Indigenous peoples to form governments in accordance with their own normative systems and the right of Indigenous women to hold local posts of authority, inherit land, and have control over their own bodies, the movement entered a contested terrain. How have Zapatista women shaped and been shaped by indigeneity articulation?

The EZLN became the first armed movement in Latin America to advocate and prioritize women's demands within its own political agenda. Subcomandante Marcos (1994), the EZLN's spokesman, has stated that the

Zapatistas' first uprising took place not in January 1994, when the world first learned about their existence, but in March 1993: "The first uprising was led by Zapatista women; there were no casualties and the women won." He was referring to the internal revolt caused by the introduction of the Women's Revolutionary Law, which Zapatista males did not welcome.

Even though Subcomandate Marcos thought women were the winners in the first Zapatista uprising, the fact remains that women's demands were not well received either by Zapatista males or by Mestizo society. The Women's Revolutionary Law emerged in the context of a discussion of what revolutionary laws would apply within Zapatista-controlled communities. Several commissions on justice, agrarian issues, and women's demands consulted Indigenous peoples in order to make proposals. The next step was for community members to vote such proposals into law. When, in the general assembly, Susana, a Tzotzil woman, presented the Women's Revolutionary Law, the males became nervous and started to whisper to each other in surprise. When Susana finished reading the proposal, a male member of the Supreme Committee of the EZLN reacted by commenting, "The best part is my wife does not understand Spanish." Susana replied, "You have screwed yourself, because we are going to translate the whole thing into all Mayan languages" (Comité Clandestino Revolucionario Indígena 1994, my translation). This story reflects both the conflicts and possibilities of speaking of Indigenous women's rights while simultaneously being loyal to Indigenous self-determination.

The Women's Revolutionary Law asserts the right of Indigenous women to participate in the armed struggle in any way they desire and according to their capacities. This law also protects Indigenous women's right to work and receive a just salary whenever applicable, to decide the number of children they have, to participate in the community's decision-making process, to access priority healthcare, to access education, and to freely choose a partner. In addition, this law also asserts that women cannot be physically or mentally abused by their family or strangers and that sexual assault will be severely punished (Rojas 1994, 22).

What is particularly relevant about the Women's Revolutionary Law is that these rights are not stated as claims made to the nation-state but are asserted to ensure internal regulation of the Zapatista communities. At the same time, this law is an example of how the human rights discourse is incorporated into local conceptions of justice. Merry (2006b, 58) contends that "the localization of human rights reflects the vastly unequal global distribution of power and resources that channels how ideas develop in global settings and how they are picked up or rejected in local places."

When the Women's Revolutionary Law was made public in early 1994, surprise was the most common reaction, including among feminist groups. However, surprise was quickly transformed into a heated debate on Indigenous women's rights and political participation. For reasons of space, it is difficult to provide a detailed account of the many round tables, conferences, meetings, seminars, and workshops held to elaborate upon the original proposal put forward by Zapatista women. Instead, I am interested in three interrelated aspects concerning Indigenous women's agency: (1) the contested uses of the human rights discourse, (2) the political uses of the individual rights discourse versus self-determination, and (3) the idea of the Indigenous female subject as victim.

Through the creation of regional and national organizations such as the Asamblea Estatal de Mujeres (Regional Women's Assembly) and the Congreso Nacional de Mujeres Indígenas (National Congress of Indigenous Women), Indigenous women started to articulate a discourse of rights that facilitated the creation of tense alliances with Mestiza women. At the local level, the Women's Revolutionary Law also constituted a watershed for Indigenous communities since it enabled women to adopt a language of rights and to advance the concept of personal autonomy in order to question essentialized traditions. For Indigenous women, the issue was not a matter of appealing to abstract traditions as the core of Indigenous peoples' identity but of acknowledging the gendered character of some of these practices by distinguishing between "good" and "bad" traditions. According to female research participants in Chiapas, "bad" traditions are those that discriminate against women, such as arranged marriages, lack of personal autonomy, lack of access to land and property, and domestic violence. According to these participants, "good" traditions are associated with elements such as language, beliefs, principles, religious practices, Indigenous knowledge, and community work and services. Although these women recognize and accept that customary law is binding, they challenge its static representations and demand change from within.

Several studies have documented the social context in which Indigenous women's rights, political participation, and access to land have been undermined (Rojas 1994; Hernández Castillo 2001; Sierra 2004). Because of the political uses of tradition, some Indigenous women have been prevented from occupying positions of religious-civic and agrarian authority. Although some aspects of gender discrimination, including the lack of access to land, were initially included in biased state laws, "tradition" later became the basis for continuing the practice of preventing Indigenous women from accessing land. Because of Chiapas's colonial and postcolonial history, many Indigenous communities were dispossessed. Thus land is a scarce resource not only for women but for men as well. Although Indigenous women understand this reality, they do not want to be excluded. In a working document of the meeting for the creation of the Congreso Nacional Indígena (National Indigenous Congress) in Mexico City in October 1996, Indigenous women stated their understanding of political autonomy as follows:

> Our rights as women must have a place in the recognition of the San Andrés Accords and in Indigenous autonomy, which starts with the individual ... In its economic dimension, autonomy includes our right as Indigenous women to have equal access to and control over the means of production. Political autonomy also supports women's basic political rights and representation. Physical autonomy means our right to decide about our own body and to live without violence. Socio-cultural autonomy means our right to be recognized as Indigenous and as women at the same time. (my translation)

Zapatista women have used the rights discourse to advance their interests and fight gender discrimination. In a context where Indigenous legal orders are recognized as a central component of indigeneity, the federal government has used women's rights as a measurement of Indigenous peoples' "backwardness." From this perspective, the notion of the Indigenous female victim constructs the state as saviour. In this image, the state is not the source of violence. Rather, the female subject is victimized by her own culture and invites protection by the state (Nagel 1998; Newdick 2005). The depiction of women as innocent victims transforms Indigenous men into aggressors, who need to be contained by the state (Altamirano-Jiménez 2011).

As Speed (2008) has shown, human rights have entered the realm of political practice and become a primary battleground in the struggle to advance Indigenous rights and maintain state control. However, human rights law has been problematic for Indigenous women not only in relation to the state and their male counterparts but also in relation to other women. Conflicts of representation and authority have permeated Indigenous women's interactions with non-Indigenous women in Chiapas and Mexico as a whole. Mestiza feminists have often attempted to subsume Indigenous women's interests within their own agenda, increasingly isolating Indigenous women. For example, as part of its strategy of recognizing civil society's role, the EZLN convened the Convención Estatal de Mujeres Chiapanecas (Chiapas Women's Convention) in September 1994 and invited women from different political and ethnic backgrounds to participate. The objective was to build a wider women's movement and to draft a document containing the most relevant women's demands, which would be presented by the Zapatistas during the negotiations for the San Andrés Accords. Indigenous women joined their voices to denounce the conditions of their lives and the structural racism they face and to support the Women's Revolutionary Law. Although few in number, urban Mestiza women soon monopolized the meeting and prevented Indigenous women from further expressing their views and concerns (Hernández Castillo 2001, 224).

A year later, in 1995, another meeting was organized. This was the Primer Encuentro Nacional de Mujeres (First National Women's Encounter), held by the Asamblea Nacional Indígena Plural por la Autonomía (National Indigenous Plural Assembly for Autonomy). Despite all of the attempts of urban feminists to ignore Indigenous women at this meeting, the latter had a stronger presence than previously, as reflected in the final document:

> We, the Yaqui, Mixe, Nahuatl, Tojobal, and Tlapaneca women ... come from afar to speak our word in this land of Chiapas ... We have talked about the violence we experience within our communities, at the hands of our husbands, the caciques [local strongmen], and the military; of the discrimination we are subjected to both as women and as Indians ... We want an autonomy with a woman's voice, face, and consciousness, in order that we can reconstruct the forgotten female half of our community. (cited in Gutiérrez and Palomo 1999, 67)

Indigenous women's demand for inclusion has relied on the notion of personal autonomy, which is essential to women's dignity, physical mobility, and work. Without these interrelated elements, a transformative political autonomy cannot be achieved. However, the lack of understanding between Mestiza feminists and Indigenous women was evident at this and other forums, with the debate on Indigenous women's rights revealing two polarized positions among feminists (Domínguez Reyes 2004, 215-16). The first position came from the so-called "hegemonic feminists," who questioned the Zapatista movement's political tactics and strategies, including the use of violence, which they saw as male-driven. Hegemonic feminists emphasized women's individual rights, legalization of abortion, sexual preferences, and free and voluntary maternity. These feminists also questioned the nature of Indigenous women's demands. Were these pragmatic demands part of a rhetorical strategy initiated by the Zapatista leaders? Were they oriented toward solving needs instead of empowering women? Did they justify women's participation in a patriarchal war? These were some of the questions hegemonic feminists raised. From their perspective, Indigenous collective rights undermine women's individual rights in the name of preserving the collectivity. In denying Indigenous women's agency and ability to think for themselves, hegemonic feminists revealed their own racist attitudes.

The second position came from the so-called "fieldwork feminists," who had worked within Indigenous communities and claimed to have a better understanding of Indigenous women's identities. Fieldwork feminists basically supported the Zapatista movement and argued that it was the first revolutionary project to consider Indigenous women's demands. Nevertheless, this group of feminists considered Indigenous women's demands to be limited in scope. This group claimed its duty was to contribute to the creation of an Indigenous feminist platform. Although sympathetic, fieldwork feminists also assumed the attitude that "they knew better" what was best for Indigenous women.

In the middle of this cacophony, Indigenous women asserted their right to advance their own political agenda based on their Indigenous and gender identities. In responding to hegemonic feminists' opposition to the recognition of Indigenous legal systems on the grounds that they worsen gender discrimination, Indigenous women pointed out that gender discrimination is not exclusive to Indigenous communities but exists within all of Mexican society. Moreover, gender does not exist in isolation but intersects with race, colonialism, and class, producing the specific forms of domination that Indigenous women face.

When Zapatista women make claims for women's liberation, they seek to transform gender relations but not all of their cultural norms and practices. In my view, this distinction signals their acceptance of the binding nature of their legal order and also a dynamic understanding of how this legal system can be negotiated and adapted to include women's aspirations. Against essentialist discussions of authenticity, Indigenous women have argued that the so-called Indigenous customary laws are not written in stone but evolve to adapt to the environment. Clearly, Indigenous women's perspectives differ from those of Mestiza feminists, who tend to approach gender equality only in terms of individual rights. Indigenous women do not necessarily understand equality in the way Mestiza feminists do. Female research participants in Chiapas emphasized that they are not against gender difference. Rather, they are looking at revaluing difference and the activities women perform, including nurturing, economic subsistence activities, household activities, and their contributions to the moral economy of reciprocity.

Indigenous women's rights and aspirations have been difficult to defend. Indigenous women have expressed their frustration with an Indigenous movement that does not acknowledge its sexism and continues to use a politics of tradition to justify gender discrimination; with hegemonic feminism, which does not understand Indigenous women's complex identity; and with the government and other sectors of the Mexican society, which have used the argument of gender discrimination to entirely reject Indigenous autonomy.

Despite the Zapatistas' efforts to develop a wider movement in Mexico, neocolonial relations and racial and class cleavages continue to limit such attempts. According to Belausteguigoitia (2001, 234), after the Zapatista uprising, Indigenous peoples, particularly women, were considered to be premodern subjects still located in the realm of tradition but entering the national political arena, which was defined in terms of a discourse and language of modernity. One of the clearest expressions of this phenomenon has been a slogan commonly used by civil society, "We all are Marcos," in reference to the Mestizo spokesman for the EZLN. This situation implies that to successfully enter the national political arena and to be accepted by civil society, Indigenous peoples, particularly women, have to fit representations of victimhood and of the crying, helpless "Indian." Zapatista women demand, instead, to be recognized as agents of their own political transformation, a demand that Mestizo society is not yet ready to accept.

Indigenous women's adoption of the concept of personal autonomy to address their individual rights has provoked internal challenges as well. In a context of conflicts and low-intensity war, the presence of the military and paramilitaries near Indigenous communities has often prevented women from exercising any real personal autonomy. Moreover, the fear of internal divisions among the Zapatistas and the need to represent a united front have, to some extent, limited the scope of Indigenous women's activism. The impact of the Zapatista movement, particularly the Women's Revolutionary Law, has been uneven among most Indigenous women. Although a discourse of women's rights and autonomy has been adopted and although the Zapatistas insist that the future is only possible with women's participation in the process of constructing a better world (Subcomandante Marcos, cited in Rovira 2007, 133), gender discrimination continues to be used for contradictory purposes. For instance, the spaces for women's participation, including the creation of textile co-operatives and community gardens, have been targeted for keeping women's participation somehow separate from the overall movement. At the same time, to many Indigenous women, these spaces are about networks and sharing experiences among themselves.

In 2001 when the Zapatistas had the historical opportunity to address Mexico's National Congress, many people were expecting Subcomandante Marcos to speak. However, an Indigenous female addressed Congress:

> My name is Esther but that does not matter. I am Zapatista but that does not matter either. I am female and Indigenous, and that is what counts. I want to reply to those who are against the recognition of Indigenous autonomy, because it would legalize female discrimination and marginalization. I want to explain to you the situation in which we Indigenous women live in our communities, nowadays that respect for women is supposedly guaranteed in the constitution. We are Indigenous women, the ones who feel the pain of giving birth, who see our children die of malnutrition, of lack of healthcare and other basic services. We Indigenous women have suffered scorn and marginalization since we were born ... We suffer family violence and we cannot make decisions, we suffer discrimination because non-Indigenous people ridicule us because of our language, our skin colour, our dress and our religions. We do not have the same opportunities men do; they have the right to make decisions and to have access to land and other resources. In this sense, we are in an unequal relation. This is life and death for us in our communities. And now you are telling us the San Andrés Accords to recognize Indigenous autonomy would marginalize us; but you know the current law already does. (*La Jornada* 2001, my translation)

This statement clearly speaks of how Indigenous women see themselves. They suffer and are discriminated against, yet they are not victims but political subjects seeking to effect political change and to regain dignity. Zapatista women's politics are embedded in the material lives they are attempting to change. Indigenous women are agents producing and being produced by the politics of place.

## Indigeneity as Place-Centred

Chapter 1 argued that indigeneity has different dimensions. The concept has been used to define a variety of peoples and the terms in which their rights are recognized. Indigeneity refers to the politics and the many actors surrounding and shaping the collective social, political, cultural, and economic interests of Indigenous peoples. Indigeneity is also about different modes of being Indigenous, which is place-specific and relational. According to Alfred (2005), indigeneity is a struggle. As a site of colonialism, power, knowledge, and modes of being in the world, indigeneity requires us to ask how we can move away from static and state-centred definitions.

According to Mignolo (2007), place and resistance are not enough to displace meta-narratives of coloniality, understood as the hegemony of imperial reason. To him, it is necessary to think politically and to intervene in the organization of knowledge itself in order to control identity production. What he calls identity "in politics" involves sites of contestation and relations between hegemonic and counterhegemonic discourses and between forces and relations of domination, subjection, and resistance. Controlling identity and rebuilding human dignity are processes involving complex symbolic meanings, norms, and practices that are implicated in sources of knowledge, social networks, economic relations, physical settings, envisioned desires, and hopes. According to Mignolo (2007), the Zapatista movement has been aimed not at fitting a spectrum of social identities but at controlling identity by thinking politically and intervening in the organization of knowledge itself. Although I agree with Mignolo that the Zapatista struggle is reorganizing knowledge, this movement is not completely delinked from global narratives. Rather, it has selectively drawn on and critiqued different sources of knowledge over time.

In 1994 the Zapatistas announced their intention to reorganize in thirty-eight municipalities in response to the federal government's attempt to entrap this movement. In early 1995 these municipalities were proclaimed autonomous (EZLN 1995). In 1997, when the federal government failed to ratify the San Andrés Accords, the Zapatista further institutionalized the de facto autonomous municipalities. In 1998 both the federal and state governments tried to dismantle these municipalities by creating new ones in the Zapatista region. In taking their political project further, the Zapatistas have articulated an inclusive understanding of indigeneity.

According to Stephen (1996, 15-16), the Zapatista movement constructed a model of redefined nationalism projected from below, which permitted a conjectural coalition of diverse movements. This redefinition allowed this movement to locate itself within a mobile field of political and cultural discourse that asserts Indigenous self-determination and occupies a political space both nationally and internationally. The Zapatistas' de facto autonomous municipalities have grounded their political actions in national and local history and Indigenous laws. For example, the rebel municipalities have been equated with the free municipalities that revolutionary heroes such as Emiliano Zapata and Ricardo Flores Magón fought for during the Mexican Revolution (Monjardín and Rebolledo Millán 1999). From this perspective, the notion of the free municipality means the restoration of people's ability to control place without interference from the state.

The Zapatistas also asserted the people's right to create their own forms of government as stated in Article 39 of the Mexican Constitution. Although the rebel autonomous municipalities found legitimacy in the Constitution, the new local political and governance structures were conceived of as being firmly rooted in Mayan governance and laws. In this regard, an Indigenous leader affirmed in an interview for this book, "Here we do things differently. Indigenous customary law is not grounded in national laws. We solve our conflicts and we govern ourselves according to our traditions and customs, our own laws" (Chiapas Highlands, January 2003; my translation). Indigenous legal systems have been central to the Zapatistas as a source of indigeneity and legitimacy. In 1998, when the Zapatista municipalities entered a period of "strategic silence," they focused on rebuilding local governance and networks. In 2003, when the Zapatistas created the regional Juntas de Buen Gobierno (Councils of Good Government), they did so based on Indigenous laws. Comprising clusters of autonomous municipalities (Stahler-Sholk 2005), the *caracoles* have focused on a self-referential identity, Indigenous peoples as social subjects, horizontal networks, and a moral economy of reciprocity that replaces state assistance.

According to the Zapatistas, their Mayan ancestors highly appreciated the *caracol* (snail) because "it represented the entrance to the heart and knowledge. It also represented what came out of the heart when one walks in the world." To the Zapatistas, the Mayan "*caracol* represents the collectivity, which acts with only one heart after words have come from everybody, after everyone as a whole has reached an agreement. The snail helped our ancestors to listen to even the most distant words" (EZLN 2003, my translation). In asserting the right of the Indigenous peoples of Chiapas to exercise their political autonomy, the Zapatistas have turned the physical spaces of the *caracoles* into centres for the rearticulation of their movement and of their collective memory of resistance.

In doing so, the Zapatistas have made a critical assessment of their diversity and internal conflicts. For instance, in some communities people were divided based on who was affiliated with the EZLN. In other communities, parallel de facto autonomous and official governments coexisted, producing jurisdictional disputes that in some instances ended up in violence. Religious divisions have also been part of the equation, contributing to a long history of conflicts in Chiapas, where Catholic liberation theology, Protestantism, and more recently, Islam have aligned with local power structures. The Zapatista *caracoles* have attempted to give all of these segments of the Indigenous population a political space for reconstructing their identity and solidarity along lines that cut across religion, party politics, and governments. For example, Indigenous nonsupporters who prefer health services in their own Indigenous languages often use the service provided by the Zapatistas.

The thirty-eight Zapatista autonomous municipalities have been grouped into five *caracoles:* Caracol la Realidad, Caracol de Morelia, Caracol de la Garrucha, Caracol de Roberto Barrios, and Caracol Oventic. The *caracoles* comprise Juntas de Buen Gobierno formed by one or two delegates of each autonomous municipality of the region and have the following responsibilities: (1) contributing to the even development of the autonomous municipalities; (2) mediating conflicts among communities; (3) protecting human rights; (4) promoting and improving the autonomous municipalities' participation in outside events; (6) establishing relationships with the international and national civil society; (7) collecting a 10 percent tax on financial assistance given to a municipality and redistributing this tax among other municipalities; and (8) consolidating the Zapatista radio station, Radio Insurgente, Voz del EZLN. The autonomous municipalities' governments, on the other hand, continue to exercise power in jurisdictions such as justice, community health, education, housing, land distribution, work, trade, culture, information, and local transit and roads.

The Zapatista *caracoles* represent a way of living and working based on the communal practices that Indigenous peoples have used to resist colonialism and marginalization. Indigenous governance traditions are synthesized in the command "govern by obeying," which implies that to govern is to serve people and that power resides in the people. More important, it implies that government is not a privilege or a job but a service. The transformation of the autonomous municipalities into *caracoles* has expanded the area of regional autonomous control by creating networks of autonomous municipal governments to oversee larger regions, by building autonomous capacity, including practices, discourses, and systems outside of hegemonic powers, and by creating a "radical" commercial corridor. In this sense, autonomy has become a project rooted in both place and resistance, where the terms on which relationship-building occurs are redefined (Hollon and Lopez 2007, 52).

Building a model of autonomy separate from the state has been challenging. The *caracoles* are subsistence, peasant-type communities, in which economic "autonomy" from the state and from the global market has entailed the revival of the moral economy of reciprocity. As explained in Chapter 1, the moral logic driving the economy of reciprocity means that all that is received must be reciprocated at some point with goods or services of similar value. Everything that is given must be given back. Reciprocity does not happen without individuals exercising responsibility toward their community and the world they live in.

Although the Zapatistas insist that there is no blueprint for this journey and that as they walk, they ask questions and learn, this place-based project is not completely isolated from the global. Rather, it selectively engages with the world. Selective engagement has been envisioned as the creation of horizontal networks involving NGOs, local producers, and fair traders based on relationships of reciprocity and solidarity. Since 1994 Zapatista communities have been engaged in various self-sufficient production, exchange, and social-service projects such as collective gardens, rabbit raising, beekeeping, candle making, boot making, textile-weaving co-operatives, locally controlled schools, and clinics offering Indigenous medicine and modern healthcare. Zapatista women are in charge of various economic collectives, including communitarian vegetable gardens, bread making, and artisan co-operatives, which have been an important yet limited source of revenue for the Zapatista communities.

The financial assistance of NGOs has continued to be important to this autonomous experience; however, Indigenous practices such as community work, which requires that families contribute time and work to the community projects, have been crucial to building a sense of collective ownership and self-sufficiency. In the past, the assistance of NGOs proved to be as divisive as government aid. NGOs provided assistance to some communities while marginalizing others. Since the creation of the *caracoles*, the regional Juntas de Buen Gobierno and municipal councils have been the entities in charge of reviewing and approving NGO projects. In doing so, these entities control where and how the assistance is allocated. The ability of the Juntas de Buen Gobierno to tax 10 percent for projects implemented within the Zapatista-controlled regions means that the autonomous municipalities have a modest revenue for undertaking their own projects and for escaping from the autonomy-without-resources trap (Stahler-Sholk 2007, 57). More important, all of these practices are aimed at challenging power asymmetries of state and global relations by building alternative models of development (Earle and Simonelli 2005, 17).

Reaction to the creation of the *caracoles* in Mexico has been diverse. To some, this initiative is historical because, with the creation of this political project, the Zapatistas have institutionalized their cultural, economic, social, and political alternatives. To some NGOs, the creation of the *caracoles* has enabled the Zapatistas to control the pace and the direction of their autonomous experience and the level of civil society's participation in the political project. For many, the *caracoles* are unconstitutional and need to be dismantled. To many NGOs, intellectuals, and human rights activists, the *caracoles* are compatible with the Mexican Constitution and with international laws such as the International Labour Organization's Convention 169 (ILO 2003). To various Indigenous organizations such as the Congreso Nacional Indígena, the Zapatista *caracoles* deserve not only to be supported but also to be extended to other regions of the country. Indeed, other Indigenous projects have been created in other regions. The Mexican government's response, on the other hand, has been to rhetorically acknowledge that a variety of forms of governments may exist and to continue implementing its conservationist development with the support of the military.

Because the *caracoles* constitute a model of state disengagement and the establishment of a self-sufficient alternative based on the right of each community to define its own relations with the outside world and its own source of political legitimacy, rather than accepting state law and rights, the long-term viability of this model of state disengagement in a context of further capitalist expansion remains likely. The resiliency of the Zapatistas' resistance in the face of a massive counterinsurgency has made this movement a powerful symbol of Indigenous global resistance to neoliberalism.

## Conclusion

This chapter has explored how the Zapatistas have constructed place and articulated indigeneity in response to the larger, abstract, intersecting phenomena of colonialism, neoliberalism, and environmentalism. I have argued that indigeneity, human rights law, and environmentalism have been critical for neoliberal interventions in Chiapas. These interventions reorganize Indigenous economies according to their ecosystems and levels of social organization. In asserting that the world they want is one "where many

worlds fit," the Zapatistas have articulated a meaning of indigeneity and difference that is outside of the neoliberal grid. In doing so, the Zapatista
movement has sought to reformulate a non-state-driven model of indigeneity that selectively engages with various types of knowledge and with the
various possibilities of coexisting in difference. The Zapatista critique is informed by local understandings of place and of being Indigenous in the
world. In this process, different landless communities of Mayan descent
articulate indigeneity in relation to "authentic Indians," Mestizos, and civil
society.

In constructing an autonomous project that is outside of the rule of the
state, the Zapatistas have sought to escape economic globalization and
power asymmetries and to construct a governable space that does not draw
upon liberalism, notions of progress, development, and "universal standards"
but upon Indigenous history, memory, practices, and the moral economy
of reciprocity. In doing so, the Zapatistas have challenged the nation-state
as a legitimate source of law and of recognition of Indigenous collective
identities.

Rather than adopting neoliberal multiculturalism, which misrecognizes
Indigenous peasants, the Zapatistas have developed an alternative model of
development grounded in both Indigenous laws and principles. By questioning, redefining, and articulating their practices and philosophies,
Zapatista communities are contesting fixed constructions of indigeneity.
Unlike the geo-economic strategies of governments and international institutions for opening up spaces, Zapatista *caracoles* are about closing local
spaces and about selectively engaging with the global. Although this inward
strategy has so far been useful in addressing immediate needs without government intervention, the long-term, transformative project has yet to be
completed.

Although the Zapatista movement has opened the space for envisioning
more egalitarian relations within communities, Mayan women continue to
challenge gender discrimination in the process of constructing alternative
ways of inhabiting the world. Whereas the rights discourse has been crucial
to asserting self-determination and making women's aspirations visible, this
discourse has also been limited by the fact that it perpetuates the very situations it aims to challenge. Mayan women have used the rights discourse to
assert themselves as political subjects, knowers, and agents of change who
are seeking to transform gender relations and their material conditions of
life. At the same time, this rights rhetoric has been used to measure the
backwardness of Indigenous culture and patriarchy.

An examination of the Nunavut, Nisga'a, and Zapatista experiences demonstrates that autonomy as an expression of Indigenous peoples' self-determination has different connotations and is shaped by how colonialism developed in specific places. Whereas the Mayan Zapatistas in Chiapas have articulated a model of autonomy disengaged from the Mexican nation-state, the Inuit and the Nisga'a have negotiated their own land claims agreements with the Canadian government. The shift away from state-conditioned support for community self-sufficiency has limited the Zapatistas' ability to provide basic services such as education, health, and economic infra-structures in order to sustain the Zapatistas' well-being. Thus relying on external networks of solidarity has been a necessary means of compensating for the absence of the state. The Inuit and the Nisga'a, in contrast, exchanged their Indigenous rights for the right to govern their homelands. Although the Inuit adopted a public model of government and the Nisga'a instated an Indigenous model of citizenship, these experiences were shaped by different forms of capital circulation and understandings of the environment.

# 6

## Indigeneity, Land, and Gender in Oaxaca

There are many stories of the wind. There are old Zapotec stories that tell about the south wind being female and about the strong north wind, the Tehuano, being male. There are also newer stories to tell about the wind. It was December 2009. I was riding the bus from Mexico City to Juchitán. It was early in the morning, and as I woke up I looked through the window and saw them, a whole bunch of them forever changing the landscape. For years, people had been talking about them, about the economic opportunities they would bring, and about the conflicts, jealousy, divisions, and resistance they have caused. These were only rumours, as the wind turbines were not yet part of the landscape. Now they are there, perfectly aligned and moving with the wind. A few seats behind me, someone said, "These turbines look like gigantic white soldiers." Someone else said, "We are finally producing sustainable energy, are we?"

In 2010, at the climate change negotiations in Cancún, Mexico, leaders of the global wind-power industry issued a declaration calling on governments and decision makers to "take urgent action to avert dangerous climate change." The declaration states that "the wind industry fully embraces its responsibility to lead the way towards a sustainable energy future" and that "wind power is a key solution to combating climate change." According to the declaration, "the industry stands ready to produce more than 12% of the electricity needed globally by 2020." Moreover, it notes that wind power attracts considerable private investment and provides revenue to local landowners (Global Wind Energy Council 2010). Similarly, at the inauguration ceremony of La Venta Wind Park, Mexican president Felipe Calderón ratified his commitment to developing alternative energy in order to reduce carbon emissions. He argued that wind projects are a clear example of how the government protects the environment while promoting prosperity for rural communities (Revista Eólica y del Vehículo Eléctrico 2012). If wind power is a sustainable solution to climate change, the energy crisis, and unemployment, why are people upset and divided? Why are Zapotec peasants fighting the wind industry?

This chapter discusses the contradictions emerging from bringing together a specific definition of indigeneity, self-government, women's rights, and natural-resource management in Oaxaca state. There are several relevant questions in this context. First, how does the Oaxaca Indigenous Law reorganize Indigenous societies' interactions with their environments, and what are the implications for communal ownership? Second, how is indigeneity defined, and how are women's rights constructed? Third, how does environmental knowledge shape the uneven reorganization of Indigenous economies and livelihoods? By exploring the Oaxaca Indigenous Law and the struggle of the Zapotecs in the Tehuantepec Isthmus, I show that although applauded for recognizing existing Indigenous normative systems, the Oaxaca Indigenous Law articulates a fixed and highly exclusive understanding of indigeneity. Moreover, by linking self-government, rights, indigeneity, and "protection of the environment," this law naturalizes new governing practices that target some Indigenous communities while disavowing others. This limited recognition of indigeneity, combined with a "rational" management of resources, is integral to the neoliberal economy and has specific effects in places where social relations and gender are imbued with power.

Unlike Chiapas, more than 70 percent of Oaxaca is covered by forested and agricultural lands, 82 percent of which are communally owned by Indigenous communities (SEMARNAT 2010). As in the case of Chiapas, government policies in Oaxaca have sought to reorganize Indigenous places and local economies. Indigenous forest dwellers have been targeted because of the knowledge they possess of their habitats and because they are considered the "strongest allies in the conservation process" (World Bank 2000, 12). Indeed, Oaxaca is well known within the conservation community for being a leader in certifying Indigenous and Mestizo community forest reserves (Bray et al. 2008). In contrast, Indigenous agricultural communities have resisted the incorporation of their lands into protected government areas. What does this difference tell us? First, that under neoliberalism, landscapes are not constructed as equal. Second, that in different places the intersection of environment, economy, conservation, and cultural rights has specific effects on peoples' livelihoods. Since struggles over nature and livelihoods are connected to the politics of indigeneity, resistance cannot be understood in the Tehuantepec Isthmus without a historical analysis and without paying attention to the role that the Zapotec organization Coalición de Obreros, Campesinos y Estudiantes del Istmo (COCEI) has played in Juchitán, the first self-declared Indigenous autonomous municipality in Mexico.

First, I explore how Zapotecs negotiated, resisted, and adapted to colonialism in ways that have helped them to maintain their lands and communal ownership. Second, I use the Oaxaca Indigenous Law to analyze how neoliberalism and environmental governance are shaping the reconfiguration of Indigenous territories and livelihoods. Third, I explore the struggle of the Zapotecs and the COCEI for political autonomy and show that Zapotecs have articulated different meanings of indigeneity over time. Fourth, I demonstrate the role that two constructions of Indigenous women have played in concealing structural gender inequalities. Finally, I analyze how the restructuring of the Indigenous economy is based upon rational development, environmental concerns, and understandings of nature that have an uneven impact on different groups of people within Indigenous communities.

## Colonialism, Land, and Resistance

Based on an examination of different colonial geographies, this section considers how colonialism has been shaped by distinct social contexts. As a mode of governance, colonialism has been differentiated with regard to its formation, practices, policies, and structures. Although extractive colonialism did not target land but mainly exploited labour, it also played a historical role in the reorganization of place. Thus attention to colonial relations and how they continue to shape the present is crucial to understanding the singularities of colonialism and the ways that local landscapes have been rendered *distinctively* visible.

During the first three centuries of Spanish colonialism, the production and diffusion of colonial knowledge, practices of domination and resistance, and territorial negotiations were part of the landscape. Extractive colonialism relied on different spatialized modalities that enabled the colonial state to exploit labour and a web of Indigenous socio-natural relationships. Unlike settler colonialism, which conquered land, extractive colonialism appropriated labour and nature's gifts yet relied on Indigenous peoples' relations to place. Economic and social imperatives, the colonized's reactions, and the resources available to the colonizers shaped how colonialism was experienced in practice in different places.

Oaxaca is located in south-western Mexico, next to the states of Puebla, Chiapas, Guerrero, and Veracruz. Oaxaca is Mexico's most culturally diverse state and has the nation's largest Indigenous population. According to official data from the Consejo Nacional de Población (National Population Council) (2000), 48.8 percent of the population belong to one of the twenty-one Indigenous peoples inhabiting this state. Oaxaca has 570 municipalities, more than any other state in the country. The Tehuantepec Isthmus is the narrowest part of the land in southern Mexico between the Gulf of Mexico and the Pacific Ocean.

When the Spaniards first arrived in what today is known as Oaxaca, they did not find a singular hegemonic Indigenous city-state like that of the Mexicas (or Aztecs). Rather, different city-states competed for the control of the territory. Zapotecs settled in Monte Albán more than 2,000 years ago. This sedentary, agricultural city-state was hierarchically organized. After the collapse of Monte Albán, the Zapotec and Mixtec inhabitants of this large mountainous region were divided into hundreds of independent village-states and settled in different areas. The Zapotecs conquered and settled in the Tehuantepec Isthmus, which was inhabited by the Huave, Mixe, and Zoque peoples. In the entangled political webs of Mesoamerica, migration and power changes were rather common. Conquests could bring extensive resource rewards and personal prestige to the Indigenous ruling class (Zeitlin 2005, 3).

After gaining control of the Tehuantepec Isthmus, the Zapotecs built a new polity in the middle of centripetal forces. Facing the military expansion of the Mexicas and the integration of dominated Indigenous communities, the Zapotecs created *barrios* (neighbourhoods) organized according to people's occupations and characterized by a clearly differentiated allocation of rights and responsibilities. The new Zapotec chiefdom became an adaptable society that maintained its political independence. As enemies of the Mexicas, Zapotec rulers allied with Spanish colonizers to secure their territorial title in perpetuity (Taylor 1972; Zeitlin 2005). Because of this control over their lands, Zapotec communities and institutions had the time to adapt gradually to the impact of colonialism (Zeitlin and Thomas 1992, 286). Zapotec communities managed to control more lands than the Spaniards themselves (Romero Frizzi 1996, 137), in striking contrast to the Indigenous peoples of Chiapas. Unlike in Chiapas, land conflicts in Oaxaca during the early colonial period developed among Indigenous communities rather than between the Spaniards and Indigenous communities. Unlike Chiapas's colonial economic development, which was dominated by cattle, coerced consumption, and commercial production, Oaxaca's economic development initially focused on trading and small-scale agriculture.

By the end of the sixteenth century, the Spanish Crown had shifted the terms under which the Indigenous communities of the Tehuantepec Isthmus retained their political autonomy. The imposition of the Iberian model of *cabildos* (municipal governments) and religion brought additional challenges to Indigenous communities. As the Zapotec chiefdom was weakened, Indigenous communities used colonial courts to reclaim territorial rights that, in some cases, had never existed. In this changing environment, Zapotec rulers struggled to preserve their privileges; commoners, in contrast, saw these changes as an opportunity to relieve social, political, and economic constraints within their own societies. Indigenous participation in the colonial economy contributed to reinforcing more horizontal relations among community members (Zeitlin 2005, 166). Despite these internal conflicts, the ruling elite continued to play a role as broker within the colonial system, shielding Zapotec communities and their lands from the kinds of devastating effects that the colonial economy produced in Chiapas (Romero Frizzi 1996, 184).

In the Tehuantepec Isthmus, as in other parts of the country, the indigenization of both Catholicism and governance practices resulted in a resignification of the so-called "cargo system." Within Indigenous communities, the cargo system commonly concerns community service and reciprocity. Under the cargo system, any religious and civil work is considered a service to the community and a service that everybody must fulfil. This system of service and reciprocity was and continues to be crucial to the sustenance of the moral economy of reciprocity. As noted earlier, this economy can be considered a set of social practices and economic interactions that foster obligations and relationships and that are guided by reciprocity principles and laws.

In the mid-seventeenth century, Spanish administrators attempted to override colonial legislation aimed at protecting Indigenous lands and communities (Sluyter 2002). Although Indigenous peoples agreed to pay tribute to the Spanish colonizers, Indigenous communities had clear expectations of colonial rule regarding their territories and autonomy. Indigenous peoples were capable of putting an enormous amount of energy into work when they saw the purpose, including the payment of tribute to sustain the ruling class, artists, artisans, and others. What they did not share was the Spanish practice of accumulating goods without providing reciprocal benefits to others (McCreery 2000, 15).

Similar to what happened in Chiapas but to a lesser extent, the introduction of the *repartimiento de efecto* (forced sale of goods) brought a new economic logic of consumption. Indigenous communities were forced to produce goods and then to buy them back from Spanish officials. At the same time, communities had to participate in the cash-generating production of cochineal financed by merchants in Mexico City. Unlike in Chiapas, this system of domination was based upon advances of money, seeds, and instruments that cultivators had to repay with the agricultural product. As the entire burden was placed on Indigenous growers, including direct production, the extraction of wealth did not involve dispossession of land but rather depended upon Indigenous labour and livelihoods. During the eighteenth century, the *repartimiento de efecto* became a major source of profit for the Spaniards and of resentment among Indigenous communities (Knight 2002, 155-56).

In other regions, Indigenous agricultural communities were dispossessed on the humid north and east sides of the Tehuantepec Isthmus. Similar to the case of Chiapas, the granting of *mercedes* (ranching lands) to the Spaniards in these areas increased dramatically toward the end of the seventeenth century. In contrast, the perceived low productivity of the south and west lands of the Tehuantepec Isthmus as well as the persistence of cash crops made it possible for Zapotecs to retain their communal lands (Beals 1975). Conflicts arose over land boundaries, abusive *repartimientos,* factionalism within communities, regional trading networks, and more important, Spanish interference within the affairs of Indigenous communities.

In her study of Zapotec politics, Zeitlin (2005) shows that rebellions occurred in the Tehuantepec Isthmus mostly when Indigenous communities perceived that the Spanish justice system had been unfair to them. In a similar vein, Nader (1998, 27) contends that Indigenous peoples in Oaxaca developed a legal-political strategy she calls the "ideology of harmony," which was aimed at exercising law and resisting colonial power and, later, nation-state intervention. Injustices and abuses against Indigenous peoples provoked numerous rebellions, including the Tehuantepec rebellion in 1660, which was aimed at defending political autonomy and natural resources. The Zapotecs allied with Zoques and Huaves and for several months controlled the region. After a year, a dramatic repression was orchestrated by colonial authorities and merchants from Mexico City and Oaxaca City. In 1715 the Zapotecs rebelled again with the overwhelming participation of women, who were the most affected by the *repartimiento de efecto* since they were continuously forced to produce more goods than stipulated. Through the eighteenth century, the Zapotecs, Huaves, and Zoques also pursued legal action to recover their lands and defend their salt mines (Díaz Polanco and Burguete 1996).

Later, as the colonial space gave way to the creation of an independent country, Zapotecs continued to defend their territorial rights. Although the independence movement took place in the name of "the people," the new independent government that came to power in Oaxaca and elsewhere in Mexico was committed to building a "modern nation," which largely excluded Indigenous peoples, who comprised up to 87 percent of the population in states such as Oaxaca (Reina 1988, 45). The new political community that was envisioned rested upon liberal principles, which asserted the collective existence of only *one people* as the subject of morality-shaping interventions in the economy, the law, and social organization. In Oaxaca, for example, the Agrarian Law of 1826 removed the right of Indigenous authorities to represent their communities in court, a relatively successful strategy in the colonial period. Moreover, the Leyes de Reforma (Reform Laws) radically reorganized rural land tenure by endorsing private ownership and individualism (Berry 1981; Stephen 1996).

As part of the Leyes de Reforma, the state government opened the door for the privatization of the saltwater lagoons and the salt pans lining the seacoast of the Tehuantepec Isthmus. In response to this initiative, the Zapotecs rose up in arms not only against privatization but also against taxes imposed by the central government. Although the conflict was initially motivated by the implementation of the Leyes de Reforma, it soon escalated into a movement to secede from Oaxaca state. The conflict that started in 1842 subsided with negotiations in 1845, when the national government offered to recognize the Zapotecs' territorial rights. However, the government did not follow through with its offer because Mexico was attempting to contain the invasion of the United States and because the Tehuantepec Isthmus was considered too important to be left to the "Indians." In 1848, when Benito Juárez took office as governor of Oaxaca state, he was determined to stabilize what he saw as "chaos" in the Isthmus. He appointed a Zapotec local leader of the previous resistance, José Gregorio Meléndez (also known as Che Gorio Melendre), to lead the militia in enforcing state power. Meléndez refused to represent the state government and, instead, declared the separation of the Isthmus from Oaxaca and the creation of the Territory of Tehuantepec. For two years, the Zapotecs defied state authority and implemented self-government, reappropriated the salt pans, and continued to cultivate disputed lands. The movement was repressed when Juárez, determined to reinforce his liberal agenda of privatizing the disputed lands and the salt pans, asked the Mexican army to intervene in Juchitán (Chassen-Lopez 2004, 325-26).

As the statement below shows, when Juárez was the state governor, he demanded that the federal government suppress the creation of the new territory based on the "natural" geography of the region and on the Zapotecs' alleged incapacity to govern themselves:

> When the Isthmus territory was separated from Oaxaca, more harm than good was done to the peoples of that region which recognized Oaxaca as their centre ... The Tehuantepec Isthmus will be great one day, but today the small population, the lack of culture and people's capacity to govern themselves make it imperative for our government to take care of the people, their development and progress. By separating the Tehuantepec Isthmus from Oaxaca, the natural geographical division has been altered and the possibilities of having a central government responding to people's needs disrupted. These are the reasons to demand the suppression of this territory and to annex it to Oaxaca. (Gobierno del Estado de Oaxaca 1856, my translation)

The federal government ordered the suppression of the Territory of Tehuantepec, and the Government of Oaxaca regained control of the Tehuantepec Isthmus. Because Indigenous communities had retained most of their lands, the impact of liberal reforms in Oaxaca and the suppression of the territory was not as devastating as the impact of similar reforms in Chiapas, where many Indigenous peoples became landless (Harvey 1999, 59).

During the Mexican Revolution of 1910, Oaxaca's Indigenous communities became involved in the movement to control place as a space of social reproduction in the middle of political transformations that were reshaping local, regional, and national power. In 1911 a regional rebellion erupted once again in Juchitán to overthrow an imposed mayor, who had arrived in Juchitán with hundreds of soldiers. Resistance to central power also came from the Government of Oaxaca, which was losing power. As has been suggested, Mexican federalism was not born as a result of a foundational pact but as a result of regional discontent due to Mexico City's political obsession with centralized power (Merino 2004). The sovereignty movement did little to endear Oaxaca to the national revolutionary government. Although one of the most important objectives of the Mexican Revolution was to restitute common lands and create *ejidos* (land plots), petitions for land in this state were not always successful (Ruiz Cervantes 1988, 390). Oaxaca distanced itself from the revolutionary national government and pushed for the incorporation of the notion of the "free municipality" as a third level of government in the Mexican Constitution to reflect regional and Indigenous demands for local autonomy. As noted earlier, although the *cabildo* (municipality) was a colonial imposition, Indigenous peoples reappropriated this institution to maintain their political autonomy. This situation explains why Oaxaca, with only 5 percent of Mexico's population, has 20 percent of the country's municipalities. The creation of new municipalities and the struggle to expand their jurisdictions have historically been means to prevent external intervention.

Although struggles for local autonomy remained, the political dynamics in Oaxaca slowly changed. In the mid-1930s, under the Lázaro Cárdenas government (1934-40), the state government and the communities of the central valleys became more sympathetic to the federal government. Cárdenas succeeded in implementing his corporatist and indigenist policies focused on Indigenous bilingual education, through which national ideologies of development and integration entered the local circuits of the Zapotec communities' history (Stephen 2002, 233). Aware that territorial rights were the centre of the autonomous movement in Oaxaca, Cárdenas created a number of *ejidos* for landless communities and restored stolen communal lands to several Indigenous communities. Land distribution and restitution created a new scenario for the social reconstruction of numerous communities, whose lands had been taken away or partitioned (Velásquez Cepeda 2000, 51). Taken together, Cardenist policies were clearly aimed at undermining the sovereignist movement and integrating Indigenous peoples into the Mexican political system.

In the Tehuantepec Isthmus, the Zapotecs' promotion of their language and culture was a response to these integration efforts. Through the so-called "*rezapotequización* movement," the Zapotec elite sought to maintain economic control and political power, which were being challenged by the Mestizo elite and *dxu* (outsiders) (Cruz 1983; Miano Borruso 2002, 99). The state's corporatist scheme was not able to penetrate the Tehuantepec

Isthmus until the 1960s, when the Zapotec political elite began to garner support for the nation-state because it had finally left the Isthmus alone (Rubin 1994, 118).

Beginning in the 1960s, as agricultural programs were dismantled without offering new alternatives for peasant and Indigenous communities, pressure to sell their lands increased. To maintain their communal lands and fulfil their community obligations, Indigenous peoples inserted themselves into the wage economy and migrated to the United States, sending remittances back home. In fact, a major difference between Oaxaca and Chiapas has been the role of international migration. Whereas regional migration had been persistent in Chiapas, Oaxaca had been a pipeline to the United States since the Bracero Program was first started in the 1940s. By the 1980s many Indigenous regions' livelihood strategies combined subsistence agriculture, artisanal production, seasonal wage labour, and remittances from transnational migration.

In the 1970s the conditions of life, the lack of opportunities, and the lack of municipal autonomy experienced by rural and, particularly, Indigenous communities were among the most important elements contributing to the rearticulation of the Indigenous movement in Oaxaca. Previously focused on defending natural resources and political autonomy, the Indigenous movement gradually yet unevenly started to articulate other discourses. One of the most important Indigenous organizations formed in the 1970s was the Zapotec COCEI. Through the establishment of a grassroots movement, this organization succeeded in addressing diverse issues, including territorial claims, loans, wages, benefits, and broader municipal powers (Rubin 1997, 250). The Zapotecs made inroads in local electoral politics and pro-democracy movements aimed at gaining control over municipal governments and political processes. Like the Nisga'a in Canada, the Zapotecs made important alliances with leftist political parties.

In attempting to diminish the radicalization of Indigenous organizations, the Mexican government was instrumental in disseminating the human rights discourse. The federal government channelled most of its resources to Oaxaca, opening important spaces for Indigenous teachers to become brokers between the state and Indigenous communities. In this context, several organizations were created that demanded the recognition of Indigenous collective rights, of Indigenous languages as official languages, and of ancestral Indigenous customary laws (Hernández Díaz 1992, 47). This development shows that the Mexican government was already willing to recognize some cultural rights but not political autonomy. In separating cultural rights from political autonomy, the Mexican government created a division between pro-state and independent Indigenous organizations, hoping to isolate radical movements.

In the early 1980s, the government's promotion of Indigenous rights had unexpected consequences since other organizations used a more politicized version of the human rights discourse to rearticulate old claims. In this context, organizations such as the Asamblea de Productores Mixes (Assembly of Mixe Producers) and the Servicios del Pueblo Mixe (Services of the Mixe People), the Organización en Defensa de los Recursos Naturales y Desarrollo Social de la Sierra Juárez (Organization for the Defence of Natural Resources and Social Development in the Juárez Highland), and the Comité por la Defensa de los Recursos Naturales y Derechos Culturales Mixes (Committee for the Defence of the Mixe Natural Resources and Cultural Rights) fought for control of their natural resources, challenged the power of local *caciques* (strongmen), and demanded the recognition of Indigenous customary laws.

Unlike in Chiapas, some Indigenous demands were accommodated in Oaxaca. Although the demand for the recognition of Indigenous legal systems started in the 1970s, the government considered this claim only in the early 1990s in the context of the neoliberal reforms implemented in Mexico and the resulting Chiapas uprising. What explains the difference between the two states? Some scholars argue that the formation of an educated Indigenous elite and its successful inclusion in government agencies created the space for negotiations between the government and Indigenous communities (Rubin 1994; Hernández Díaz 2001). Others have pointed out that unlike in Chiapas, de facto political autonomy and control over communal lands have given Indigenous communities in Oaxaca some currency when bargaining with the nation-state (Stephen 2002). Although I think these arguments are important, it is necessary to question the type of accommodation of Indigenous demands that has been implemented and its implications for the diversity of Indigenous peoples living in Oaxaca state.

### Neoliberalism and the Oaxaca Indigenous Law

On 21 March 1994, three months after the Zapatista uprising in Chiapas, the governor of Oaxaca presented a proposal containing two important initiatives, one to recognize Indigenous traditional forms of electing authorities and customary law and the other to pass the Oaxaca Indigenous Law. These initiatives were passed in 1995 and 1998, respectively, by the local Congress. For some, the law responded to the demands of Indigenous organizations from the north and the Sierra Mazateca (Mazatec Highland)

(Gijsbers 1999, 9). For others, the law was aimed at stopping the Partido Revolucionario Institucional (PRI) from abusing the electoral system and from imposing its representatives upon Indigenous communities. Why was the local Constitution reformed at this time? What does this law recognize? What kind of recognition does it guarantee, and what kind of exclusion does it create?

A superficial account of these constitutional reforms in Oaxaca would limit this event to the Oaxaca government's efforts to maintain political stability. Additional factors also influenced these reforms. First, as shown in this chapter, Oaxaca has had a long history of Indigenous mobilizations for political autonomy. Second, the electoral reform to recognize Indigenous traditional forms of electing authorities was aimed at formalizing an already existing traditional mechanism and at stopping or at least decreasing the influence of the opposition's political parties, particularly the Partido de la Revolución Democrática (PRD), within Indigenous municipalities (Recondo 2001, 94). Third, the recognition of Indigenous legal orders not only maintained economic development but also explicitly supported conservation-driven development.

Since this law was passed, at least 412 out of 570 Indigenous municipalities have decided to be ruled by their traditional normative systems, and none has returned to the multiparty electoral process (Velásquez Cepeda 1998, 109). Most of the 412 municipalities that adopted or formalized their customary laws were small. In contrast, larger municipalities in the Tehuantepec Isthmus have maintained the partisan system. To some, the Oaxaca Indigenous Law is comprehensive in its recognition of Indigenous peoples' political and cultural rights, particularly those involving local and municipal governance. The sixty-three articles of the law deal with matters such as general provisions defining Indigenous peoples and communities, autonomy, culture and education, internal normative systems, the rights of Indigenous women, and the right of communities to determine their membership criteria according to their own customs. In other words, the law deals with self-government but is limited regarding Indigenous jurisdiction over natural resources. The law defines Indigenous autonomy as follows:

> Autonomy is the expression of the right to self-determination of Indigenous peoples. As part of Oaxaca state, they can make their own decisions, according to their worldviews, on Indigenous territories, natural resources, socio-political organization, justice administration, education, languages, health, and culture. Within Indigenous territories, the Mexican state will

exercise its sovereignty, Oaxaca state will exercise its autonomy, and the Indigenous peoples will exercise their forms of social organization, their normative systems, and their traditions. (Gobierno del Estado de Oaxaca 1998, Chapter 3, my translation)

Internal normative systems are defined in the law as a "set of oral judicial norms of customary character that Indigenous peoples and communities recognize as valid and use to regulate public life and that authorities apply in the regulation of conflicts" (Gobierno del Estado de Oaxaca 1998, Article 3, Section VIII, my translation).

Many celebrated the recognition of Indigenous legal systems. Some observers rightly pointed out that the Oaxaca Indigenous Law establishes a pluralistic legal regime (Esteva 2000, 216). At issue is the extent to which self-governance without resources can guarantee social reproduction. In my view, this definition of normative systems ignores that Indigenous legal orders are closely connected to land/territory and the social reproduction of the community. Regarding natural resources, the law states, "The Indigenous peoples and the state, through the State Institute of Ecology and according to the applicable law, will decide the measures to protect the environment. Economic projects promoted by the state and private corporations that affect Indigenous peoples and their natural resources will be consulted and agreed upon with these peoples" (Gobierno del Estado de Oaxaca 1998, Chapter 7, Article 52, my translation).

I argue that by limiting Indigenous normative systems to some form of self-government, the law has reframed Indigenous jurisdiction over natural resources in some cases and denied them in others. As noted in Chapter 2, when Article 27 of the Mexican Constitution was reformed in 1992 to legalize the sale and leasing of *ejidos,* such reforms carefully excluded forested lands. Communities that sell off agricultural lands cede their forested lands to the state, which then become state property. Under the modified Constitution, as long as forest dwellers keep their lands under communal ownership and are ruled by Indigenous laws, they can continue to retain legal rights to their forest (Haenn 2006, 144). Moreover, it is the responsibility of communities to build their capacity to manage their forests according to conservation concerns. This type of community-driven conservation does not require communities to relinquish their communal ownership but rather to manage their forest in specific ways. Thus, from the perspective of Indigenous forest communities, the incentive to maintain or shift to Indigenous customary law is closely connected to the new livelihood strategies open to them. Years of neoliberal restructuring in Mexico's countryside have had profound consequences for Indigenous peoples. The slow erosion of Indigenous livelihood strategies has left people with no choice but to rely on forests as a commodity. As Agrawal, Chhatre, and Hardin (2008) have suggested, growing and competing demands for environmental services, timber, biofuels, and food are posing a challenge to the governance of forests worldwide because it requires land-use changes that are driven by these contradictory global demands.

Thus the connection between natural resources, protection of the environment, and economic projects is embedded in specific understandings of nature and society. In a 1994 report, the World Bank recommended changes to land use in Mexico, specifically the exploitation of forests' commercial value. The report stated that despite the number of people living in forested areas, the rural economy was *unfortunately* dominated by agriculture (World Bank 1994; SEMARNAT 2010). Moreover, the separation of forests from people facilitates the transformation of different ecological elements into commodities produced for a global market and creates new livelihood strategies driven by cash rather than subsistence. As a female Mixe activist stated in an interview for this book,

> Look, when I was a little girl, I used to go with my family to my grandfather's little ranch. We used to go harvest coffee beans and to eat whatever was out there. We ate tortillas with salt and black beans, we ate mandarins, mangoes, squash, beans, and fresh corn. I remember we did not have much money, but we did not feel poor. Now we have somehow become poor, and we women are even poorer. You guys call this globalization, do you not? (Matías Romero, Oaxaca, November 2003; my translation)

From this research participant's point of view, economic globalization has deprived people of control over their subsistence practices. At present, for instance, many Indigenous communities need to buy the corn they once produced for self-sustenance. Before the implementation of the North American Free Trade Agreement (NAFTA), Indigenous communities were self-sufficient. Although a number of scholars have claimed that Oaxaca represents a unique case whose communal property and community-managed forests exist on a scale and at a level of maturity unmatched elsewhere in the world (Bray et al. 2003; Chapela 2005; Bray et al. 2008), forest management is not driven by local use values but by a northern global market that is inserting Indigenous communities into a neocolonial green capitalist economy that benefits from Indigenous social organization and govern-ance. Thus it is important to pay attention to the implications of adopting these livelihood strategies in practice.

Unlike Indigenous agricultural lands, which were liberalized, forested lands were re-regulated to address conservation concerns. By thinking about neoliberalism as a process that produces spaces, states, subjects, and the environment in complex ways, we can ask what makes certain resource re-gimes possible and how indigeneity is being articulated in the context of social and economic devaluation of local livelihoods. I come back to these questions in the last section of this chapter.

## Zapotec or Indigenous?
The Zapotec people from Juchitán in the Tehuantepec Isthmus have long been represented in mass media, painting, and literature. For some people, Juchitán is a land of women and *muxes* (males who live as women) and of elastic attitudes toward sex and gender. This place is also peculiar in that it was the first Indigenous municipality to rise up against the state party in the 1980s and to chip away its power, whereas other segments of the population chose other alternatives. Unlike the forest-dwelling Indigenous communities described above, Juchitán is a town that serves as the munici-pal seat for the surrounding communities, a busy economic centre where regional products, craft trading, agriculture, services, and wage labour are significant. The Zapotec's defence of their political autonomy and the im-agery of the strong Zapotec matriarchs have reinforced local cultural pride. Questioning how political autonomy has been shaped by neoliberal policies is relevant here. This section analyzes the emergence of the Zapotec organ-ization COCEI, its struggle for political autonomy, and how political auton-omy has been reshaped by neoliberalism.

The emergence in the 1970s of the COCEI can partially be understood as an expression of this people's longstanding struggle for autonomy. Despite the economic transformations experienced in the early twentieth century due to the construction of the railway and later the oil refinery in Salina Cruz, land tenure and subsistence practices in the Tehuantepec Isthmus were not an issue until the late 1950s. The construction of the Benito Juárez Dam in 1958 and the land survey implemented prior to its construction were used as justifications by the federal government to unilaterally decree that all irrigation lands in Juchitán would become *ejidos* and therefore property of the Mexican state instead of communal lands. As explained in Chapter 1, Article 27 of the Mexican Constitution of 1917 opened the space for land distribution in the form of *ejidos,* which granted usufruct rights to *ejido* holders. Transforming communal lands into *ejidos* would have replaced communal ownership with usufruct rights to the land. The Zapotec elite, old-style bosses, peasants, and entrepreneurs mobilized to reverse the decree and to defend property against the government's plans during the 1960s (Rubin 1994, 111). Communal land ownership and years of internal, informal land sales had resulted in the overlapping of land-tenure systems, in which natural-resource uses, social stratification, inter-elite conflict, and gendered practices were being negotiated and contested.

The construction of infrastructure in the region stimulated urban commercialization and further transformed natural-resource uses (Campbell 1990, 189). Brosius, Tsing, and Zerner (1998) argue that concepts such as community, customs, and land rights are fragile and vary according to political contexts. Slowly, the movement of Zapotec people against external intervention gave way to a class-based alliance of some Zapotecs against other Zapotecs who had competing visions of identity, social practices, culture, and political and economic projects. Whereas wealthier Zapotecs allied with Mestizos to protect private property, the emergence in the 1970s of the COCEI connected the concerns and demands of the other sectors of Zapotec society, including territorial claims, loans, wages, benefits, and broader municipal powers (Rubin 1997, 250). The Zapotecs made inroads in local electoral politics and pro-democracy movements aimed at gaining control over municipal governments and political processes at a time when Mexican politics were dominated by one party, the PRI.

When asked to reflect on what had caused these conflicts, a research participant said, "We had land because we worked hard. Those who sold their lands and later wanted them back, saying lands were communal, were just lazy people who were poor because they did not work. They wanted all without effort. Those 'communists' said they were going to take away our land. Of course, we were not going to allow them to do so" (Juchitán, Oaxaca, November 2003; my translation).

Threats and fear of land expropriation by the COCEI caused anxiety among affluent Zapotecs who feared land expropriation. The COCEI was accused of being a communist organization and of fighting for "lazy people." However, in the words of a research participant,

> It was a matter not only of resisting the market forces' domination and exploitation but also of battling oligarchs. The most important feature of our identity is the Zapotec language. We are very proud of being Binnizá [People

of the Clouds], so the political movement was also to promote our culture and language and to make it the official language in the municipal government and business. ((Juchitán, Oaxaca, November 2003; my translation)

From this point of view, people identified not only as Zapotecs but also as people who were exploited in specific ways by both the local and the external political and economic elite. Similar to the commoners' resistance to Zapotec rulers in the colonial period, the COCEI articulated a political project aimed at relieving social hierarchies and class distinctions among the Zapotecs. Although the COCEI articulated a Zapotec identity in resistance to both government domination and capitalist development (Campbell 1990, 215), a female activist noted in an interview that the COCEI's goals were more complex: "We struggled against Oaxaca state power. Everything is decided there: what laws are passed, who governs, who is punished. We are part of Oaxaca because they decided so. Our desires, aspirations did not count" (Oaxaca City, November 2003; my translation).

These statements show that this movement sought not only to defend communal lands and combat class distinctions but also to carve out a locus where ordinary Zapotecs could have some control over place, the space of social reproduction. In reconstructing a coherent subject, political leaders moved between addressing class distinctions and representing the cohesiveness of the political movement. In doing so, they revitalized cultural roots and concepts to recreate spaces of identity and political claims.

The role of Zapotec intellectuals was certainly decisive in the creation of the COCEI and its political project. To Hernández Díaz (2001, 15), the emergence of these intellectuals as political leaders was linked to the flow of Zapotec students to educational centres in both Oaxaca City and Mexico City and their participation in the student movement in 1968. To Reina Aoyama (1997), in contrast, Zapotec intellectuals had been playing a crucial role in the revitalization of Zapotec culture since at least the late nineteenth century. She argues that these intellectuals' self-identification as Zapotecs shows that, unlike other Indigenous people in Mexico, educated Zapotecs have maintained their identity instead of being assimilated into the Mestizo culture. Although both arguments are important, I contend that the roles intellectuals played in the late-nineteenth-century resistance movement and in the emergence of the COCEI differ in some ways. Whereas the resistance movement constructed a local nationalism aimed at unifying a socially differentiated *people* to defend the Zapotecs' resources against outsiders' intervention, the COCEI movement emerged in a context of changing notions of property and the incorporation of rural areas into the national political economy, shaping contested understandings of community, social identity, and power relations. From this point of view, the COCEI was focused not only on revitalizing culture and defending land but also on building a more inclusive political project.

The demands for reform of the political system in which the COCEI emerged facilitated political alliances with the Mexican Communist Party, later the PRD. In 1981 after several years of struggle, the COCEI became the first Indigenous organization to succeed in municipal elections and to be recognized by the Partido Revolucionario Institucional. Juchitán became the only autonomous municipality in Mexico to be governed by a leftist Indigenous government. During a reign of two and a half years by what was called the Ayuntamiento Popular (Popular Municipal Council), the COCEI embarked on an ambitious program centred on gaining control of the lands that had been lost to Mestizo large stakeholders, organizing Zapotec peasants, students, and labourers, and implementing programs through *tequio* (communal work). The COCEI also invested heavily in the revival of Zapotec culture by sponsoring the development of arts, literature, and music.

Building this political space was not easy. The Oaxaca state government consistently attempted to subordinate the Ayuntamiento Popular by taking away its functions. In 1983, for example, the state government removed all municipal powers, throwing the COCEI out of office. In response, a referendum was held, and 30,000 Zapotecs opted for the continuation of the COCEI government. In December federal police officers evacuated the municipal building, arrested COCEI supporters and leaders, and dissolved the government. In an attempt to build a wider support basis, the COCEI started to downplay its Zapotec identity and to appeal to other Indigenous communities in the region. It began to emphasize a political project open to modernity yet firmly rooted in Indigenous traditions. From this perspective, the movement vindicated individual and collective autonomous capacity to control economic and socio-cultural development and the nature of state-society relations (Miano Borruso 2002, 36).

In the COCEI's view, electoral politics were not enough to control the pace of development and the nature of state-society relations, so it adopted a more radical stand and promoted civil disobedience. In response, this organization met government repression. By combining different political strategies – which included channelling massive resources to the region, creating space for democratic elections, promoting the creation of more culturally driven Indigenous organizations, and pushing for the ascendancy of well-educated Indigenous leaders into government offices – the federal government expected to dismantle the autonomist project (Rubin 1994, 124-25).

This organization came back to power in 1986 through a strategic coalition with the local PRI. This alliance was heavily criticized but proved to bring more resources and tranquility to Juchitán. Later, in 1988, the fragile political environment in which the federal government of Carlos Salinas de Gortari came to power forced it to implement a new controversial strategy for dealing with opposition movements and parties: the Pacto de Concertación Social (Social Dialogue Pact). "Concertación social" was a fancy term to describe efforts aimed at transforming the state's relations with Indigenous peoples under neoliberalism. Through this project, opposition parties were offered economic support in exchange for the cessation of civil disobedience and for peaceful coexistence with the federal government. Perhaps tired of political repression, the COCEI chose to align itself with the Salinas government and to adopt a more conciliatory position when it came back to power in 1989. Although funding was channelled to Juchitán to improve services and increase employment, the COCEI slowly started to lose support.

What COCEI leaders called the construction of a "new political culture" rooted in Zapotec culture, history, and dialogue resulted in some leaders and supporters distancing themselves from this organization. The COCEI concentrated on reconstructing a local nationalism that drew on local understandings of being. Juchitecos (Zapotecs of Juchitán) distanced themselves from surrounding Indigenous communities and instead focused on a local cultural project that drew upon a great past. A research participant explained, "We [Zapotecs] do not accept to be called Indigenous; we are Zapotecs and very proud of who we are. Indigenous people are those who are ashamed of who they are ... Our ancestors were the Binnigulaza [Ancient People of the Clouds], who were great, wise warriors. We have in our veins the desire to be a free people, a people that struggle and oppose injustices" (Juchitán, Oaxaca, December 2003; my translation).

Although this desire to be a "free people" and to "oppose injustices" was commonly articulated by COCEI leaders, this organization was perceived by other Indigenous organizations in the region as being "self-centred" and "opportunistic." As mentioned earlier, the COCEI appealed to other Indigenous peoples in the region during harsh times but distanced itself from these communities when it started dialoguing with the federal government. When different meetings were held to oppose the Puebla Panama

Plan and later the Mesoamerican Biological Corridor, the COCEI was either absent or reluctant to take a clear position. Entering into dialogue with the federal government and embracing economic development had clearly brought benefits to Juchitán in the form of jobs and services.

Unlike the redefined nationalism of the Zapatistas in Chiapas, which is ethnically inclusive, the Zapotecs' local nationalism is characterized by the perception of difference between Zapotecs and outsiders (i.e., anyone who is not Zapotec). This identity downplays class differentiation and emphasizes reciprocal relationships and practices embedded in the *guendalisá* (obligations to one's relationships).

Important divisions among COCEI supporters and between the COCEI and other Indigenous organizations in the Tehuantepec Isthmus have occurred. In 2002, after twenty years in government, the COCEI lost elections because of allegations of leaders' abuses of power and internal divisions. In 2005 the COCEI was back in power and dismantled its alliance with the PRD. In 2007 it won elections once again by making alliances with the Partido del Trabajo (Labour Party). However, the COCEI's political influence has diminished. Although it has institutionalized a Zapotec cultural project and secured a place in electoral politics, it has opened the isthmus to economic development. Since the Pacto de Concertación Social was embraced by the COCEI in the late 1980s, Juchitán has slowly "welcomed" supermarkets, burger chains, and wind parks. Although Zapotecs of all walks of life embrace their identity and celebrate their autonomy, this type of economic development has had uneven impacts among them. This situation is generating, once again, a space in which competing understandings of land ownership, natural-resource uses, community, livelihoods, and identity are put forward, as I show in the last section of this chapter. Before doing so, I wish to concentrate on another divide that separates Zapotecs from other Indigenous peoples.

### The Female Subject versus the Strong Matriarch

As argued earlier, the recognition of Indigenous normative systems in Oaxaca has been very controversial. For some, this recognition is an expression of legal pluralism. For others, Indigenous normative systems work against Indigenous women's civil and political rights. Indigenous women's increasing demands for the democratization of gender relations within Indigenous communities and for the elimination of practices that discriminate against them have led some non-Indigenous feminists, politicians, academics, and international organizations to frame Indigenous normative systems as a serious challenge to democracy and individual rights. From this perspective, Indigenous women's experiences of violence, poverty, and discrimination are exclusively understood as cultural problems hindering women's ability to exercise agency. Moreover, this understanding of culture naturalizes inequalities and essentializes the notion of the "female subject as victim" (Newdick 2005, 75). This section explores two constructions of the Indigenous woman in relation to indigeneity: the female victim and the strong matriarch. I argue that both conceal structural gender inequalities.

Article 46 of the Oaxaca Indigenous Law (Gobierno del Estado de Oaxaca 1998) states that the state government will promote, within the framework of Indigenous traditional norms, women's recognition in their communities and women's full participation in activities not contemplated by "tradition." In addition, Article 45 reinforces women's roles in reproducing Indigenous communities. Article 48, on the other hand, states that Indigenous women have the right to be trained and to receive a bicultural education. Although the debate on the Oaxaca Indigenous Law has focused on the negative consequences of customary laws for women, little has been said about how the law itself reinscribes gendered power relations.

An important body of legal-anthropological literature (Collier 1995; Hernández Castillo 2001; Sierra 2004) on Indigenous law and women in different regions in Mexico has shed some light on how conflict resolution is based on negotiation and compromise rather than on punishment. As well, these studies have shown that compromise neither benefits all equally nor is passively accepted. Although conflict resolution based on Indigenous law shows how power is based on cultural values and perspectives that construct gender relations (Sierra 2004, 120), the ideology of harmony contributes to the implementation of mechanisms oriented toward maintaining local loyalty and concealing conflicts and difference.

Analyses specific to Oaxaca show that Indigenous women's positions within their communities vary. The majority of civic and religious positions are open to women, and women can vote in communal assemblies in 76 percent of the 412 municipalities ruled by Indigenous normative systems (Velásquez Cepeda 1998, 13). In some communities, women participate in the community's political life through their husbands. In others, married women have lost their right to hold land and to participate in politics. Having access to both communal and individual *ejidos* (land plots) is, in many Indigenous communities, the realization of full citizenship. Deere and León (2000) argue that there is a fundamental relation between gender, property rights, and empowerment. From their perspective, land/property rights are fundamental for women when negotiating economic and social rights. Although this argument is important, I think the relationship between land/property rights and the ability to negotiate economic and social rights is not necessarily a cause-effect relationship within neoliberal governance. Scholars who have considered the gender implications of privatization and marketization of land have argued that during the transition from Indigenous rule to private property, women tend to lose the few rights they enjoy. For example, Ahlers's (2005) study of the privatization of land and water rights in Mexico shows that new livelihood projects and an emphasis on the value of land have led to gender conflicts and inequalities. Similarly, Nightingale (2009) argues that gender itself is reinscribed through practices, policies, and responses associated with specific knowledge and practices. From these perspectives, those practices, policies, and responses that go beyond the household are also crucial to understanding how property rights are part of how nature is produced in gendered ways.

Moreover, in her study comparing Oaxaca and Nunavut, Gowan (2003, 69) argues that the situation in Oaxaca urges us to look beyond women's direct participation in formal decision making and to consider the scope of women's participation in community life. Gowan, drawing upon Lynn Stephen's arguments regarding Indigenous women's indirect participation, notes that although women cannot hold civil posts in the cargo system in some communities, they have other means to influence local politics. Since the household unit is crucial to the local system of governance and to the moral economy of reciprocity, this system cannot function without the work of both men and women. I think this argument is relevant to understanding the overlapping of two governance systems and spheres of politics.

In this context, we can ask whether women are necessarily more disadvantaged and/or disenfranchised in autonomous communities and municipalities ruled by Indigenous law than in those that are not. The relationship between land/territory and identity constitutes the central element of the articulation of political autonomy, governance, and citizenship/membership. Although controlling Indigenous women's access to community land is a way to control their rights, Indigenous laws have also evolved. When I asked a Mixe female activist about her experience accessing land, she said,

> In my community, they tell me that because I am a woman, I cannot participate in the communitarian assemblies and I cannot hold land. I inherited my dad's *ejido* because my older brother died a long time ago. The men in the community did not want to acknowledge this inheritance and wanted

to redistribute this piece of land, but I refused and refused. After a lot of fighting and discussion, the men told me, "You will have that land if you can show us you can work as hard as a man in the *tequio*." (San Juan Guixicovi, Oaxaca, January 2004; my translation)

Indigenous norms and practices are immersed in conflict and internal divisions located within a particular equilibrium between resistance, on the one hand, and social and power relations, on the other, as seen in any other legal order. Indigenous women's resistance and challenge to gender-discriminatory practices are concealed by constructions of the female subject as victim, who is helpless and who needs outside intervention. Land/territory, gender, and citizenship reveal the power relations surrounding not only Indigenous political autonomy but also the construction of Indigenous "cultures" as "retrograde." For Indigenous peoples to maintain rights to their forested lands, they must continue to be ruled by Indigenous law, yet Indigenous normative systems are often represented as culturally and inherently gender-biased and backward.

In striking contrast to the representations of the female subject as victim, Zapotec women in Juchitán have a contradictory role in the nationalist imagery. For many famous travellers, painters, and academics, Zapotec culture is a "matriarchal society" where women rule. In the nationalist tourism industry, the image of the Zapotec woman has become the symbol of the exotic, modern, Indigenous woman. Unlike other Indigenous women, Zapotec women inherit and own land and property, hold religious posts in *velas* (community-wide celebrations to distribute wealth and reinforce kinship), and are at the centre of these celebrations. Reina Aoyama (1997) notes that Zapotec women's participation in the local and regional economy is not new but a centuries-old practice. In the 1980s women actively participated in the COCEI's struggle for political autonomy. Women's participation was decisive in repelling soldiers, defending the authorities' offices, and voting to overthrow the PRI. Women, particularly older ones, became involved in political campaigns and in convincing undecided voters. Since women controlled the local market, political leaders often organized meetings in the market and addressed the women instead of the men. When I asked a male research participant to reflect on the role of women in Juchitán, he noted, "Women walk beside men and work as hard as men do. Zapotec women are strong, are powerful and beautiful. Nothing moves without women" (Juchitán, Oaxaca, November 2003; my translation). Although the COCEI has drawn upon the daily practices of women, it has reproduced gendered forms of political and social practices. In this sense, women are not outside of social relations but are produced through specific social relations (Mohanty 1994, 203). As a female research participant noted, "Outsiders like to say that Juchitán is a matriarchal society. To me a matriarchy means that women rule over men. I do not think that is what happens here. Women are strong and have power because we work hard. Work is very important to us, but a matriarchy? I do not think so" (Oaxaca City, November 2003; my translation).

Despite Zapotec women's high status and economic power, with some exceptions, they have not assumed political leadership roles in government or grassroots movements (Rubin 1997, 230-33). I agree with other scholars who contend that Juchitán cannot accurately be described as a "matriarchy" (Miano Borruso 2002; Stephen 2002). In actuality, the romanticizing of a Zapotec "matriachial culture" conceals gendered violence and women's inability to negotiate power within the contemporary political sphere, notwithstanding that women do participate in public and ritual life in ways that would be considered unusual in other parts of the country. Zapotecs of all classes have acted to preserve their identity, the autonomy it has fostered, and the economic benefits it has brought (Rubin 1997, 37). Unlike other Indigenous women in Mexico, Zapotec women dominate the family economy and the local and regional markets. Juchitán's economy is female-centred and is based on a clear division of work with respect to the provision of goods and services for community rituals, festivals, and gift giving.

However, as Kellogg (2005, 110) notes, although Zapotec women make important economic contributions and are both authoritative and powerful, this power and authority are exercised in the Indigenous sphere of governance. Thus not only does women's strong presence in the local and regional economy clash with contemporary understandings of private-public, or domestic-political, divisions of the world, but discourses of women's power also ground them firmly in the domestic realm as reproducers of the nation, a sphere that is no longer valued. A female research participant associated with a community-celebration committee explained this situation:

> In women you can see that our culture is strong. When a child is born, we talk to him in Zapotec; all maternal love is expressed in Zapotec, the language of our ancestors. Unlike men, women have not lost their traditional clothes. You are a Zapotec, so you know that we have forms of modernizing our *trajes* [clothing]. Men no longer use their traditional clothes. (Juchitán, Oaxaca, December 2003; my translation)

Since Zapotec women are already considered to be in an outstanding position, the disparity between their economic contributions and political power is seldom questioned. The image of the strong matriarch perpetuated by Zapotecs themselves, academics, and intellectuals alike represents a modern version of indigeneity and pride. However, it also silences the inequalities that result from negotiating a balance between modernization and tradition. More important, it conceals the burden of reproducing culture. Zapotec women's presence in the public sphere through the economy and community celebrations and their limited political participation are immersed in different layers of memory, gender roles, and understandings of community. Increasing class stratification among this people and the centrality of the civil political space have made it more difficult for women to transform power and economic wealth, which are closely associated with the moral economy of solidarity, into formal political power (Kellogg 2005, 109). Although tradition is reflected through women's roles as a *guzana* (the one who gives birth) and a *guzana gola* (great mother), the names of the positions that men use in community celebrations are borrowed from formal politics. Terms such as "president" and "secretary" are common. As in the Nisga'a case, the image of the strong matriarch is central to a modern yet traditional articulation of indigeneity.

## Land and Wind Stories

Chapter 1 argued that identity, resistance, and belonging are grounded in places where colonial entanglements and international forces are implicated in shaping the political economy in which the articulation of indigeneity takes place. Chapter 2 noted that neoliberalism has often been portrayed as a monolithic force that transforms places from the outside. However, neoliberalism materializes differently in different locations and is driven by specific actors, institutions, networks, governments, organizations, and discourses operating on different scales and underpinning its materialization in different places.

Changes to Article 27 of the Mexican Constitution and the passing of the Oaxaca Indigenous Law have had uneven effects on different groups of people. If we think of neoliberalism as a process that produces spaces, states, subjects, and the environment in complex ways, we can ask what makes certain resource regimes possible, what kind of exclusion is produced, and how indigeneity is being articulated in the context of the social and economic devaluation of local livelihoods.

I argue that the Oaxaca Indigenous Law recognizes Indigenous normative systems as essential to indigeneity; however, this law excludes other
peoples from protection. Unlike Indigenous forest dwellers, who are targeted because of the knowledge they possess of their habitats and because they
are considered the "strongest allies in the conservation process" (World
Bank 2000, 12), agricultural Indigenous communities have resisted the incorporation of their lands into protected government areas. At present,
these peoples find themselves engaging with global articulations of indigeneity in their attempts to control place.

The Tehuantepec Isthmus is part of an expansive development project
that is considered emblematic of neoliberalism in Mexico: the Mesoamerican
Biological Corridor. In Oaxaca's development agenda, which is consistent
with measures recommended in the World Bank report *Mexico: Southern
States Development Strategy* (2003), the Mesoamerican Integration and
Development Project is aimed at economically reorganizing spaces and providing "viable" opportunities for Indigenous peoples to engage in the capitalist economy. Accordingly, increasing productivity and economic viability
means moving away from "nonviable" and "nonproductive" Indigenous subsistence practices and toward new livelihood strategies, including ecotourism, power generation, and exploitation of natural resources such as forests,
minerals, and biodiversity. This mega development project is constructed as
a "viable," "sustainable," "secure" way for Indigenous peoples to participate
in the global economy.

In the Tehuantepec Isthmus, the implementation of this development
agenda depends upon a distinction between Indigenous-government and
peasant-government relations and ideas of land management. This region
has been represented as an area that needs outside intervention and governance. Deforestation, low productivity, and poverty have all characterized
this region even though, according to the Instituto Nacional de Estadística y
Geografía (National Institute of Statistics and Geography), this area is not
considered poor or marginal. The Mexican government, the Comisión
Federal de Electricidad (Federal Electricity Commission), the Global Wind
Energy Council, and the Sistema de Interconexión Eléctrica de los Países de
América Central (Central American Electrical Interconnection System)
have all concluded that wind parks are essential to reversing these problems
and contributing to the North American Clean Development Mechanism.

However, Indigenous communities are resisting. At first glance, the resistance of local communities and communal and *ejido* landholders seems

counterintuitive or even reactionary since it stands against the prevailing global concern with environmentally clean energy. The deference between what government gives to multinational corporations dictating the terms of wind-park construction and the treatment that Indigenous landowners have received reveals a more complex picture.

International corporations were first introduced to individual landholders by representatives of the Oaxaca government in the mid-1990s. Instead of addressing either communal or *ejidal* assemblies, these corporations went door to door convincing individuals to sign contracts that leased their lands for up to twenty-five years. Their strategy succeeded with some of the poorest communities, which lack most services. La Venta I and La Venta II wind parks were constructed in the area of the Juchitán municipality in 2003 and are currently the biggest wind-power projects in Mexico. However, the goal is to eventually build 3,000 windmills, which will completely cover the narrow isthmus (Oceransky 2008-09). Six more parks are being planned, and the goal is to have fourteen parks functioning by 2014. Although the Mexican government supports this economic-development project, these wind parks are being financed by the World Bank and the Inter-American Development Bank. These financial institutions are interested in promoting private investment and preventing the Mexican government from creating another state-based energy corporation, as required by the Mexican Constitution.

The promise of development spread quickly to other communities, causing divisions among members over who had the authority to speak on behalf of whom: the individual landholder or either the communal or *ejidal* assemblies. In conversations with members of my Zapotec community, I learned that many thought they would actually get a lot of money. Rumours spread quickly about some people getting rich. Anxiety over the mixed information people were getting did not help. Government representatives acted as the "experts" who had the knowledge and often used a highly technical language when talking to members of Indigenous communities. In different forums, discussions, and meetings, Indigenous communities have addressed several questions that are crucial to understanding the nature of the proposed development. What is the purpose of the Mesoamerican Integration and Development Project? Why is energy not produced for local people but for a global market? Since companies are leasing only a part of communities' lands, what are other community members supposed to do? If the development projects are supposed to benefit them, why have communities not been consulted?

In many cases, community members were misinformed when they signed tenancy contracts of up to fifty years in exchange for promises and amounts of money that were never stated in the contracts. When I asked a female landholder about her motivations for signing a lease contract, she sadly explained, "I am a widow. I grow corn but that is not enough anymore to survive. When the company came, they promised me help and money. Now they say I signed a contract leasing my land for thirty years in exchange for receiving 1,500 pesos [roughly $150] annually for each of my three hectares. Now I am told I cannot even grow my corn" (my translation).

Like this woman, many feel betrayed and frustrated. Many have denounced as arbitrary the annual rent offered to land owners, explaining that it does not compensate for the negative consequences that wind parks have for farmers' livelihoods. As a result of these pressures, payments have been increased in some contracts. However, they continue to be a fraction of what energy companies pay to farmers annually in Canada or in Spain. This variation in the terms of the contracts has led some people to conclude that the companies offer as little as possible for the land of poor, illiterate *campesinos* (peasants). Contracts include restrictions on their use of land and grant usufruct rights over the land to the companies.

Wind power is also attractive to industries that have heavily polluted the Tehuantepec Isthmus in the past. When I was a little girl, I heard many times about the river that traverses my community, the Rio de los Perros (River of Dogs), but I never saw any dogs there. It was not until later that I found out that what people called *bicu niza* in Zapotec were in fact river otters, which inhabited this river until the early 1960s. As part of the development trend of the time, a cement plant was built in the isthmus, and although it provided some jobs, it contaminated and overused the water sources feeding the river until they almost dried up. CEMEX, the cement company, is now concerned with reducing its environmental footprint and adopting more sustainable practices. Thus this corporation decided to join the wind-power industry and generate green energy. CEMEX's wind-power park was completed in 2009 and now supplies 25 percent of its clean energy to CEMEX, which in turn offers carbon credits to the Clean Development Mechanism (CEMEX 2009).

At the inauguration ceremony for La Venta II, Mexican president Felipe Calderón confirmed the efforts made to develop alternative energy in order to reduce carbon emissions. However, the Mexican energy ministry called upon wind-power investors to consider instead the biodiesel option for agricultural communities, as it would indeed generate more benefit for them (Secretaría Nacional de Energía 2011). These contradictory positions suggest a lack of planning and, more important, a lack of meaningful consultation with the affected communities.

Zapotec peasants have accused the COCEI of being co-opted and of selling out the Tehuantepec Isthmus to transnational corporations (López Morales 2007). Peasants noted that the COCEI has long abandoned its political goals and is no longer interested in justice. Zapotec peasants have created the Movimiento Alternativo del Istmo (Isthmus Alternative Movement) and the Asamblea de Pueblos Indígenas del Istmo en Defensa de la Tierra y el Territorio (Isthmus Indigenous Peoples' Assembly for the Defence of Land and Territory). These organizations have demanded information about how these projects landed in the region without meaningful consultation. The Asamblea de Pueblos Indígenas del Istmo is closely working with the Centro de Derechos Humanos Tepeyac (Tepeyac Human Rights Centre), located in Tehuantepec.

Unlike the COCEI, which draws on local nationalism, the Asamblea de Pueblos Indígenas del Istmo embraces the terms "Indigenous" and "Indigenous rights," partly because no domestic legislation protects Zapotec lands against the challenges Zapotec peasants are facing. Neither the Mexican Indigenous Law nor the Oaxaca Indigenous Law offer protection for Indigenous peoples' lands or for the overlapping land-tenure systems that exist in this region. This situation speaks of the complexity of implementing neoliberal policies and recognizing Indigenous rights in different regions of the world and illustrates the power dynamics that exist on different scales.

According to the Centro de Derechos Humanos Tepeyac, wind-power parks have not only been imposed on the Indigenous peoples but have also displaced them from their lands. The centre notes that the Mexican government is in violation of the International Labour Organization's Indigenous and Tribal Peoples Convention, known as Convention 169 (ILO 2003), which clearly states that Indigenous communities must be consulted prior to any development project affecting their lands. Based on this legal argument, some Indigenous communities and a team of lawyers have filed a collective lawsuit to cancel 185 lease contracts. Nongovernmental organizations that focus on the environment or human rights have expressed criticism of wind-energy projects in the isthmus. Greenpeace Mexico, for instance, has stated, "We do not want corporations to build wind farms that expel communities from their lands. This is not the development that the country needs; we need to develop clean energies together with the communities that own the lands so that they are part of the wind farms, so that they make decisions" (cited in Quecha Reyna 2008, my translation).

According to a 2003 Environmental Impact Report commissioned by the Comisión Federal de Electricidad itself, the greatest danger of these wind parks is to the bird population (Henestrosa Orozco 2009). Wind power is central to attracting manufacturing plants and supermarkets and to creating a type of development in which Zapotecs provide cheap labour to foreign-owned companies. Indigenous peasants do not oppose wind power itself; rather, they demand to have a share of the benefits as well as to be consulted collectively. Unlike the COCEI, the incipient Zapotec movement against the wind-power industry has engaged with international legal tools and global articulations of indigeneity. Unlike the COCEI, which has called upon notions of class and indigeneity, this emergent movement appeals to Zapotec landowners to defend the collective nature of their lands. Does this mean that the Zapotecs have moved from a peasant to an Indigenous identity? To respond to this question in the affirmative would be very simplistic. The Zapotecs have historically emphasized local conceptions of indigeneity (or being Binnizá), autonomy, and responsibility. At present, however, not all community members depend upon the same livelihoods. As a communal landholder put it in an interview, "We must all find a way to prosper and survive as Zapotecs" (Matías Romero, Oaxaca, November 2003). The tendency to see places as homogeneous locations prevents us from seeing how both resistance and engagement simultaneously unfold *in* place.

## Conclusion

Places are loci of collective memory and political identities. When people mobilize their identity into a force of solidarity, they depend upon the specificities that construct and maintain these identities. Zapotecs have articulated different understandings of indigeneity at different times in relation to regional and national powers. The new development taking place in the Tehuantepec Isthmus is based on external constructions and on global wants. The reorganization of Indigenous economies in accordance with new livelihood strategies to meet these global wants has different consequences for different groups of people and for different Indigenous communities.

The growing resistance to the economic project unfolding in the Tehuantepec Isthmus is not against development per se but against the type of development affecting the livelihoods of Zapotec *campesinos*. Unlike the traditional commodification of nature involving raw materials, the new geo-economic strategies rest not only on the liberalization of the natural environment per se but also on uneven constructions of nature. The conservation economy and green economic growth may be conceived of as reducing environmental impacts; however, ecological commodification and marketization further depend on nature and further separate Indigenous peoples from their lands and compromise their relationships with place. At stake here is not the implementation of a greener capitalism but how place is transformed in accordance with neocolonial divisions of labour.

By analyzing the roles of the Indigenous female victim and the strong matriarch, I have shown that these constructs have served specific functions. The image of the Indigenous female victim has been used to oppose Indigenous normative systems, and the notion of the strong matriarch has been used to conceal gender differentiation and to represent an image of the modern Indigenous woman. Gender and the inequalities between men and women are closely connected to how nature is produced and reinscribed by struggles over resources and through a variety of socio-economic processes.

# Conclusion
---
## Toward Spaces of Indigenous Repossessions

In these pages I have analyzed the relationships between neoliberalism, indigeneity, gender, and the environment in Canada and Mexico. I have shown that the articulation of indigeneity is shaped by colonial structures, by the economic, social, and political interests of the sites of articulation, and by gendered senses of place, all of which operate on different scales and make certain political visions (im)possible. The discourses, practices, and strategies embedded in the articulation of indigeneity are neither homogeneous nor representative of the only Indigenous response. Indigenous places are heterogeneous locations where both resistance and engagement develop. Understanding Indigenous peoples' specific responses to global wants starts with a consideration of how places have been shaped and reorganized by colonialism. Global discourses of rights, environmentalism, and development are locally engaged, contested, and transformed through articulatory practices, producing diverse understandings of indigeneity that both challenge hegemonic views and are modified by them.

Neoliberal understandings of the self, difference, the economy, and the environment have shaped state practices and articulations of indigeneity. By fixing specific meanings of indigeneity and defining the economic opportunities open to Indigenous peoples, the state and multiple sites of articulation naturalize colonialism and identify *who* is entitled to rights. Unlike in the past, current economic strategies shaping the spatial and social reconfiguration of place and indigeneity rest not only on the liberalization of the natural environment per se but also on schemes aimed at commodifying "saved" ecosystems. Although Indigenous peoples have participated in the market before, the neoliberal conservation scheme drives them away from their livelihoods and encourages them to establish conservation partnerships with businesses. Land management, ecotourism, and conservation have become means of achieving economic growth for Indigenous peoples.

As shown in this book, neoliberal conservation promises respect for and protection of property rights, including communal ownership, partnerships, and economic benefits, but it devalues Indigenous livelihoods and knowledge. The cases presented in this book suggest that neoliberalism is messy and contradictory. Specifically, the introduction of neoliberal conservation is producing economies and ecosystems that are available for the global market (Igoe and Brockington 2007), not for local consumption, and that are changing Indigenous peoples' livelihoods. Knowledge of Indigenous peoples' articulations of indigeneity both in resisting and in integrating into the neoliberal project is important to understanding the complexity of their struggles and to questioning fixed notions of Indigenous identities.

In Canada land management and conservation are central to land claims and dictate the terms on which Indigenous rights can be enjoyed. Rights and development have a number of consequences for Indigenous peoples in general and even more seriously for Indigenous women. One of the serious consequences of the cartographic-legal strategy currently being employed is that nature and natural resources are almost exclusively depicted as economic potential, a depiction that does not match Indigenous peoples' understandings of their relationships with nature, natural resources, and place. The same is true in land claims negotiations and agreements as well. Natural resources and the ways that people understand and relate to them are socially constructed. The production and use of natural resources are central to creating understandings of identity and territory (Desbiens 2004).

Land claims agreements are negotiated based on Euro-Canadian neoliberal understandings of natural resources and resource production. Because neoliberalism focuses on reaching agreements that will allow Indigenous communities to become self-sufficient and participate in the larger economy through natural-resource development, Indigenous peoples are denied the opportunity to address the spatial inequalities created through colonial dispossessions of land and resources. Instead, they are placed in a neoliberal property regime that limits the space from which anyone other than large corporations can derive benefit. The focus is simply on providing Indigenous peoples with the same opportunities as non-Indigenous citizens to partici-pate in large-scale resource development.

In a place like the Arctic, for example, the conditions created by climate change are facilitating an emergent model of development that continues to see this region as a storehouse of resources. This model clashes with con-servation initiatives that have produced contradictory consequences for the hunting rights of the Inuit and their ability to profit from these rights, rais-ing questions about the meaning of conservation and Indigenous rights under neoliberalism. The Nisga'a, on the other hand, have been recognized for sustainably managing their resources and celebrated for embracing pri-vate property. In representing themselves as both conservationists and entre-preneurs, the Nisga'a have taken advantage of the conservation economy.

In Mexico neoliberal conservation has created distinctions between Indigenous communities based upon their livelihoods and social organiza-tion. Whereas "peasants" are represented as a nostalgic, unproductive, and unsustainable group, "Indigenous" people are identified as being allies of conservation. In Chiapas and Oaxaca, for example, community-driven con-servation projects have depended upon communal forest ownership and Indigenous social organization for their success. In contrast, the members of Indigenous peasant communities, both the landless and landowners, are encouraged to change their livelihoods and to participate in the labour force or wind-power generation, a "sustainable" development project that has dis-placed Zapotec peasants from their lands. In Chiapas a static, essentialist, and highly exclusive definition of indigeneity has benefited a few Indigenous communities, and many business-driven conservation projects have bene-fited corporations and foreign tourists, who pay for a "real" Indigenous experience (Igoe and Brockington 2007, 437). Those who have been dispos-sessed of their lands are constructed as land invaders, whose livelihoods are disposable and a threat to conservation. Zapatista communities are building a community-driven project that is outside of the state's power and neo-liberal recognition.

How do we understand these differences? Neoliberalism is rooted in specific colonial histories. Colonial governance was not uniform across countries or across places. The distinction between land-based settler col-onialism and labour-based extractive colonialism is useful in explaining why some Indigenous peoples maintained their communal lands in Mexico and shows how Indigenous communities negotiated, adapted to, and resisted the reorganization of colonial space and later the emerging nation-states. In

Canada, because the colonial process was driven predominantly by land, many Indigenous peoples were dispossessed of their territories. To survive as distinctive peoples, they engaged with capitalism. The distinction between settler and extractive colonialism is useful in understanding how Indigenous peoples' dispossession and resistance have unfolded differently in various places. This distinction is also useful in exploring the effects of the discourse of rights, the environment, and indigeneity on "Indigenous places and senses of place" (Swyngedouw 2009, 122-23). Moreover, it is useful in understanding Indigenous peoples' specific responses.

Articulations of indigeneity both in resisting and in integrating into the neoliberal project are crucial to comprehending the complexity of Indigenous peoples' struggles and to questioning fixed notions of Indigenous identities. However, indigeneity cannot be reduced to articulation. Indigenous peoples' responses, particularly the contingent nature of resistance, can be understood partly, but not exclusively, as resulting from the global articulations of indigeneity. By elucidating the different contingent spatial configurations through which the strategies of Indigenous peoples are enacted, this book shows how unities, stabilities, and tensions are negotiated and contested. Resistance is politically variable and mediated by social and power relations, negotiations, and co-operation between Indigenous peoples and different actors and among Indigenous people themselves. What actors intervene, what kinds of prescriptions they implement, and where they operate reveal the asymmetry of the power relations that shape the global economy and the complex arenas in which Indigenous peoples struggle.

In analyzing the articulation of indigeneity, I have noted four paradoxes: (1) global/state articulations of indigeneity unevenly empower Indigenous peoples; (2) not all landscapes are created equal; (3) Indigenous nationalism may lead to new internal divisions and further gender discrimination; and (4) struggles for rights increase state power.

## Global/State Articulations of Indigeneity Unevenly Empower Indigenous Peoples

In these pages I have argued that colonialism was not a homogeneous force that transformed Indigenous spaces. Colonizers wanted different things from the colonized, and the places and people they encountered were diverse. The heterogeneity of place and colonial experience resulted in a variety of practices that produced domination, resistance, negotiation, and adaptation. Historical analysis suggests that Indigenous-specific histories and experiences have shaped different processes of collective identity constructions, understandings of community, and critical practices that can never be captured by *universal* definitions of indigeneity. Such definitions are based on static and predetermined notions of culture that clash with constantly contested, imagined, and negotiated social norms and practices in place.

Settler and extractive colonialism entailed different material configurations. In Canada the colonial process rested on the concepts of terra nullius and homo nullius, justifying the removal of Indigenous peoples from their lands. Whereas the Indigenous space was constructed as a controlled and confined space that limited Indigenous movement and livelihoods, the settler space was comprised of open, vast, and unregulated lands. In contrast, extractive colonialism in Mexico was concerned more with exploiting labour and extracting wealth. The social communities, or pueblos, were reorganized to access labour easily. However, many maintained their communal lands and resources.

Efforts to reclaim certain Indigenous rights and to mobilize certain concepts have stemmed from the economic, social, political, and cultural processes that took place in the past and also from the new possibilities that have arisen due to global articulations of indigeneity. The association of indigeneity with a "primordial," fixed attachment to the land is embedded in essentialist cultural constructions that downplay Indigenous peoples' diverse ways of relating to multiple landscapes and to each other and of conferring responsibilities within their communities.

For the purposes of this book, two discursive and material consequences are particularly relevant. First, indigeneity purports that Indigenous peoples have *always* been in a limited place regardless of their complex genealogies of simultaneously travelling the waters and inhabiting the land. Place and belonging revolve around a fixed habitation that functions to erase interconnections, coexistence, and relationships. Second, Indigenous territories and landscapes become a separate body of resources used for fixed, isolated, Indigenous practices that need to be adapted in accordance with the conservation economy. Producing nature as separate from the social reinscribes geographies of gendered inequalities and injustices and reveals the inadequacy of rights-based projects that seek to create opportunities for Indigenous peoples under neoliberalism. Moreover, when Indigenous peoples demand a fairer share of the economic projects taking place in their homelands, they are perceived as being less Indigenous and less concerned with "conserving" nature and "preserving" their cultural identity. We forget that entrepreneurial Indigenous citizenship is also a product of the neo-liberal landscape.

In the historical exploration of the cases treated in this book, I have shown that the mobilization of concepts such as land title, land rights, and Indigenous law has not necessarily led to local empowerment and the fulfillment of local aspirations. In Canada, by requiring diverse Indigenous peoples to show that they were exclusively involved in subsistence activities regardless of the nature of their social organization and by equating hunting with land use, the state continues to disregard difference, the role of women, and the habitation of multiple landscapes as well as the complex legal and social systems organizing relationships in place.

In this framework, land claims have become economic transactions through which Indigenous peoples recover their lands only to cede them to Canada in exchange for self-government rights and compensation. Corporations and the Canadian government are heavily involved in shaping the local economy. Indigenous communities are encouraged to develop leadership, partnerships, local ventures, and self-sufficiency. Ironically, the combination of the rights discourse and colonial narratives about land title and about "traditional," "cultural" economic activities has further limited both the Inuit's and the Nisga'a's ability to maintain their livelihoods and benefit from the land.

Drawing on notions of entrepreneurialism, the self, and the environment, the Nisga'a have attempted to increase the flow of capital into their communities. They have embraced private property and conservation-driven businesses to take advantage of the global economy. This position, however, is not new. For example, since its early days, the Nisga'a Tribal Council has advocated extending the notion of rights beyond "traditional" fishing to include "industrial" practices. The Inuit, on the other hand, have embraced resource development to generate jobs for people who can no longer depend exclusively upon their traditional livelihoods. Although apparently contradictory, these articulations of indigeneity facilitate different types of capital circulation and commodification of nature. As in the case of the Inuit, the Nisga'a see engagement with the economy as empowering, but the government has not fulfilled this vision. Twenty other modern agreements that the Government of Canada has signed have not been fully implemented. Although the government has stated that land claims agreements are more than just "real estate transactions," (quoted in Land Claims Agreements Coalition 2008), it has tended to block their implementation by finding ongoing legal and technical disagreements about the specific meanings of land claims.

In Mexico, on the other hand, the neoliberal reorganization of Indigenous economies and livelihoods has focused on the uneven fragmentation of local production and consumption. By simultaneously liberalizing Indigenous peasants' control over their *ejidal* lands and by protecting communal ownership of forested communities, this strategy has been aimed at simultaneously weakening kin systems and the moral economy of reciprocity in some places and at valuing its contribution to the conservation economy in others. In this context, the formal recognition of Indigenous laws has been transformed into a cultural right to self-government. From this perspective, overcoming injustice is about cultural recognition, not about having control over territory and resources. By limiting collective rights to self-government, neoliberalism has made Indigenous lands vulnerable *in practice* when governments or foreign investors are allocated lands. Moreover, by associating indigeneity exclusively with Indigenous legal orders, neoliberalism has excluded many Indigenous peoples. Neoliberal promises of protection for land rights go hand in hand with conservation-driven businesses. Although Indigenous forest dwellers are targeted for their knowledge and forests, Zapotec peasants are encouraged to abandon their "unproductive," "unsustainable" livelihoods. The Zapatista strategy, on the other hand, redefines Indigenous legal orders and decentres the nation-state as the source of power and people's sovereignty. In doing so, this strategy has given the Zapatistas an Indigenous law to control place.

In both the Canadian and Mexican approaches, policies aimed at accommodating Indigenous claims revolve around more government support and intervention. I have argued that in designing and implementing these policies, nation-states have used politics, the law, and colonial narratives to justify who is entitled to hold land and to profit from it and its resources.

**Not All Landscapes Are Created Equal**
In the current neoliberal context, nature is being valued not only for the resources it provides but also for the "gifts" or "services" we have taken for granted. Clean air, water sources and filtration, carbon storage, biodiversity, human bodies, and other socio-natural entities are now part of the global economy. These ecological services are considered sources of "natural capital" that provide economic opportunities for conservation around the world. Under the current neoliberalism, not all landscapes are created equal. Resource-dependent Indigenous communities are encouraged to exploit

the services locked up in their ecosystems and their knowledge of the natural environment. In contrast, Indigenous peasants and hunters are encouraged to abandon their "unproductive occupations."

Unlike past narratives, the current geo-strategies focus on economics and conservation as justifications for (re)making Indigenous space and reorganizing Indigenous livelihoods. However, these neoliberal strategies are not homogeneous. According to Bakker (2010, 722) different processes of neoliberalization are applied to different kinds of socio-natures depending on their biophysical characteristics, their connection to labour, their consumption practices, and the effectiveness of existing property regimes. This book has shown how nature is produced differently in places. In cases like Nunavut, extracting resources and taking advantage of climate change seem more profitable than commodifying socio-natures. Competing sovereignties in the Arctic and land claims have limited the Inuit's ability to benefit from development and retain control of their homeland. Nunavut's demand for more power is also a demand to expand the notion of indigeneity to include seawater rights. Indigenous peoples inhabit and relate to different landscapes; their livelihoods are embedded in a web of power relations that shape how the Inuit are renegotiating meanings of identity, sharing their practices, and revalorizing country food.

In Chiapas and Oaxaca processes of neoliberalization have identified Indigenous forest dwellers with consumption and Indigenous peasants with the labour force. In the Tehuantepec Isthmus, Zapotec peasants have been driven to sign long-term contracts that transfer their usufruct rights to the wind industry. Peasants' subsistence practices are constructed as "unviable" and "nonsustainable," and they are encouraged to "modernize" their livelihood practices. In the emergent struggle against the wind industry, Zapotecs are articulating indigeneity and invoking the rights stated in the International Labour Organization's Convention 169 (ILO 2003) to defend their lands. In Chiapas the Zapatista-controlled territories are represented as an "illegal" and "violent" space that legitimizes the use of force to remap places by bringing this space under the rule of state law and into the market economy. Unlike the Zapotecs, the Zapatistas are building a community-driven notion of indigeneity, which is more inclusive and practice-oriented. In the Nisga'a case, neoliberalism and private property have been embraced. The book has shown how places engage in articulating and producing representations of indigeneity in relation to specific circumstances. Moreover, it has demonstrated that these processes are shaped by distinct networks and alliances that produce different meanings of indigeneity, with specific consequences for the future.

Unlike previous geo-political discourses, these current geo-strategies are not about remaking self-enclosed, exclusionary spaces. They are about opening up local spaces and incorporating all Indigenous places into the global market. In this sense, the nation-state is central to amalgamating indigeneity, development, and capitalist social relations. The incorporation of "frontiers" and their "poor" inhabitants into the global economy has become part of an "optimistic" world. In contrast, opposition to this vision results in fearful images of "permanent poverty," "marginalization," and "seclusion." In this picture, Indigenous peoples and individuals have been unevenly empowered by simple answers to complex questions. It is simplistic to assume that Indigenous peoples' adoption of or support for neoliberal development is just a manifestation of their having been bought off. Instead, it is important to consider that Indigenous strategies for addressing the broader issues of historical inequalities and gender inequities are embedded in local frameworks and a broader politics of indigeneity that have naturalized certain solutions.

### Indigenous Nationalism May Lead to Internal Divisions and Further Gender Discrimination

To the extent that Indigenous nationalism is constructed to facilitate Indigenous peoples' negotiations with the state, it mimics rigid definitions of indigeneity that rest on timeless cultural interpretations. Both nationalism and global articulations of indigeneity are inherently exclusionary. Nationalism uses culture, tradition, and gender roles as border guards to construct a homogeneous national identity. Global articulations of indigeneity, on the other hand, pull Indigenous peoples away from their diverse local and spatialized practices, laws, and responsibilities as "Indigenous" communities and toward a definition that emphasizes "cultural" rights.

This articulation of indigeneity dispossesses Indigenous peoples of their relationships with place and of their historical interconnections and reduces both to a set of practices that have the potential to coexist with the capitalist economy. Land becomes a body of resources used for predetermined cultural purposes that reproduce colonial constructions of the "Other" and women. The separation of the material from the cultural has led to a convenient separation of economics from politics and culture and to new patterns of gendered inequalities and injustices.

In equating hunting with ownership, the Canadian state has, once again, disenfranchised Indigenous women. Although in both the Nisga'a and Inuit cases, women make important contributions to local economies and social organization, the transformation of complex legal systems and social organization into notions of property and land rights has fragmented the production cycle into a few subsistence practices. When the Nisga'a replaced their system of landholding *wilps* (houses) with the "common bowl" approach, women, as repositories of name titles, lineage, and land ownership, were formally marginalized.

Similarly, Inuit women's work within the production cycle was relegated to a secondary role when hunting became the central activity. As hunting has become an expensive activity, conflicts have arisen over how local understandings of being Indigenous are interpreted. Details of the social and legal embeddedness of ownership and resource allocation have revealed how colonial landscape transformations continue to reinforce the Canadian state's sovereignty over the land.

In Chiapas and Oaxaca, Indigenous peoples' ability to negotiate with and adjust to colonial and state power has generated uneven levels of institutionalization and the coexistence of different land-tenure systems secured by Indigenous law and practices. The construction of Indigenous law as a governance practice that is independent of other social and economic processes is incomplete since this construction simultaneously tends to oppose notions of modern, progressive, and liberal democratic rights. This dichotomous opposition between Indigenous law and Indigenous culture has become the target of the ad hoc liberal discourse that government employs to justify appointing itself as a liberator of Indigenous women, who are cast as victims of their own culture. However, I have shown that the contemporary situation of Indigenous women is due to the overlapping of colonial and nation-state legislation with Indigenous practices.

Unlike the Zapatistas, who have reclaimed Indigenous law to give different people of Mayan descent a law, the Zapotecs from Juchitán have constructed a local nationalism that at first rejected the term "Indigenous" and was in tension with Mestizo society. More recently, peasants have engaged with global articulations of indigeneity that clash with local understandings of being Zapotecs. From this point of view, it is not that the Zapotecs were "peasants" before identifying as "Indigenous." Rather, peasants are one segment of an Indigenous place that has been historically heterogeneous and increasingly differentiated. Unlike the Indigenous female victim, Zapotec and Nisga'a women have been a symbol of power and authority and have played a role in the complex economic and moral economy of solidarity. Nevertheless, this economic power and authority have not been translated into political power in spaces other than the women's sphere. Furthermore, these differences make us think of how the female body becomes a convenient site where discourses of power are borne and contested.

Indigenous women's struggles to access land, resources, and rights and to change unbalanced gender relations awkwardly position them between discourses of domination and subjugation. On the one hand, property rights reify class inequalities and shore up capitalism; on the other hand, land and resources have other meanings for Indigenous societies. Nature is essential not only to securing Indigenous material survival but also to reproducing kinship relations and social practices and to fulfilling obligations. In both Canada and Mexico, Indigenous women have used the discourse of rights to frame their complex identities as Indigenous persons and as women and to convey the idea that gender is produced in specific ways. This framework is further complicated when rights are used as a "universal" standard to measure different categories of people, places, and practices, thus concealing the many layers of their oppression.

**Struggles for Rights Increase State Power**
Indigenous peoples' struggles to have their rights to self-determination recognized unfold in complex national and international arenas in which nation-states, global organizations, networks, and market imperatives converge. I have argued that Indigenous claims are embedded in tensions between local needs and global wants. The transformation of diverse, local understandings of being Indigenous into a stereotyped, recognizable identity prescribes a set of needs and solutions that neither challenge the neoliberal economic project nor legitimately advance Indigenous women's rights. International organizations and states have legally recognized some degree of political autonomy, yet they have failed to address issues related to the material reproduction of Indigenous peoples and to the socio-economic well-being of Indigenous women. In this process, states have reasserted control over Indigenous populations. Unlike colonial domination, this new form of state control is not physically enforced and does not require relocation or forced labour but rather the recognition of certain cultural rights.

By recognizing these rights, international organizations and states have created the conditions in which these rights are exercised. Because this form of recognition is framed in the language of social justice and human rights, it neutralizes nonconformity and displaces blame from the colonial state to the "backwardness" of Indigenous cultures. The expectations, norms, and values associated with indigeneity are reiterated by settlers, Mestizos, academics, nongovernmental organizations, and Indigenous peoples themselves. Thus, to be able to govern themselves, Indigenous peoples must speak the language of liberal democracy and commit to "universal" standards. The cases presented in this study reveal that the political possibilities created by separating Indigenous rights into the categories of law, governance, land ownership, and culture, as well as the neoliberal ideologies that promote an acceptance of everyone's responsibility, leave little room for Indigenous *transformative* action.

Although self-government has enabled the Inuit to interact with the Canadian state and the global economy, it has leveraged Inuit rights away from resource sovereignty and toward a state-mediated model of land claims centred on economic development and neoliberal self-government. Neoliberalism has transformed Indigenous rights to self-government into an obligation to deliver services, to pay for government functions, to fight poverty, and to assume the risks of the decisions made elsewhere. This transformation of rights into obligations is extremely attractive to governments, which have been cutting off services and programs, reducing deficits, and changing the nature of their relationships with society. In a context where impacts on local livelihoods come from faraway places and where exclusive subsistence economies are no longer options, rights as duties are putting more pressure on Indigenous communities. The Inuit's demands for seawater rights and for a fair share of the resource development being implemented in their homeland have been portrayed as an anomaly. In contrast, the Nisga'a's adoption of private property is celebrated because they are taking on the responsibility to provide for themselves. In the current economic environment and under the land claims approach pursued in Canada, Indigenous rights have been effectively liberalized so that Indigenous communities can use their land as collateral to participate in the market economy. Although the Nisga'a have moved toward private property in attempting to take advantage of the global economy, neoliberal reforms in British Columbia have framed the conditions under which they can participate.

In a similar vein, the Zapotecs' participation in the electoral system has done little to vindicate their individual and collective autonomous capacity to control economic development. Although the Zapotecs' defence of political autonomy and the imagery of the strong matriarch have reinforced local pride, changing notions of property and the uneven incorporation of the Tehuantepec Isthmus into the global economy are clashing with heterogeneous understandings of community, resistance, and Zapotec identity.

Unlike the Nisga'a, Inuit, and Zapotecs, the Zapatista communities of Chiapas represent a non-state-driven autonomous project that explicitly stands against neoliberal recognition. As a result, the Zapatista nationalist movement is aimed at controlling place by moving away from nation-state recognition through the implementation of new political, social, and economic norms and practices based on the moral economy of reciprocity and community-driven recognition. By questioning, redefining, and articulating norms, practices, and philosophies, Zapatista communities are contesting hegemonic constructions of indigeneity. Unlike governments' and international institutions' geo-political strategies, Zapatista *caracoles* (administrative centres) are about closing local spaces and selectively delinking the local from the global. Although this inward strategy has so far been useful in addressing immediate needs without government intervention, a sustainable and generalized transformation remains to be seen.

By exploring the connections between neoliberalism, indigeneity, gender, and the environment in two countries and four locations, I have sought to go beyond current attempts to compartmentalize research in terms of the global South and the global North. This compartmentalization has led scholars to ask questions about some places but not about others, masking the uneven development across countries, regions, places, and social groups.

### Spaces of Indigenous Repossessions

I have argued that the making of space and place is not only about domination but also about resistance. Place is a heterogeneous space where both engagement and resistance occur. Beyond the specificities of the cases analyzed in this study, how Indigenous spatial strategies have been articulated has significant implications. Claims to Indigenous collective rights have entailed political acts aimed at representing a stereotyped indigeneity, which is exclusionary. In the first instance, this stereotyped identity, the rights discourse, and the imperatives of the market are not enough to transform neocolonial power relations. Indeed, these elements work to create exclusionary politics and to open up places not fully transformed by market forces. What is needed are alternative frameworks for articulating difference, place, and responsibility in order to address inequalities and inequities by repossessing space. The shift from spaces of dispossession to spaces of repossession is useful in recognizing that the structures of inequalities and domination are imposed not only from the outside but also from within. Thus repossessing the Indigenous self means taking responsibility for transcending internal limitations and for reacting against imposed definitions and categorizations of indigeneity by moving from a politics *of* place to a politics *in* place.

How Indigenous peoples frame resistance has consequences for the kind of future they want to engender. How Indigenous peoples define themselves creates inclusions and exclusions. Indigeneity and self-determination, as they now exist, are conditioned by hegemonic power relations aimed at containing the "Other." Local understandings of being Indigenous are better served if they are firmly rooted in place and in the different experiences contained there – that is, in notions of local history, travelling and arrival, specific understandings of work, social organization, and communal responsibilities. As has been shown, place is a meaningful site for people's everyday life practices. When these practices are superseded by meta-narratives of timeless, essentialized cultures, Indigenous peoples begin to think of themselves in relation to the colonizer and in relation to the binaries of inside versus outside and private versus public.

In my view, it is not productive to define indigeneity in reference to the colonizer or only in terms of an attachment to the land. It is not land-related activities *alone* that make people Indigenous. These subsistence activities are of little significance without the local web of social, spiritual, and economic relations in which they are embedded. A flexible conception of place as a spatial and temporal configuration and of "work" as a set of social practices can be useful in grounding a heterogeneous space of autonomy, relations, and layered Indigenous identities. From this perspective, place/territory, ethical relations to the land, work, and social practices are transversally interwoven differently in different places. They cut across multiple subsistence practices, productive units, exchanges, gift giving, sharing, crafting, consumption, and solidarity networks that depend on people's mobility and relations with each other. These transversally intersected practices are dynamic and speak of Indigenous relations *to* and *in* place. Without the responsibilities of relationships *with* and *in* place, locations are meaningless.

Global discourses shaping the ways that Indigenous peoples should see themselves and gender relations have done little to place women in the landscape. Imagining Indigenous spaces of repossession involves creating inclusive spaces of gender difference and reciprocal relationships with difference. By their heterogeneous nature, transversally intersected practices require

Indigenous women's territorial and spatial *autonomy,* eluding the inside-outside and private-public dichotomies. Men and women participate differently in the complex system of social and economic production through which they simultaneously access the private and the public, assume their subjectivity, and demarcate transversal spaces of power and authority. Relations in place involve assuming that men and women relate to landscape and space differently and that difference is not hierarchical. Indigenous peoples' layered identities, which comprise elements such as sexuality, gender, class, and location, make relationships between people and space and between people and place richer and fuller. These complexities shape not only how people physically use space and places but also how they interpret, represent, and reproduce the self and its relation to the social unit.

From this perspective, there is no clear-cut division between economic and social practices. Relations to community and attachments to place are not about immobility or about having always been in one place. Attachments to place derive from different fields of relationships with the landscape, the spiritual and nonhuman worlds, and the social unit. Attachments can be developed via birth, affiliation, adoption, allegiance, or the fulfilment of responsibilities to place and the social unit. At its core, this transversal intersection of place, social practices, and work stands against a "one size fits all" definition of indigeneity and uneven constructions of nature. Instead, place embraces a view that economic, political, cultural, and social development should occur simultaneously and be diversely crafted. Thus self-determination is not about addressing a "past" colonial harm but about infusing place with specific histories, memories, dislocations, and gendered meanings of dispossession to recreate self-determined jurisdictions.

Repossessing space involves inward localism. However, Indigenous peoples cannot assume that they should cut themselves off from the rest of the world, for they have never been isolated. Rather, repossessing space requires Indigenous peoples to selectively engage with translocal forces and to maintain control over the pace and degree of their interactions with external forces by constantly interrogating and negotiating what kinds of places they seek to engender.

# References

Abele, Frances, and Thierry Rhodon. 2007. "Inuit Diplomacy in the Global Era: The Strengths of Multilateral Internationalism." *Canadian Foreign Policy* 13 (3): 45-63.

Aboriginal Affairs and Northern Development Canada. 2010. *The Government of Canada's Statement of Support to the UNDRIP.* http://www.aadnc-aandc.gc.ca/eng/1309374239861.

Adam, Allan. 2012. "Gateway Pipeline Threatens Our Way of Life." *Edmonton Journal,* 5 May. http://climateandcapitalism.com/2012/05/08/gateway-pipeline-threatens-our-way-of-life.

Adams, W.M. 2001. *Green Development.* 2nd ed. New York: Routledge.

Adelman, Jeremy, and Stephen Aron. 1999. "From Borderlands to Borders: Empires, Nation States and the Peoples in between in North American History." *American Historical Review* 104 (3): 814-41.

Agnew, John. 2001. "The New Global Economy: Time-Space Compression, Geopolitics, and Global Uneven Development." *Journal of World System Research* 7 (2): 133-54.

Agrawal, Arun. 2007. "Forests, Governance, and Sustainability: Common Property Theory and Its Contributions." *International Journal of the Commons* 1 (1): 111-36.

Agrawal, Arun, Ashwini Chhatre, and Rebecca Hardin. 2008. "Changing Governance of the World's Forests." *Science* 320 (5882): 1460-62.

Agrawal, Bina. 1994. *A Field of One's Own: Gender and Land Rights in South Asia.* Cambridge, UK: Cambridge University Press.

Ahlers, Rhodante. 2005. "Gender Dimensions of Neoliberal Water Policy in Mexico and Bolivia: Empowering or Disempowering?" In *Opposing Currents: The Policy of Water and Gendering Latin America*, ed. Vivienne Bennet, Sonia Davila-Poblete, and Maria Nieves Rico, 53-71. Pittsburgh, PA: University of Pittsburgh Press.

Alfred, Taiaiake. 1995. *Heeding the Voices of Our Ancestors: Kahnawake Mohawk Politics and the Rise of Native Nationalism.* Toronto: Oxford University Press.

–. 1999. *Peace, Power, Righteousness: An Indigenous Manifesto.* Oxford: Oxford University Press.

–. 2005. *Wasá'se: Indigenous Pathways of Action and Freedom.* Toronto: Broadview.

–. 2009. "Colonialism and State Dependency." *Journal of Aboriginal Health* 5 (2): 42-60. http://www.naho.ca/jah/english/jah05_02/V5_I2_Colonialism_02.pdf.

Alfred, Taiaiake, and Jeff Corntassel. 2005. *Being Indigenous: Resurgences against Contemporary Colonialism.* Oxford: Blackwell.

Allen, John. 2003. *Lost Geographies of Power.* Oxford: Blackwell.

Altamirano-Jiménez, Isabel. 2004. "North American First Peoples: Slipping Up into Market Citizenship?" *Citizenship Studies* 8 (4): 349-65.

–. 2007. "Indigenous Peoples and the Topography of Gender in Mexico and Canada." In *Remapping Gender in the New Global Order*, ed. Marjorie Cohen and Janine Brodie, 131-50. Abingdon, UK: Routledge.

–. 2008a. "The Colonization and Decolonization of Indigenous Diversity." In *Lighting the Eighth Fire: The Liberation, Resurgence, and Protection of Indigenous Nations*, ed. Leanne Simpson, 176-86. Winnipeg: Arbeiter Ring.

–. 2008b. "Nunavut: Whose Homeland, Whose Voices?" *Canadian Woman Studies* 26 (3-4): 128-34.

–. 2011. "Settler Colonialism, Human Rights and Indigenous Women." *Prairie Forum* 36: 105-25.

Amagoalik, John. 1997. "What Will Gender Parity Achieve?" *Nunatsiaq News*, 31 March.

Ambus, Lisa, et al. 2007. "Market Opportunities and Benefits from Small Forest Tenures." *BC Journal of Ecosystems and Management* 8 (2): 88-99.

Anaya, James. 1996. *Indigenous Peoples in International Law.* Oxford: Oxford University Press.

Anderson, Benedict. 2000. *Imagined Communities: Reflections on the Origin and Spread of Nationalism.* London: Verso.

Archibald, Linda, and Mary Crnkovich. 1999. "If Gender Mattered: A Case Study of Inuit Women, Land Claims and the Voisey's Bay Nickel Project." http://www.swc-cfc.gc.ca.pubspr/0662280024/199911_06622800_e.pdf.

Arctic Council. 2009. *Arctic Human Development Report.* http://library.arcticportal.org/589.

Axtell, James. 1992. *Beyond 1492: Encounters in Colonial North America.* New York: Oxford University Press.

Baitenmann, Helga. 1997. *Rural Agency and State Formation in Post-revolutionary Mexico: The Agrarian Reform in Central Veracruz (1915-1992).* New York: New School of Social Research.

Baker, Joanne. 2006. "Gender, Sovereignty, and the Discourse of Rights in Native Women's Activism." *Meridians: Feminism, Race, Transnationalism* 7 (1): 127-61.

Bakker, Karen. 2010. "The Limits of 'Neo-liberal Natures': Debating Green Neo-liberalism." *Progress in Human Geography* 34 (6): 715-35. http://phg.sagepub.com/content/34/6/715.full.pdf.

Baldwin, A. 2009. "Carbon Nullius and Racial Rule: Race, Nature and the Cultural Politics of Forest Carbon in Canada." *Antipode* 41: 231-55.

Banting, Keith. 1996. "Social Policy." In *Border Crossings: The Internationalization of Canadian Public Policy*, ed. Bruce Doern, Les Pal, and Brian Tomlin, 27-54. Don Mills, ON: Oxford University Press.

Bargh, Maria. 2001. "Romance and Resistance in the Pacific: Neoliberalism and Indigenous Resistance in the Pacific." *Revue Juridique Polynésienne* 1 (118): 251-74. http://194.214.253.172/IMG/pdf/15_Bargh_.pdf.

–, ed. 2007. *Resistance: An Indigenous Response to Neoliberalism*. Wellington, NZ: Huia.

Bargh, Maria, and Jacob Otter. 2009. "Progressive Spaces of Neo-liberalism in Aotearoa: A Geneaology and a Critique." *Asia Pacific Viewpoint* 50 (2): 154-65.

Barker, John. 1998. "Tangled Reconciliations: The Anglican Church and the Nisga'a of BC." *American Ethnologist* 25 (3): 433-51.

Bashevkin, Sylvia. 2002. *Welfare Hot Buttons: Women, Work and Social Policy Reform*. Toronto: University of Toronto Press and University of Pittsburgh Press.

Beals, Leon. 1975. *The Peasant Marketing System of Oaxaca*. Mexico, Berkeley, and Los Angeles: University of California Press.

Belausteguigoitia, Marisa. 2001. "Descaradas y deslenguadas: el cuerpo y la lengua india en los umbrales de la nación." *Debate Feminista* 12 (24): 230-52.

Benjamin, Thomas. 1996. *A Rich Land, a Poor People: Politics and Society in Modern Chiapas*. Albuquerque: University of New Mexico Press.

Bennett, Mark. 2005. "'Indigeneity' as Self Determination." *Indigenous Law Journal* 4: 71-115.

Benwell, Bethan, and Elizabeth Stokoe. 2006. *Discourse and Identity*. Edinburgh: Edinburgh University Press.

Berry, Charles R. 1981. *The Reform in Oaxaca, 1856-76 : A Microhistory of the Liberal Revolution*. Lincoln: University of Nebraska Press.

Blackburn, Carole. 2007. "Producing Legitimacy: Reconciliation and the Negotiation of Aboriginal Rights in Canada." *Journal of the Royal Anthropological Institute* 13 (3): 622-38.

–. 2009. "Differentiating Indigenous Citizenship: Seeking Multiplicity in Rights, Identity and Sovereignty in Canada." *American Ethnologist* 36 (1): 66-78.

Blaser, Mario. 2004. "Life Projects: Indigenous Peoples' Agency and Development." In *In the Way of Development: Indigenous Peoples, Life Projects, and Globalization*, ed. Mario Blaser, Harvey Feit, and Glenn McRae, 26-44. London/Ottawa: Zed Books/IDRC.

Blaser, Mario, Harvey Feit, and Glenn McRae. 2004. "Introduction." In *In the Way of Development: Indigenous Peoples, Life Projects, and Globalization*, ed. Mario Blaser, Harvey Feit, and Glenn McRae, 1-12. London/Ottawa: Zed Books/IDRC.

Blaut, J.M. 1993. *The Colonizer's Model of the World*. New York: Guilford.

Bodenhorn, Barbara. 1990. "'I'm Not the Great Hunter, My Wife Is': Iñupiat and Anthropological Models of Gender." *Études/Inuit/Studies* 14 (1-2): 55-74.

Bohaker, Heidi, and Franca Iacovetta. 2009. "Making Aboriginal People 'Immigrants Too': A Comparison of Citizenship Programs for Newcomers and Indigenous Peoples in Postwar Canada, 1940s-1960s." *Canadian Historical Review* 90 (3): 427-561.

Borrows, John. 2002. *Recovering Canada: The Resurgence of Indigenous Law.* Toronto: University of Toronto Press.

Bourgeois, Annette. 1997. "Nunavut Rejects Equity Plan: Eastern Arctic Residents Vote Down Proposal to Elect a Man and a Woman from Each Riding." *Winnipeg Free Press*, 27 May.

Brading, David. 1985. *The Origins of Mexican Nationalism.* Cambridge, UK: Cambridge University Press.

Braun, Bruce. 2002. *The Intemperate Rainforest: Nature, Culture and Power on Canada's West Coast.* Minneapolis: University of Minnesota Press.

Bray, David B., et al. 2003. "Mexico's Community-Managed Forests as a Global Model for Sustainable Landscapes." *Conservation Biology* 17 (3): 672-77.

–, et al. 2008. "A New Conservation and Development Frontier: Community Protected Areas in Oaxaca, Mexico." *Current Conservation* 2 (2): 7-9.

Brennan, Timothy. 1990. "The National Longing for Form." In *Nation and Narration*, ed. Homi Bhabha, 44-70. London: Routledge.

Brodie, Janine. 2010. "Globalization, Canadian Family and Policy, and the Omission of Neo-liberalism." *North Carolina Law Review* 88 (5): 1559-91.

Brosius, Peter. 1999. "Analysis and Interventions: Anthropological Engagements with Environmentalism." *Current Anthropology* 40: 277-309.

Brosius, Peter, Anna Tsing, and Charles Zerner. 1998. "Representing Communities: Histories and Politics of Community-Based Natural Resource Management." *Society and Natural Resources* 11: 157-68.

Brown, Richard Harvey. 1993. "Cultural Representation and Ideological Domination." *Social Forces* 71 (3): 657-76.

Brown, Wendy. 2001. *Politics out of History.* Princeton, NJ: Princeton University Press.

Brumbach, Hetty Jo, and Robert Jarvenpa. 2002. "Gender Dynamics in Native Northwestern North America: Perspectives and Prospects." In *Many Faces of Gender: Roles and Relationships through Time in Indigenous Northern Communities*, ed. Lisa Frink et al., 195-210. Boulder: University Press of Colorado and University of Calgary Press.

Bryan, Joe. 2009. "Where Would We Be without Them? Knowledge, Space and Power in Indigenous Politics." *Futures* 41: 24-32.

Buell, Mark. 2006. *Resource Extraction Development and Well-Being in the North: A Scan of the Unique Challenges of Development in Inuit Communities.* Ottawa: Ajunnginiq Centre, National Aboriginal Health Organization.

Bull, Gary Q. 2010. "Forest Carbon, Business and Politics: Nisga'a Hope to Profit from Carbon." http://forest300.blogspot.com/2010/08/nisgaa-hope-to-profit-from-carbon.html.

Butler, Caroline F., and Charles Menzies. 2000. "Out of the Woods: Tsimshian Women and Forestry Work." *Anthropology of Work Review* 21 (2): 12-17.

Butler, Judith. 1999. *Gender Trouble: Feminism and the Subversion of Identity.* New York: Routledge.

Campbell, Howard. 1990. "Zapotec Ethnic Politics and the Politics of Culture in Juchitán, Oaxaca (1350-1990)." PhD diss., Department of Anthropology, University of Wisconsin.

Canadian Constitution Foundation. 2007. *Annual Report.* http://www.canadian constitutionfoundation.ca/files/1/2007 20Annual 20Report.pdf.

Cardinal, Harold. 1977. *The Rebirth of Canada's Indians.* Edmonton: Hurtig.

Carey, David, Jr. 2006. "Empowered through Labor and Buttressing Their Communities: Mayan Women and Coastal Migration, 1875-1965." *Hispanic American Historical Review* 86 (3): 501-34.

Cassidy, Frank. 1993. "Troubled Hearts: Indigenous People and the Crown in Canada." In *Becoming Visible: Indigenous Politics and Self-Government,* ed. Terje Brantenberg, Janne Hansen, and Henry Minde. Tromsø, Norway: University of Tromsø Centre for Sámi Studies. http:/www.sami.uit.no/girji/n02/en/203cassi. html.

Castree, Noel. 2004. "Differential Geographies: Place, Indigenous Rights and 'Local' Resources." *Political Geography* 23: 133-67.

–. 2005. *Nature.* New York: Routledge.

–. 2009. "The Time-Space of Capitalism." *Time and Society* 18 (1): 26-61.

Castro, Peter, and Erik Nielsen. 2001. "Indigenous People and Co-management: Implications for Conflict Management." *Environmental Science and Policy* 4 (4-5): 229-39.

CBC North. 2005. "In Nunavut, Exploration Frenzy Continues." 4 February. http://www.cbc.ca/news/canada/north/story/2005/02/04/exploration-permits-02042005.html.

CEMEX. 2009. "Mexican President Inaugurates First Phase of EURUS Wind Farm." http://www.cemex.com/MediaCenter/PressReleases/PressRelease20090122.aspx.

Chabot, Marcelle. 2003. "Economic Changes, Household Strategies, and Social Relations of Contemporary Nunavik Inuit." *Polar Record* 39 (208): 19-34.

Chapela, Francisco. 2005. "Indigenous Community Forest Management in the Sierra Juárez." In *The Community Forests of Mexico: Managing for Sustainable Landscapes,* ed. David Barton Bray, Leticia Merino Pérez, and Deborah Barry, 92-112. Austin: University of Texas Press.

Chapin, Mac. 2004. "A Challenge to Conservationists." *World Watch,* November-December, 17-31.

Chassen-Lopez, Francie R. 2004. *From Liberal to Revolutionary Oaxaca: The View from the South, 1867-1911.* University Park: Pennsylvania State University Press.

Christie, Gordon. 2011. "Indigeneity and Sovereignty in Canada's Far North: The Arctic and Inuit Sovereignty." *South Atlantic Quarterly* 110 (2): 329-46.

Clifford, James. 2001. "Indigenous Articulations." *Contemporary Pacific* 13 (2): 468-90.

Colchester, Marcus. 2002. "Indigenous Rights and the Collective Conscious." *Anthropology Today* 18 (1): 1-3.

Collier, Jane Fishburne. 1995. *El derecho zinacanteco: Procesos de disputar en un pueblo indígena de Chiapas.* Mexico City: CIESAS and UNICACH.

Comaroff, Jean, and John Comaroff. 1991. *Of Revelation and Revolution: Christianity, Colonialism and Consciousness in the South.* Chicago: University of Chicago Press.

Comité Clandestino Revolucionario Indígena – Comandancia General del Ejército Zapatista de Liberación Nacional. 1994. *Segunda Declaración de la Selva Lacandona.* 10 June. http://palabra.ezln.org.mx/comunicados/1994/1994_06_10_d.htm.

Condon, Richard G., and Pamela R. Stern. 1991. "Gender Preference, Gender Identity and Gender Socialization amongst Contemporary Inuit Youth." *Ethos* 21 (4): 384-416.

Conference Board of Canada. 2001. *Nunavut Economic Outlook.* Ottawa: Conference Board of Canada.

Connor, Walker. 2004. "The Timelessness of Nations." *Nations and Nationalism* 10 (1-2): 35-47.

Consejo Nacional de Población. 2000. *Censo Nacional.* http://www.conapo.gob.mx/micros/pronturio/08.pdf.

Conservative Party of Canada. 2006. *Stand Up For Canada.* Federal election platform.

Corntassel, Jeff. 2003. "Who Is Indigenous? 'Peoplehood' and Ethnonationalist Approaches to Rearticulating Indigenous Identity." *Nationalism and Ethnic Studies* 9 (1): 75-100.

Coulthard, Glen. 2010. "Place against Empire: Understanding Indigenous Anti-colonialism." *Affinities: A Journal of Radical Theory, Culture, and Action* 4 (2): 79-83.

Crenshaw, Kimberlé. 1989. "Demarginalizing the Intersection of Race and Sex: A Black Feminist Critique of Antidiscrimination Doctrine, Feminist Theory and Antiracist Politics." *University of Chicago Legal Forum:* 139-67.

Cruz, Víctor de la. 1983. *La rebelión de Che Gorio Melendre.* Juchitán: Ayuntamiento Popular.

Dahl, Jens. 1997. "Gender Parity in Nunavut?" *Indigenous Affairs* 3-4: 42-47.

Daly, Richard. 2005. *Our Box Was Full: An Ethnography for the Delgamuukw Plaintiffs.* Vancouver: UBC Press.

de Certeau, Michel. 1984. *The Practice of Everyday Life.* Berkeley: University of California Press.

Deere, Carmen Diana, and Magdalena León. 2000. *Ciudadanía y derechos económicos: La importancia de la tierra para las mujeres latinoamericanas.* Bogotá, Colombia: Tercer Mundo and Universidad Nacional de Colombia.

Delaney, David. 2002. "The Space That Makes Race." *Professional Geographer* 54 (1): 6-14.

Deloria, Vine, Jr. 1992. *God Is Red: A Native View of Religion.* Golden, CO: Fulcrum.

DeLuca, Kevin. 1999. "Articulation Theory: A Discursive Grounding for Historical Practice." *Philosophy and Rhetoric* 32 (4): 334-48.

Department of Justice Canada. 2000. *Nisga'a Final Agreement.* http://laws-lois. justice.gc.ca/eng/acts/N-23.3.

Desbiens, Caroline. 2004. "Producing North and South: A Political Geography of Hydro Development in Québec." *Canadian Geographer* 48 (2): 101-18.

–. 2007. "Speaking the Land: Exploring Women's Historical Geographies in Northern Quebec." *Canadian Geographer* 51 (3): 360-72.

Dewar, Barry. 2009. "Nunavut and the Nunavut Land Claims Agreement: An Unresolved Relationship." *Policy Options* 30 (7): 74-79. http://www.tunngavik. com/wp-content/uploads/2010/04/nlca-nunavut-dewar-2009.pdf.

Dhillon, C., and M.C. Young. 2010. "Environmental Racism and First Nations: A Call for Socially Just Public Policy Development." *Canadian Journal of Humanities and Social Sciences* 1 (1): 25-39.

Díaz Polanco, Héctor, and Araceli Burguete. 1996. "Sociedad colonial y rebelión in- dígena en el Obispado de Oaxaca (1660)." In *El fuego de la inobediencia: Autonomía y rebelión india en el obispado de Oaxaca,* ed. Hector Díaz Polanco, 17-52. Oaxaca City: CIESAS Istmo.

Dobson, A. 1990. *Green Political Thought: An Introduction.* London: Unwin Hyman.

Dodds, Klaus-John, and James Derrick Sidaway. 1994. "Locating Critical Geopolitics." *Environment and Planning D: Society and Space* 12 (5): 515-24.

Dodson, Michael. 1994. "The End of the Beginning: Re(de)finding Aboriginality." *Australian Aboriginal Studies* 1: 2-13.

Domínguez Reyes, Edmé. 2004. "Feminismo, clase y etnicidad: Hegemonía o toler- ancia." In *Mujeres, Ciudadanía y Participación Política en México,* ed. Edmé Domínguez Reyes, 205-44. Göteborg, Sweden: Göteborg University and Red Haina.

Drucker, Philip. 1963. *Indians of the Northwest Coast.* Garden City, NY: Natural History Press.

Earle, Duncan, and Jeanne Simonelli. 2005. *Uprising of Hope: Sharing the Zapatista Journey to Alternative Development.* Walnut Creek, CA: Altamira.

Engle, Karen. 2010. *The Elusive Promise of Indigenous Development: Rights, Culture, Strategy.* Durham, NC: Duke University Press.

Enloe, Cynthia. 1993. *Sexual Politics at the End of the Cold War: The Morning After.* Berkeley and Los Angeles: University of California Press.

Escobar, Arturo. 2001. "Culture Sits in Places: Reflections on Globalism and Subaltern Strategies of Globalization." *Political Geography* 20: 139-74.

–. 2005. *Mas allá del Tercer Mundo: Globalización y differencia.* Bogotá, Colombia: Instituto Colombiano de Antropología e Historia.

Esteva, Gustavo. 2000. "The Revolution of the New Commons." In *Aboriginal Rights and Self-Government: The Canadian and Mexican Experience in North American Perspective,* ed. Curtis Cook and Juan Lindau, 186-217. Montreal and Kingston: McGill-Queen's University Press.

Esteva-Fabregat, Claudio. 1995. *Mestizaje in Ibero-America.* Tucson: University of Arizona Press.

Evans, Julie. 2009. "Where Lawlessness Is Law: The Settler-Colonial Frontier as a Legal Space of Violence." *Australian Feminist Law Journal* 30 (June): 3-22.

http://www.decolonizing.ps/site/wp-content/uploads/2010/03/evans-j-where
-lawlessness-is-law.pdf.

Exell, Robert. 1990. "History of Indian Land Claims in BC." *Advocate* 48, part 6
(December): 866-80.

EZLN (Ejército Zapatista de Liberación Nacional). 1995. *Tercera Declaracion de la
Selva Lacandona.* http://www.struggle.ws/mexico/ezlnco.html.

–. 2003. "El nacimiento de los Caracoles." www.laneta.apc.org/sclc/ezln/2003agosto
09.htm.

Fairweather, Joan G. 2006. *A Common Hunger: Land Rights in Canada and South
Africa.* Calgary: University of Calgary Press.

Feagan, Robert. 2007. "The Place of Food: Mapping Out the 'Local' in Local Food
Systems." *Progress in Human Geography* 31 (1): 23-42.

Feit, Harvey A. 2010. "Neoliberal Governance and James Bay Cree Governance:
Negotiated Agreements, Oppositional Struggles, and Co-Governance." In *Indigen-
ous Peoples and Autonomy: Insights for a Global Age,* ed. Mario Blaser, Ravi de
Costa, Deborah McGregor, and William Coleman, 49-79. Vancouver: UBC Press.

Findlay, Andrew. 2010. "The Nisga'a's Private Struggle." *BCBusiness,* 3 March. http://
www.bcbusiness.ca.

Finley-Brook, M. 2007. "Green Neoliberal Space: The Mesoamerican Biological
Corridor." *Journal of Latin American Geography* 6 (1): 101-24.

Fisher, Robin. 1977. *Contact and Conflict: Indian-European Relations in British
Columbia.* Vancouver: UBC Press.

Fiske, Jo-Anne. 1991. "Colonization and the Decline of Women's Status: The
Tsimshian Case." *Feminist Studies* 17 (3): 509-36.

Flores Vera, Eusebio. 2000. "Protestantismo, catolicismo y vida rural entre los
totonacos de la costa." MA thesis, Social Anthropology Department, Centro de
Investigación y Estudios Superiores en Antropología Social.

Florescano, Enrique. 1997. *Etnia, estado y nación.* Mexico City: Aguilar.

Foley, Michael. 1995. "Privatizing the Countryside: The Mexican Peasant Movement
and Neo-liberal Reform." *Latin American Perspectives* 84 (22): 59-76.

Freeman, Milton. 1979. "Traditional Land Users as a Legitimate Source of Environmental Expertise." In *The Canadian National Parks: Today and Tomorrow
– Conference II, Ten Years Later,* ed. J.G. Nelson, 345-69. Waterloo, ON: Studies
in Land Use, History and Landscape Change, University of Waterloo.

Frink, Lisa. 2002. "Fish Tales: Women and Decision Making in Western Alaska." In
*Many Faces of Gender: Roles and Relationships through Time in Indigenous
Northern Communities,* ed. Lisa Frink, Rita S. Shepard, and Gregory A. Reinhardt,
93-110. Boulder: University Press of Colorado.

–. 2007. "Storage and Status in Precolonial and Colonial Coastal Western Alaska."
*Current Anthropology* 48 (3): 349-74.

García de León, Antonio. 2002. *Fronteras interiores: Chiapas, una modernidad particular.* Mexico City: Oceano.

Geertz, Clifford. 1973. *The Interpretation of Culture.* New York: Basic Books.

Gellner, Ernest. 1983. *Nations and Nationalism.* London: Wiley-Blackwell.

–. 1988. *Naciones y nacionalismo.* Mexico City: CONACULTA and Alianza Editorial.

–. 1994. *Encounters with Nationalism*. Oxford: Blackwell.

Gerrard, Emily. 2008. "Climate Change and Human Rights: Issues and Opportunities for Indigenous Peoples." *University of New South Wales Law Journal* 31 (3): 941-52.

Gibson, Chris. 1999. "Cartographies of the Colonial/Capitalist State: A Geopolitics of Indigenous Self-Determination in Australia." *Antipodes* 31 (1): 47-79.

Gijsbers, Wim. 1999. *Usos and costumbres: Caciquismo e intolerancia religiosa.* Oaxaca City: Centro de Apoyo al Movimiento Popular Oaxacaqueño A.C.

Global Wind Energy Council. 2010. *Wind Industry Cancún Declaration*. http://dev6. semaforce.be/fileadmin/documents/Publications/Cancun Declaration.pdf.

Gobierno del Estado de Oaxaca. 1856. *Cartas del gobierno de Oaxaca al Soberano Congreso Constituyente*. Facsimilar ed. Oaxaca: Ediciones Toledo.

–. 1998. *Ley de Derechos de los Pueblos y Comunidades Indígenas del Estado de Oaxaca*. http://www.diputados.gob.mx/comisiones/asunindi/oaxregla.pdf.

Godlewska, Christina, and Jeremy Webber. 2007. "The Calder Decision: Aboriginal Title, Treaties and the Nisga'a." In *Let Right Be Done*, ed. Hamar Foster, Heather Raven, and Jeremy Webber, 1-36. Vancouver: UBC Press.

Goldman, Michael. 2001. "The Birth of a Discipline: Producing Authoritative Green Knowledge, World Bank–Style." *Ethnology* 2 (2): 191-217.

Gombay, Nicole. 2000. "The Politics of Culture: Gender Parity in the Legislative Assembly of Nunavut." *Études/Inuit/Studies* 4 (1): 125-48.

–. 2005. "The Commoditization of Country Foods in Nunavik: A Comparative Assessment of Its Development, Applications, and Significance." *Arctic* 58 (2): 115-28.

Government of British Columbia. 1877. *Report of the Government of British Columbia on the Subject of Indian Reserves*. Victoria: Government Printer.

Government of Nunavut. 1993. *Agreement between the Inuit of the Nunavut Settlement Area and Her Majesty the Queen in Right of Canada*. Iqaluit: Government of Nunavut. http://www.gov.nu.ca/hr/site/doc/nlca.pdf.

Gowan, Rebecca. 2003. "Shared Points of Departure and Battlegrounds of Meaning: Indigenous Women and Self-government in Nunavut and Oaxaca." MA thesis, Department of Political Science, Carleton University.

Green, Joyce. 2001. "Canaries in the Mines of Citizenship: Indian Women in Canada." *Canadian Journal of Political Science* 34 (4): 715-38.

Greider, Thomas, and Lorraine Garkovich. 1994. "Landscapes: The Social Construction of Nature and the Environment." *Rural Sociology* 59 (1): 1-24.

Grek Martin, Jason William. 2009. "Making Settler Space: George Dawson, the Geological Survey of Canada and the Colonization of the Canadian West in the Late 19th Century." PhD diss., Geography Department, Queen's University.

Guemple, Lee. 1986. "Men and Women, Husbands and Wives: The Role of Gender in Traditional Inuit Society." *Études/Inuit/Studies* 10 (1-2): 9-24.

Guibernau, Montserrat. 1999. *Nations without States: Political Communities in a Global Age*. Cambridge, UK: Polity.

Gupta, Akhil, and James Ferguson. 1997. "Beyond 'Culture': Space, Identity, and the Politics of Difference." In *Culture, Power, Place: Explorations in Critical Anthropology*, ed. A. Gupta and J. Ferguson, 33-51. Durham, NC: Duke University Press.

Gutiérrez, Margarita, and Nellys Palomo. 1999. "Autonomía con mirada de mujer." In *México: Experiencias de autonomía indígena,* ed. Araceli Burguete Cal y Mayor, 54-86. Copenhagen: International Working Group on Indigenous Affairs.

Gutiérrez Chong, Natividad. 2006. "Patriotic Thoughts or Intuition: Roles of Women in Mexican Nationalisms." *Nations and Nationalism* 12 (2): 339-58.

Haenn, Nora. 2002. "Nature Regimes in Southern Mexico: A History of Power and Environment." *Ethnology* 41 (1): 1-26.

–. 2006. "The Changing and Enduring Ejido: A State and Regional Examination of Mexico's Land Tenure Counter Reforms." *Land Use Policy* 23 (2): 136-46.

Hale, Charles R. 1997. "Cultural Politics of Identity in Latin America." *Annual Review of Anthropology* 26 (1): 567-90.

–. 2002. "Does Multiculturalism Menace? Governance, Cultural Rights, and the Politics of Identity in Guatemala." *Journal of Latin American Studies* 34 (3): 485-524.

–. 2005. "Dangerous Discourses: Human Rights and Multiculturalism in Neo-liberal Mexico." *PoLAR: Political and Legal Anthropology Review* 28 (1): 10-19.

Hall, Stuart. 1999. "Old and New Identities." In *Theories of Race and Racism: A Reader,* ed. Les Back and John Solomos, 144-53. London: Blackwell.

Hamilton, Sarah. 2002. "Neo-liberalism, Gender and Property Rights in Rural Mexico." *Latin American Research Review* 37 (1): 119-43.

Harcourt, Wendy, and Arturo Escobar. 2002. "Women and the Politics of Place." *Development* 45 (1): 8-13. http://www.scribd.com/doc/20244399/Escobar-and-Harcourt-Women-and-the-Politics-of-Place.

Harkin, Michael. 1993. "Power and Progress: The Evangelic Dialogue among the Heiltsuk." *Ethnohistory* 40 (1): 1-33.

Harper, Stephen. 2006. Letter to Dwight A. Dorey, National Chief, Congress of Aboriginal Peoples. 10 January. Reproduced in "Conservative Leader Promises New Deal for Urban Aboriginals." Turtle Island Native Network Forum, http://www.turtleisland.org/discussion/viewtopic.php.

Harris, Cole. 2002. *Making Native Space: Colonialism, Resistance and Reserves in British Columbia.* Vancouver: UBC Press.

–. 2004. "How Did Colonialism Dispossess? Comments from an Edge of Empire." *Annals of the Association of American Geographers* 94 (1): 165-82.

Harris, Douglas C. 2001. *Fish, Law and Colonialism.* Toronto: University of Toronto Press.

Harvey, David. 1996. *Justice, Nature and the Geography of Difference.* Malden, MA and Oxford: Blackwell.

Harvey, Neil. 1999. *The Chiapas Rebellion: The Struggle for Land and Democracy.* Durham, NC: Duke University Press.

–. 2001. "Globalisation and Resistance in Post–Cold War Mexico: Difference, Citizenship and Biodiversity Conflicts in Chiapas." *Third World Quarterly* 22 (6): 1045-61.

Haythornthwaite, Gabriel. 2000. "Tossing the Templates: B.C. Natives Reject Nisga'a Treaty Style." *Canadian Dimension* 34 (5): 33-36.

Henderson, Ailsa. 2007. "Cultural Renaissance or Economic Emancipation? Predictors of Support for Devolution in Nunavut." *Journal of Canadian Studies* 41 (2): 1-23.

Henestrosa Orozco, Ricardo. 2009. "Desarrollo del proyecto eólico en la región del Istmo de Tehuantepec." *Investigación y Ciencia* 42: 18-21.

Henheffer, Tom. 2009. "Inuit Communities Torn over Emissions Reductions." *Maclean's,* 17 December. http://www2.macleans.ca/tag/arctic/page/2.

Hernández Castillo, Aída. 2001. "Entre el etnocentrismo feminista y el essencialismo étnico: Las mujeres indígenas y sus demandas de género." *Debate feminista* 24 (12): 206-29.

Hernández Díaz, Jorge. 1992. "El movimiento indígena y la construcción de la etnicidad en Oaxaca." *Cuadernos del Sur* 2: 47-66.

–. 2001. *Reclamos de la identidad: La formación de las organizaciones indígenas en Oaxaca.* Mexico City: Miguel Ángel Porrúa and Universidad Autónoma Benito Juárez de Oaxaca.

Heynen, Nikolas, and Paul Robbins. 2005. "The Neoliberalization of Nature: Governance, Privatization, Enclosure and Valuation." *Capitalism Nature Socialism* 16 (1): 5-8.

Hicks, Jack, and Graham White. 2000. "Nunavut: Inuit Self-Determination through a Land Claim and Public Government?" In *Inuit Regain Control of Their Lands and Lives,* ed. Jens Dahl et al., 30-117. Copenhagen: International Work Group for Indigenous Affairs.

Hobsbawm, Eric. 1992. *Nations and Nationalism since 1780.* 2nd ed. Cambridge: Cambridge University Press.

Hollon, Ryan, and Karen Lopez. 2007. "Autonomous Capacity Building: Zapatista Bases of Support, Radical Commercial Corridors, and the Battle for the Horizon in the Urban US." *Affinities: A Journal of Radical Theory, Culture and Action* 1 (1): 49-68.

Holmes, Joan. 1987. *Bill C-31: Equality or Disparity? The Effects of the New Indian Act on Native Women.* Ottawa: Canadian Advisory Council on the Status of Women.

Hopson, Eben. 1978. "Hopson's Address to the London Press Corps." http://www.ebenhopson.com/papers/1978/London.html.

Horn, Rebecca. 1997. *Post-conquest Coyoacan: Nahua-Spanish Relations in Central Mexico.* Stanford, CA: Stanford University Press.

Howitt, Richard. 2003. "Scale." In *A Companion to Political Geography,* ed. John Agnew, Katharyne Mitchell, and Gerard Toal, 138-57. Oxford: Blackwell.

–. 2009. "Getting the Scale Right? A Relational Scale Politics of Native Title in Australia." In *Leviathan Undone? Towards a Political Economy of Scale,* ed. Roger Keil and Rianne Mahon, 141-58. Vancouver: UBC Press.

Hume, Stephen. 2000. "Songs of the Nass." *Canadian Geographic* 120 (1): 58-68.

Hutchinson, John. 1999. "Re-interpreting Cultural Nationalism." *Australian Journal of Politics and History* 45 (3): 392-409.

Igoe, Jim, and Dan Brockington. 2007. "Neoliberal Conservation: A Brief Introduction." *Conservation and Society* 5 (4): 432-49.

ILO (International Labour Organization). 2003. *C169 – Indigenous and Tribal Peoples Convention: A Manual.* http://www.ilo.org/ilolex/cgi-lex/convde.pl?C169.

Indian Land Committee. 1910. *Examination of Indian Agent Perry at Victoria.* http://gsdl.ubcic.bc.ca, Nass Agency.

Instituto Nacional de Estadística y Geografía. *México en cifras.* http://www3.inegi.
org.mx/sistemas/mexicocifras/default.aspx.

Inuit Tapiriit Kanatami. 2008. "Inuit Leader Sends 12 Questions to Party Leaders
in an Open Letter." https://www.itk.ca/front-page-story/inuit-leader-sends-12
-questions-party-leaders-open-letter.

–. 2009. "An Integrated Arctic Strategy." https://www.itk.ca/publication/integrated
-arctic-strategy.

–. 2011. "Inuit Ready for Oil and Gas Drilling in the Arctic." https://www.itk.ca/
inuitready-for-oil-and-gas-drilling.

Ita, Ana de. 2006. "Land Concentration in Mexico after PROCEDE." In *The Promised
Land: Competing Visions of Agrarian Reform,* ed. Peter Roset, Raj Patel, and
Michael Courville, 148-64. New York: Food First Books.

Jaimes, M. Annette, and Theresa Halsey. 1992. "American Indian Women: At the
Center of Indigenous Resistance in North America." In *The State of Native
America: Genocide, Colonization, and Resistance,* ed. M. Annette Jaimes, 311-44.
Boston: South End.

Jamieson, Kathleen. 1978. *Indian Women and the Law in Canada: Citizens Minus.*
Ottawa: Minister of Supply and Services Canada.

Jamieson, Stuart. 1968. *Times of Trouble: Labour Unrest and Industrial Conflict in
Canada,* 1900-1966. Ottawa: Privy Council Task Force in Labour Relations.

Jessop, Bob. 2002. *The Future of the Capitalist State.* Cambridge: Polity.

Johnson, Leigh. 2010. "The Fearful Symmetry of Arctic Climate Change: Accumulation by Degradation." *Environment and Planning D: Society and Space* 28 (5):
828-47.

Jung, Courtney. 2003. "The Politics of Indigenous Identity: Neo-liberalism, Cultural
Rights and the Mexican Zapatistas." *Social Research* 7 (2): 433-62.

–. 2006. "Why Liberals Should Value Identity Politics." *Daedalus* 135 (4): 32-39.

–. 2008. *The Moral Force of Indigenous Politics: Critical Liberalism and the Zapatistas.* Cambridge: Cambridge University Press.

Kabeer, Naila. 2005. "Gender Equality and Women's Empowerment: A Critical
Analysis of the Third Millennium Development Goal." *Gender and Development*
13 (1): 13-24.

Keil, Roger, and Rianne Mahon. 2009. "Introduction." In *Leviathan Undone? Towards
a Political Economy of Scale,* ed. Roger Keil and Rianne Mahon, 3-16. Vancouver:
UBC Press.

Kellogg, Susan. 1997. "From Parallel and Equivalent to Separate and Unequal:
Tenochca Mexica Women, 1500-1700." In *Indian Women of Early Mexico:
Identity, Ethnicity and Gender Differentiation,* ed. Susan Schroeder, Stephanie
Wood, and Robert Kaskett, 123-44. Norman: University of Oklahoma Press.

–. 2005. *Weaving the Past: A History of Latin America's Indigenous Women from
the Pre-Hispanic Period to the Present.* New York: Oxford University Press.

Kemmis, D. 1990. *Community and the Politics of Place.* Norman: University of
Oklahoma Press.

Kilbane Gockel, Catherine, and Leslie C. Gray. 2011. "Debt-for-Nature Swaps in
Action: Two Case Studies in Peru." *Ecology and Society* 16 (3): n.p. http://www.
ecologyandsociety.org/vol16/iss3/art13.

King, Ynestra. 1997. "Managerial Environmentalism, Population Control and the New National Insecurity: Towards a Feminist Critique." *Political Environments* 5. http://www.cwpe.org/node/135.

Knight, Alan. 2002. *Mexico: The Colonial Era*. Cambridge: Cambridge University Press.

Kobayashi, Audrey. 1994. *Women, Work, and Place*. Montreal and Kingston: McGill-Queen's University Press.

Kobayashi, Audrey, and Abigail B. Bakan. 2003. *Nunavut: Lessons of an Equity Conversation for Anti-racist Activists*. Toronto: Canadian Race Relations Foundation.

Kohn, Hans. 2008. *The Idea of Nationalism: A Study in its Origin and Background*. New Jersey: Transaction.

Komisaruk, Catherine. 2009. "Indigenous Labor as Family Labor: Tributes, Migration, and Hispanicization in Colonial Guatemala." *Labor: Studies in Working-Class History of the Americas* 6 (4): 41-46.

Kusugaq, Jose. 2000. "The Tide Has Shifted: Nunavut Works for Us, and It Offers a Lesson to the Broader Global Community." In *Inuit Regain Control of Their Lands and Lives*, ed. Jens Dahl et al., 20-30. Copenhagen: International Work Group for Indigenous Affairs.

*La Jornada*. 2001. "Comandante Esther Palabra Zapatista, Ejército Zapatista de Liberación Nacional." 29 March.

Laclau, Ernesto, and Chantal Mouffe. 1985. *Hegemony and Socialist Strategy: Towards a Radical Democratic Politics*. London: Verso.

Laghi, Brian. 1997. "Eastern Arctic Residents Reject Gender-Equal Plan: Supporters Said It Would Reflect Balance of Work in Traditional Inuit Society." *Globe and Mail*, 27 May.

Land Claims Agreements Coalition (LCAC). 2008. "Submission to the Standing Senate Committee on Aboriginal Peoples of the Parliament of Canada." http://www.landclaimscoalition.ca/coalition-documents.

–. 2011. "Schedule of Modern Land Claims Agreements." http://www.landclaims coalition.ca/coalition-documents.

Larner, Wendy. 2003. "Neoliberalism?" *Environment and Planning D: Society and Space* 21 (5): 509-12. http://www.envplan.com/epd/editorials/d2105ed.pdf.

Larson, Brooke, and Robert Wasserstrom. 1983. "Coerced Consumption in Colonial Bolivia and Guatemala." *Radical History Review* 27 (1): 49-78.

Laurie, Nina, Robert Andolina, and Sarah Radcliffe. 2002. "The Excluded 'Indigenous'? The Implications of Multi-ethnic Policies for Water Reform in Bolivia." In *Multiculturalism in Latin America: Indigenous Rights, Diversity and Democracy*, ed. Rachel Sieder, 252-76. New York: Palgrave Macmillan.

LaViolette, Forrest E. 1973. *The Struggle for Survival: Indian Cultures and the Protestant Ethic in British Columbia*. Toronto: University of Toronto Press.

Lawrence, Bonita, and Kim Anderson. 2005. "Introduction to 'Indigenous Women: The State of Our Nations.'" *Atlantis* 29 (2): 1-8.

Leach, Melissa. 2007. "Earth Mother Myths and Other Ecofeminist Fables: How a Strategic Notion Rose and Fell." *Development and Change* 38 (1): 67-85.

Lewis, Nick. 2009. "Progressive Spaces of Neo-liberalism?" *Asia Pacific Viewpoint* 50 (2): 113-19.

Leyva, Xochitl, and Gabriel Ascencio. 1996. *Lacandonia al filo del agua*. Mexico City: Centro de Investigación y Estudios Superiores en Antropología Social.

Littlefield, Lorraine. 1987. "Women Traders in the Maritime Fur Trade." In *Native People, Native Lands: Canadian Indians, Inuit and Métis*, ed. Bruce Alden Cox, 173-83. Ottawa: Carleton University Press.

López Morales, Alberto. 2007. "Amagan para impedir votación." *El Universal*, 4 October.

Loukacheva, Natalia. 2004. "Security Challenges and Legal Capacity of Greenland and Nunavut Jurisdictions." Paper presented at the Third Northern Research Forum, Yellowknife, 15-18 September. http://www.nrf.is/Publications/The Resilient North/List of authors.htm.

–. 2007. *The Arctic Promise: Legal and Political Autonomy of Greenland and Nunavut*. Toronto: University of Toronto Press.

Macnaghten, Phil. 2003. "Embodying the Environment in Everyday Life Practices." *Sociological Review* 51: 62-84.

Magnusson, Warren. 2009. "Scaling Government to Politics." In *Leviathan Undone? Towards a Political Economy of Scale*, ed. Roger Keil and Rianne Mahon, 105-20. Vancouver: UBC Press.

Manuel, George, and Michael Posluns. 1974. *The Fourth World: An Indian Reality*. New York: Free Press.

Martin, Patricia. 2005. "Comparative Topographies of Neoliberalism in Mexico." *Environment and Planning A* 37 (2): 203-20.

Martínez Cobo, José R. 1986. *Study on the Problem of Discrimination against Indigenous Populations*. http://www.un.org/esa/socdev/unpfii/en/spdaip.html.

Martínez Luna, Jaime. 2010. "The Fourth Principle." In *New World of Indigenous Resistance: Noam Chomsky and Voices from North, South and Central America*, ed. Lois Meyer and Benjamín Maldonado Alvarado, 85-101. San Francisco: City Lights Books.

Marx, Karl, and Friedrich Engels. 1978. *The Marx-Engels Reader*. New York: W.W. Norton.

Massey, Doreen. 1994. "A Global Sense of Place." In *Space, Place and Gender*, 146-56. Minneapolis: University of Minnesota Press.

Mathews, Andrew S. 2009. "Unlikely Alliances: Encounters between State Science, Nature Spirits, and Indigenous Industrial Forestry in Mexico, 1926–2008." *Current Anthropology* 50 (1): 75-101.

McAfee, Kathleen. 1999. "Saving Nature to Sell it? Biodiversity and Green Developmentalism." *Environment and Planning D: Society and Space* 17 (2): 133-54.

McAfee, Kathleen, and Elizabeth N. Shapiro. 2010. "Payment for Ecosystem Services in Mexico: Nature, Neoliberalism, Social Movements and the State." *Annals of the Association of American Geographers* 100 (3): 1-21.

McCarthy, J., and S. Prudham. 2004. "Neoliberal Nature and the Nature of Neoliberalism." *Geoforum* 35: 275-83.

McClintock, Anne. 1993. "Family Feuds: Gender, Nationalism and the Family." *Feminist Review* 44: 61-80.

McCreery, David. 2000. *The Sweat of Their Brow: A History of Work in Latin America*. New York: M.E. Sharp.

McKillop, Heather. 2006. "In Search of Maya Sea Traders." *Journal of Latin American and Caribbean Anthropology* 11 (1): 231-33.

McKinley, E. 2007. "Postcolonialism, Indigenous Students, and Science Education." In *Handbook of Research on Science Education*, ed. S.K. Abell and N.G. Lederman, 199-226. Mahwah, NJ: Erlbaum.

Memmi, Albert. 2003. *The Colonizer and the Colonized.* Oxford: Earthscan.

Merino, Mauricio. 2004. *Los gobiernos municipales de México.* Mexico City: CIDE.

Merlan, Francesca. 2009. "Indigeneity: Global and Local." *Current Anthropology* 50 (3): 303-33.

Merry, Sally Engle. 2006a. *Human Rights and Gender Violence: Translating International Law into Local Justice.* Chicago: University of Chicago Press.

–. 2006b. "Human Rights and Transnational Culture: Regulating Gender Violence through Global Law." *Osgoode Hall Law Journal* 44 (1): 53-75.

Miano Borruso, Marinella. 2002. *Hombre, mujer y muxe en el Istmo de Tehuantepec.* Mexico City: CONACULTA, INAH, and Plaza y Valdés Editores.

Mifflin, Michael. 2008. "Canada's Arctic Sovereignty and Nunavut's Place in the Federation." *Policy Options* 29 (7): 86-90.

Mignolo, Walter. 2007. "The De-colonial Option and the Meaning of Identity in Politics." *Anales Nueva Epoca* 9-10: 43-72.

Millennium Partners. 2002. *Building Nunavut through Decentralization: Evaluation Report.* Iqaluit: Evaluation and Statistics Division, Department of Executive and Intergovernmental Affairs, Government of Nunavut.

Minogue, Sara. 2005. "Two Girls for Every Boy at the GN." *Nunatsiaq News,* 27 May. http://www.nunatsiaqonline.ca/archives/50527/news/nunavut/50527_01.html.

Mitchell, Marybelle. 1996. *From Talking Chiefs to a Native Corporate Elite: The Birth of Class and Nationalism among Canadian Inuit.* Montreal and Kingston: McGill-Queen's University Press.

Mohanram, Radhika. 2002. *Imperial White: Race, Diaspora and the British Empire.* Minneapolis: University of Minnesota Press.

Mohanty, Chandra. 1991. "Cartographies of Struggles: Third World Women and the Politics of Feminism." In *Third World Women and the Politics of Feminism,* ed. Chandra Mohanty, Ann Russo, and Lourdes Torres, 51-80. Bloomington: Indiana University Press.

–. 1994. "Under Western Eyes: Feminist Scholarship and Colonial Discourses." In *Colonial Discourse and Postcolonial Theory: A Reader,* ed. Laura Chrisman and Patrick Williams, 196-220. New York: Harvester Wheatsheaf.

–. 2003. *Feminism without Borders: Decolonizing Theory, Practicing Solidarity.* Durham, NC: Duke University Press.

Monjardín, Adriana, and Dulce María Rebolledo Millán. 1999. "Los municipios autónomos zapatistas." *Revista Chiapas* 7, http://membres.multimania.fr/revistachiapas.

Monture, Patricia M., and Patricia D. McGuire, eds. 2009. *First Voices: An Aboriginal Women's Reader.* Toronto: INANNA Publications and Education.

Monture-Angus, Patricia. 1995. *Thunder in My Soul: A Mohawk Woman Speaks.* Halifax: Fernwood.

Moore, Donald S. 1998. "Subaltern Struggles and the Politics of Place: Remapping Resistance in Zimbabwe's Eastern Highlands." *Cultural Anthropology* 13 (3): 344-81.

Morkenstam, Ulf. 2005. "Indigenous Peoples and the Right to Self-determination: The Case of the Swedish Sami People." *Canadian Journal of Native Studies* 25 (2): 433-61.

Mulrennan, Monica E., and Colin H. Scott. 2000. "Mare Nullius: Indigenous Rights in Saltwater Environments." *Development and Change* 31 (3): 681-708.

Mulroney, Brian. 1985. "Notes for an Opening Statement to the Conference of First Ministers on the Rights of Aboriginal Peoples." In *The Quest for Justice: Aboriginal Peoples and Aboriginal Rights*, ed. Menno Boldt and J. Anthony Long, 157-65. Toronto: University of Toronto Press.

Murray, Peter. 1985. *The Devil and Mr. Duncan*. Victoria, BC: Sono Nis.

Muszynski, Alicja. 1996. *Cheap Wage Labour: Race and Gender in the Fisheries of British Columbia*. Montreal and Kingston: McGill-Queen's University Press.

Nadasdy, Paul. 2005. "Anti-Politics of TEK: The Institutionalization of Co-management Discourse and Practice." *Anthropologica* 47 (2): 215-32.

Nader, Laura. 1998. *Ideología armónica: Justicia y control en un pueblo de la montaña zapoteca*. Oaxaca City: Instituto Oaxaqueño de las Culturas, Fondo Estatal para la Cultura y las Artes, and CIESAS.

Nagel, Joane. 1998. "Masculinity and Nationalism: Gender and Sexuality in the Making of Nations." *Ethnic and Racial Studies* 21 (2): 242-69.

Napoleon, Val. 2005. "Aboriginal Self Determination: Individual Self and Collective Selves." *Atlantis* 29 (2): 31-46.

Nash, June. 1993. "Maya Household Production in the World Market: The Potters of Amatenango del Valle, Chiapas, Mexico." In *Crafts in the World Market: The Impact of Global Exchange in Middle American Artisans*, ed. June Nash, 127-55. Albany: State University of New York Press.

Nast, Heidi. 2006. "Loving ... Whatever: Alienation, Neoliberalism and Pet-Love in the Twenty First Century." *ACME: An International E-Journal for Critical Geographies* 5 (2): 300-27.

Natcher, David C. 2001. "Land Use Research and the Duty to Consult: A Misrepresentation of the Aboriginal Landscape." *Land Use Policy* 18: 113-22.

National Round Table on the Environment and the Economy. 2003. *Securing Canada's Natural Capital: A Vision for Nature Conservation in the 21st Century*. Ottawa: Renouf.

Neumann, Roderick P. 2004. *Imposing Wilderness: Struggles over Livelihoods and Nature Preservation*. Los Angeles: University of California Press.

Newdick, Vivian. 2005. "The Indigenous Woman as Victim of Her Culture in Neoliberal Mexico." *Cultural Dynamics* 17 (1): 73-92.

Newell, Dianne. 1993. *Tangled Webs of History: Indians and the Law in Canada's Pacific Coast Fishery*. Toronto: University of Toronto Press.

Nietschmann, Bernard. 1995. "Defending the Miskito Reefs with Maps and GPS: Mapping with Sail, Scuba, and Satellite." *Cultural Survival Quarterly* 18 (4): 34-37.

Niezen, Ronald. 2003. *The Origins of Indigenism: Human Rights and the Politics of Identity*. Berkeley: University of California Press.

–. 2005. "Recognizing Indigenism: Canadian Unity and the International Movement of Indigenous Peoples." *Comparative Studies in Society and History* 42 (1): 119-48.

Nightingale, Andrea. 2002. "Participating or Just Sitting In: The Dynamics of Gender and Caste in Community Forestry." *Journal of Forestry and Livelihoods* 2: 17-24.

–. 2009. "The Nature of Gender: Work, Gender, and Environment." *Environment and Planning D: Society and Space* 24 (2): 165-85.

*Nisga'a Final Agreement: Implementation Report 2006-08.* 2008. http://www.gov.bc.ca/arr/firstnation/nisgaa/implement/down/nisgaa_fa_implementation_report_2006-08.pdf.

*Nisga'a Final Agreement 2001/2002 Annual Report.* 2002. http://www.aadnc-aandc.gc.ca/DAM/DAM-INTER-HQ/STAGING/texte-text/al_ldc_ccl_fagr_nsga_nfar_nfar_1300283751725_eng.pdf.

Nisga'a Lisims Government. 1998. "Understanding the Nisga'a Treaty: Land Title." http://www.kermode.net/nisgaa/treaty/title.htm.

Nisga'a Tribal Council. 1980. *Citizens Plus.* New Aiyansh, BC.

North Sky Consulting Group. 2009. *What We Heard Report.* http://www.gov.nu.ca/reportcard/What We Heard.pdf.

*A Northern Vision: A Stronger North and a Better Canada.* 2007. http://www.anorthernvision.ca/northernvision.html.

Nugent, Daniel. 1995. "Northern Intellectuals and the EZLN." *Monthly Review* 47 (3): 124-38.

Nunavut Implementation Commission. 1994. "Two-Member Constituencies and Gender Equality: A Made in Nunavut Solution for an Effective and Representative Legislature." In *Footprints in the New Snow.* Iqaluit: Government of Nunavut.

Nunavut Tunngavik. 2006. "NTI Launches Lawsuit against Government of Canada for Breach of Contract." http://www.tunngavik.com/blog/2006/12/06/nti-launches-lawsuit-against-government-of-canada-for-breach-of-contract.

Nuttall, Mark. 1992. *Arctic Homeland: Kinship, Community and Development in Northwest Greenland.* Toronto: University of Toronto Press.

Obama, Barack. 2011. *Statement of Support to the UNDRIP.* http://indigenousfoundations.arts.ubc.ca/?id=1097.

Oceransky, Sergio. 2008-09. "Wind Conflicts in the Isthmus of Tehuantepec: The Role of Ownership and Decision-Making Models in Indigenous Resistance to Wind Projects in Southern Mexico." *The Commoner* 13: 203-22. http://www.commoner.org.uk/N13/14-Oceransky.pdf.

Otero, Gerardo. 2004. *¿Adiós al campesinado? Democracia y formación politica de classe en el México rural.* Mexico City: Miguel Ángel Porrúa, Universidad Autonóma de Zacatecas, and Simon Fraser University.

Palmater, Pamela. 2011. *Beyond Blood: Rethinking Indigenous Identity.* Winnipeg: Purich.

Palmer, Lisa. 2007. "Interpreting 'Nature': The Politics of Engaging with Kakadu as an Aboriginal Place." *Cultural Geographies* 14: 255-73.

Parlee, Brenda, et al. 2005. "Health of the Land, Health of the People: Case Study on Gwich'in Berry Harvesting in Northern Canada." *Eco Health* 2: 127-37.

Parnaby, Andrew. 2008. *Citizen Docker: Making a New Deal on the Vancouver Water Front, 1919-1939.* Toronto: University of Toronto Press.

Patterson, E. Palmer. 1992. "Kincolith's First Decade: A Nisga'a Village (1867-1878)." www2.brandonu.ca/library/cjns/12.2/Patterson.pdf.

Peck, Jamie. 2004. "Geography and Public Policy: Constructions of Neoliberalism." *Progress in Human Geography* 28 (3): 392-405.

Peet, R., and M. Watts. 1996. "Liberation Ecology: Development, Sustainability, and Environment in an Age of Market Triumphalism." In *Liberation Ecologies: Environment, Development, and Social Movements,* ed. R. Peet and M. Watts, 1-45. New York: Routledge.

Peluso, Nancy Lee. 1995. "Whose Woods Are These? Counter-Mapping Forest Territories in Kalimantan, Indonesia." *Antipode* 27 (4): 383-406.

Penrose, Jan. 2002. "Nations, States and Homelands: Territory and Territoriality in Nationalist Thought." *Nations and Nationalism* 8 (3): 277-97.

Perreault, Thomas, and Patricia Martin. 2005. "Geographies of Neoliberalism in Latin America." *Environment and Planning A* 37 (2): 191-201.

Povinelli, Elizabeth A. 2002. *The Cunning of Recognition: Indigenous Alterities and the Making of Australian Multiculturalism.* Durham, NC, and London: Duke University Press.

Quecha Reyna, Iván. 2008. "Critica Greenpeace proyecto eólico en el Istmo, Oaxaca." *El Universal* (Mexico City), 5 June. http://estadis.eluniversal.com.mx/notas/512513.html.

Raibmon, Paige. 2006. "The Practice of Everyday Colonialism: Indigenous Women at Work in the Hop Fields and Tourist Industry of Puget Sound." *Labor: Studies in Working-Class History of the Americas* 3 (3): 23-56.

Ramirez, Renya. 2007. "Race, Tribal Nation, and Gender: A Native Feminist Approach to Belonging." *Meridians: Feminism, Race, Transnationalism* 7 (2): 22-40.

Ramos, Alcida Rita. 1998. *Indigenism: Ethnic Politics in Brazil.* Madison: University of Wisconsin Press.

Ranchod-Nilsson, Sita, and Mary Ann Tétreault. 2005. "Gender and Nationalism: Moving beyond Fragmented Conversations." In *Women, States and Nationalism: At Home in the Nation?* ed. Sita Ranchod-Nilsson and Mary Ann Tétreault, 1-17. New York: Taylor and Francis e-Library.

Raunet, Daniel. 1984. *Without Surrender, Without Consent: A History of the Nishga Land Claims.* Vancouver: Douglas and McIntyre.

Ray, Dorothy Jean. 1976. *The Eskimos of Bering Strait, 1650-1898.* Seattle: University of Washington Press.

Recondo, David. 2001. "Usos y costumbres, procesos electorales y autonomía indígena en Oaxaca." In *Costumbres, leyes y movimiento indio en Oaxaca y Chiapas,* ed. Lourdes De León Pasquel, 91-112. Mexico City: CIESAS and Miguel Ángel Porrúa.

Reina, Leticia. 1988. "De las reformas borbónicas a las leyes de reforma." In *Historia de la cuestión agraria mexicana: Estado de Oaxaca,* vol. 1, *Prehispánico-1924,* ed. Leticia Reina, 181-269. Mexico City: Juan Pablos Editor.

Reina Aoyama, Leticia. 1997. "Las zapotecas del Istmo de Tehuantepec en la reelaboración de la identidad étnica en el siglos XIX." Paper presented at the 20th

International Congress of the Latin America Studies Association, Guadalajara, 17-19 April.

Revista Eólica y del Vehículo Eléctrico. 2012. "Eólica en México: El Presidente Calderón inauguró tres centrales eólicas." 8 March. http://www.evwind.com/2012/03/08/eolica-en-mexico-el-presidente-calderon-inauguro-tres-centrales-eolicas.

Robbins, Paul. 2004. *Political Ecology: A Critical Introduction.* Oxford: Blackwell.

–. 2006. "Carbon Colonies: From Local Use Value to Global Exchange in 21st Century Postcolonial Forestry." In *Colonial and Postcolonial Geographies of India,* ed. S. Raju Kumar and S. Corbridge, 279-97. New Delhi: Sage.

Rojas, Rosa. 1994. *Chiapas ¿y las mujeres qué?* Vol. 1. Mexico: Ediciones la Correa Feminista.

Romero Frizzi, María de los Ángeles. 1996. *El sol y la cruz: Los pueblos indios de Oaxaca colonial.* Mexico City: CIESAS.

Rose, Alex. 2001. *Spirit Dance at Meziadin: Chief Joseph Gosnell and the Nisga'a.* Vancouver: Harbour.

Rossiter, David. 2004. "The Nature of Protest: Constructing the Spaces of British Columbia's Rainforests." *Cultural Geographies* 11: 139-64.

–. 2007. "Lessons in Possession: Colonial Resource Geographies in Practice on Vancouver Island, 1859-1865." *Journal of Historical Geography* 33 (4): 770-90.

Rossiter, David, and Patricia K. Wood. 2005. "Fantastic Topographies: Neo-liberal Responses to Aboriginal Land Claims in British Columbia." *Canadian Geographer* 49 (2): 352-66.

Roth, Christopher F. 2002. "Without Treaty, Without Conquest: Indigenous Sovereignty in Post-Delgamuukw British Columbia." *Wicazo Sa Review* 17 (2): 143-65.

Rovira, Giomar. 2007. *Mujeres de maíz.* Mexico City: Editorial Era.

Rubin, Jeffrey. 1994. "COCEI in Juchitán Grassroots Radicalism and Regional History." *Journal of Latin America Studies* 26: 109-36.

–. 1997. *Decentering the Regime: Ethnicity, Radicalism and Democracy in Juchitán, Mexico.* Durham, NC: Duke University Press.

Ruiz Cervantes, Francisco José. 1988. "De la bola a los primeros repartos." In *Historia de cuestión agraria mexicana: Estado de Oaxaca,* vol. 1, *Prehispánico-1924,* ed. Leticia Reina, 332-423. Mexico City: Juan Pablos Editor.

Rundstrom, Robert. 1991. "Mapping, Postmodernism, Indigenous Peoples and the Changing Direction of North American Cartography." *Cartographica* 28: 1-12.

Rus, Jan. 1983. "Whose Caste War? Indians, *Ladinos* and the Chiapas 'Caste War' of 1869." In *Spaniards and Indians in Southeastern Mesoamerica: Essays on the History of Ethnic Relations,* ed. Murdo J. Macleod and Robert Wasserstrom, 127-69. Lincoln: University of Nebraska Press.

Rutherford, Stephanie. 2007. "Green Governmentality: Insights and Opportunities in the Study of Nature's Rule." *Progress in Human Geography* 31 (3): 291-307.

Rynard, Paul. 2000. "'Welcome In, but Check Your Rights at the Door': The James Bay and Nisga'a Agreements in Canada." *Canadian Journal of Political Science* 33: 211-43.

Said, Edward. 1994. *Orientalism.* London: Pandora.

Saladin d'Anglure, Bernard, and Françoise Morin. 1992. "The Inuit People between Particularism and Internationalism: An Overview of Their Rights and Powers in 1992." *Études/Inuit/Studies* 16 (1-2): 13-19.

Sánchez, Consuelo. 1999. *Los Pueblos indígenas: Del indigenismo a la autonomía.* Mexico City: Siglo XXI.

Sanders, Douglas. 1995. "State Practice and the United Nations Draft Declaration on the Rights of Indigenous Peoples." In *Becoming Visible: Indigenous Politics and Self-Government,* ed. Terje Brantenberg, Janne Hansen, and Henry Minde. Tromsø, Norway: University of Tromsø Centre for Sámi Studies. http://www.sami.uit.no/girji/n02/en/102sandd.html.

Saunders, Barbara. 1997. "From a Colonized Consciousness to Autonomous Identity: Shifting Relations between Kwakwaka'wakw and Canadian Nations." *Dialectical Anthropology* 22: 137-58.

Schroeder, Richard A. 1997. "'Re-claiming' Land in the Gambia: Gendered Property Rights and Environmental Intervention." *Annals of the Association of American Geographers* 87: 487-508.

Scott, Heidi. 2008. "Colonialism, Landscape and the Subterranean." *Geography Compass* 2 (6): 1853-69.

Searles, Edmond. 2002. "Food and the Making of Inuit Identities." *Food and Foodways* 10: 55-78.

"A Seat of One's Own: Nunavut MP Says Attitudes about Women in Politics Need to Change." 2001. *Nunatsiaq News,* 9 November.

Secretaría Nacional de Energía. 2011. "Proyecta Sener inversión para generar más energía limpia." http://www.noticiasnet.mx/portal/principal/72386-proyecta-sener-inversion-para-generar-mas-energia-limpia.

Seed, Patricia. 2001. *American Pentimento: The Invention of Indians and the Pursuit of Riches.* Minneapolis: University of Minnesota Press.

SEMARNAT (Secretaría de Medio Ambiente y Recursos Naturales). 2010. *El ambiente en números: Selección de estadísticas ambientales para consulta rápida.* Mexico City: SEMARNAT.

Shadian, Jessica. 2006. "Remaking Arctic Governance: The Construction of an Arctic Inuit Polity." *Polar Record* 42: 249-59.

–. 2007. "In Search of an Identity Canada Looks North." *American Review of Canadian Studies* 37 (3): 323-53.

–. 2010. "From States to Polities: Reconceptualizing Sovereignty through Inuit Governance." *European Journal of International Relations* 16 (3): 485-510.

Shannon, Kerrie Ann. 2006. "Everyone Goes Fishing: Understanding Procurement for Men, Women and Children in an Arctic Community." *Études/Inuit/Studies* 30 (1): 9-29.

Sidaway, James. 1994. "New Theoretical Directions in Political Geography." *Geoforum* 25 (4): 487-503.

Sierra, María Teresa. 2004. "Derecho indígena y mujeres: Viejas costumbres, nuevos derechos." In *Voces disidentes: Debates contemporáneos en los estudios de género en México,* ed. Romano Pérez-Gil, 113-49. Mexico City: Cámara de Diputados, CIESAS, and Miguel Ángel Porrúa.

Silliman, Stephen. 2001. "Theoretical Perspectives on Labor and Colonialism: Reconsidering the California Missions." *Journal of Anthropological Archaeology* 20: 379-407.

Sluyter, Andrew. 2002. *Colonialism and Landscape : Postcolonial Theory and Applications.* Lanham, MD: Rowman and Littlefield.

Smith, Andrea. 2005. "Native American Feminism, Sovereignty and Social Change." *Feminist Studies* 31 (1): 116-32.

Smith, Anthony. 1995. *National Identity.* Reno: University of Nevada Press.

–. 2001. *Nationalism: Theory, Ideology, History.* Cambridge: Polity.

Smith, Neil. 2009. "Nature as Accumulation Strategy." http://neil-smith.net/wp-content/uploads/2009/10/nature-as-accumulation-strategy.pdf.

Speed, Shannon. 2008. *Rights in Rebellion: Indigenous Struggle and Human Rights in Chiapas.* Stanford, CA: Stanford University Press.

Spivak, Gayatri C. 1989. "Response to the Difference Within: Feminism and Critical Theory." In *The Difference Within: Feminism and Critical Theory,* ed. Elizabeth Meese and Alice Parker. Amsterdam: Benjamins.

Stahler-Sholk, Richard. 2000. "A World in Which Many Worlds Fit: Zapatista Responses to Globalization." Paper presented at the *Globalization in the New Millennium?* panel, Latin American Studies Association 22nd International Congress, Miami, Florida, 16-18 March.

–. 2005. "Time of the Snails: Autonomy and Resistance in Chiapas." *NACLA Report on the Americas* 38 (5): 34-40.

–. 2007. "Resisting Neoliberal Homogenization: The Zapatista Autonomy Movement." *Latin American Perspectives* 34 (2): 48-63.

Standing Senate Committee on Aboriginal Peoples of the Parliament of Canada. 2008. *Honouring the Spirit of Modern Treaties: Closing the Loopholes.* www.parl.gc.ca/Content/SEN/Committee/392/abor/rep/rep05may08-e.pdf.

Stasiulis, Daiva K. 1999. "Relational Positionalities of Nationalisms, Racisms and Feminisms." In *Between Woman and Nation: Nationalisms, Transnational Feminisms, and the State,* ed. Caren Kaplan, Norma Alarcón, and Minoo Moallem, 182-218. Durham, NC: Duke University Press.

Steele, Jackie, and Manon Tremblay. 2005. "Paradise Lost? The Gender Parity Plebiscite in Nunavut." *Canadian Parliamentary Review* (Spring): 34-39.

Stephen, Lynn. 1996. "Redefined Nationalism in Building a Movement for Indigenous Autonomy in Mexico: Oaxaca and Chiapas." Paper presented at the Annual Meeting of the American Anthropological Association, San Francisco, 20-24 November.

–. 2002. *¡Zapata Lives! Histories and Cultural Politics in Southern Mexico.* Berkeley and Los Angeles: University of California Press.

Sterritt, Neil J., et al. 1998. *Tribal Boundaries in the Nass Watershed.* Vancouver: UBC Press.

Stewart-Harawira, Makere. 2005. *The New Imperial Order: Indigenous Responses to Globalization.* London: Zed Books.

Stocks, Anthony. 2003. "Mapping Dreams in Nicaragua's Bosawas Reserve." *Human Organization* 62 (4): 344-56.

–. 2005. "Too Much for Too Few: Problems of Indigenous Rights in Latin America." *Annual Review of Anthropology* 34: 85-104.

Stoymenoff, Alexis. 2012. "Government Labels Environmentalists 'Terrorist Threat' in New Report." *Vancouver Observer,* 10 February. http://www.vancouverobserver. com/sustainability/2012/02/10/are-canadian-environmentalists-terrorist-threat.

Strang, Veronica. 2009. *Gardening the World: Agency, Identity and Ownership of Water.* Oxford and New York: Berghahn.

Stuart Pupcheck, Leanne. 2001. "True North: Inuit Art and Canadian Imagination." *American Review of Canadian Studies* 31 (1-2): 191-208.

Subcomandante Marcos. 1994. "El primer alzamiento, en marzo de 1993." *La Jornada* (Mexico City), 26 January.

Sullivan, Sian. 2008-09. "An Ecosystem at Your Service?" *The Land* (Winter): 21-23.

Sunseri, Lina. 2010. *Being Again of One Mind: Oneida Women and the Struggle for Decolonization.* Vancouver: UBC Press.

Suzack, Cheryl, Shari M. Huhndorf, Jeanne Perreault, and Jean Barman, eds. 2010. *Indigenous Women and Feminism: Politics, Activism, Culture.* Vancouver: UBC Press.

Swyngedouw, Erik. 2009. "Producing Nature, Scaling Environment: Water, Network and Territories in Fascist Spain." In *Leviathan Undone? Towards a Political Economy of Scale,* ed. Roger Keil and Rianne Mahon, 121-40. Vancouver: UBC Press.

Swyngedouw, Erik, and Nikolas Heynen. 2003. "Urban Political Ecology, Justice and the Politics of Scale." *Antipode* 35 (5): 898-918.

Sylvain, Renée. 2005. "Disorderly Development: Globalization and the Idea of 'Culture' in the Kalahari." *American Ethnologist* 32 (3): 354-70.

Taylor, William. 1972. *Landlord and Peasant in Colonial Oaxaca.* Stanford, CA: Stanford University Press.

Tennant, Paul. 1990. *Aboriginal Peoples and Politics: The Indian Land Question in British Columbia, 1849-1989.* Vancouver: UBC Press.

Thornberry, Patrick. 2002. *Indigenous Peoples and Human Rights.* Manchester: Manchester University Press.

Tokar, Brian. 2005. "Genetics, 'Natural Rights,' and the Preservation of Biodiversity." In *Rights and Liberties in the Biotech Age: Why We Need a Genetic Bill Of Rights,* ed. Sheldon Krimsky and Peter Shorett, 11-15. Lanham, MD: Rowman and Littlefield.

Trask, Haunani-Kay. 1996. "Feminism and Indigenous Hawaiian Nationalism." *Signs: A Journal of Women in Culture and Society* 21 (4): 906-16.

Tsing, Anna. 2003. *Friction: An Ethnography of Global Connections.* Princeton, NJ, and Oxford: Oxford University Press.

Tuathail, Gearoi O. 1996. *Critical Geopolitics: The Politics of Writing Global Space.* Minneapolis: University of Minnesota Press.

Tully, James. 2004. "Exclusion and Assimilation: Two Forms of Domination in Relation to Freedom." In *Political Exclusion and Domination: NOMOS XLVI,* ed. Melissa Williams and Stephen Macedo, 191-230. Cambridge, MA: Harvard University Press.

Turner, Dale, and Audra Simpson. 2008. "Indigenous Leadership in a Flat World." Research Paper for the National Centre for First Nations Governance. fngovernance. org/ncfng_research/turner_and_simpson.pdf.

United Nations. 2007. *Declaration on the Rights of Indigenous Peoples.* http://www. un.org/esa/socdev/unpfii/documents/DRIPS_en.pdf.

Usher, Jean. 1974. *William Duncan of Metlakatla: A Victorian Missionary in British Columbia.* Ottawa: Native Museums of Canada.

Valdivia, Gabriela. 2005. "On Indigeneity, Change, and Representation in the Northeastern Ecuadorian Amazon." *Environment and Planning A* 37 (2): 285-303.

Velásquez Cepeda, María Cristina. 1998. *El nombramiento: Antropología jurídica de los usos y costumbres para la renovación de los ayuntamientos de Oaxaca.* Oaxaca: Instituto Estatal Electoral de Oaxaca.

–. 2000. *El nombramiento: La elección por usos y costumbres en Oaxaca.* Oaxaca: Instituto Estatal Electoral de Oaxaca.

Veraccini, Lorenzo. 2011. "Introducing Settler Colonial Studies." *Settler Colonial Studies* 1: 1-12.

Washbrook, Sarah. 2007. "Enganche and Exports in Chiapas, Mexico: A Comparison of Plantation Labour in the Districts of Soconusco and Palenque, 1876-1911." *Journal of Latin American Studies* 39 (4): 797-825.

Watts, J.M., and R. Peet. 2004. "Liberating Political Ecology." In *Liberation Ecologies: Environment, Development, and Social Movements,* 2nd ed., ed. R. Peet and J.M. Watts, 3-47. London: Routledge.

White, Graham. 2006. "Traditional Aboriginal Values in a Westminster Parliament: The Legislative Assembly of Nunavut." *Journal of Legislative Studies* 12 (1): 8-31.

Wilford, Rick. 1998. "Women, Ethnicity and Nationalism." In *Women, Ethnicity and Nationalism: The Politics of Transition,* ed. Rick Wilford and Robert Miller, 1-22. New York: Taylor and Francis.

Wilmer, Franke. 1993. *The Indigenous Voice in World Politics.* Thousand Oaks, CA: Sage.

Wimmer, Andreas. 2002. *Nationalist Exclusion and Ethnic Conflict: Shadows of Modernity.* Cambridge: Cambridge University Press.

Wolfe, Patrick. 1999. *Settler Colonialism and the Transformation of Anthropology: The Politics and Poetics of an Ethnographic Event.* London: Cassell.

–. 2006. "Settler Colonialism and the Elimination of the Native." *Journal of Genocide Research* 8 (4): 387-409.

World Bank. 1994. *Mexico: Second Decentralization and Regional Development Project Report.* Washington, DC: World Bank.

–. 2000. *Mesoamerican Biological Corridor: Project Appraisal Document.* Washington, DC: World Bank.

–. 2003. *Mexico: Southern States Development Strategy.* Washington, DC: World Bank.

–. 2011. "The Mesoamerican Biological Corridor." *Regional Program Review* 5 (2). http://siteresources.worldbank.org/EXTGLOREGPARPROG/Resources/MBC_ rpr.pdf.

Wright, Miriam. 2008. "'Building the Great Lucrative Fishing Industry': Aboriginal Gillnet Fishers and Protests over Salmon Fishery Regulations for the Nass and Skeena Rivers, 1950s-1960s." *Labour/Le Travail* 61. http://journals.hil.unb.ca/ index.php/LLT/article/view/9328.

Wunder, Sven. 2005. "Payment for Environmental Services: Some Nuts and Bolts." http://www.cifor.org/publications/pdf_files/OccPapers/OP-42.pdf.

Wyndham, Felice S. 2009. "Spheres of Relations, Lines of Interaction: Subtle Ecologies of the Rarámuri Landscape in Northern Mexico." *Journal of Ethnobiology* 29 (2): 271-95.

Young, Nathan, and Ralph Matthews. 2007. "Resource Economies and Neo-liberal Experimentation: The Reform of Industry and Community in Rural British Columbia." *AREA: Journal of the Royal Geographical Society* 39 (2): 176-85.

Young, Neil. 2008. "Radical Neoliberalism in British Columbia: Remaking Rural Geographies." *Canadian Journal of Sociology* 33 (1): 1-36.

Youngblood Henderson, James (Sa'ke'j). 2002. "Sui Generis and Treaty Citizenship." *Citizenship Studies* 6 (4): 415-41.

–. 2008. *Indigenous Diplomacy and the Rights of Peoples: Achieving UN Recognition.* Winnipeg: Purich.

Yuval-Davis, Nira. 1996. "Women and the Biological Reproduction of 'The Nation.'" Women Studies International Forum 19: 17-24.

–. 2002. *Gender and Nation.* London: Sage.

Yuval-Davis, Nira, and Floya Anthias. 1989. "Introduction." In *Woman-Nation-State,* ed. Nira Yuval-Davis and Floya Anthias, 1-15. London: Macmillan.

Zeitlin, Judith Francis. 2005. *Cultural Politics in Colonial Tehuantepec: Community and State among the Isthmus Zapotec, 1500-1750.* Stanford, CA: Stanford University Press.

Zeitlin, Judith Francis, and Lillian Thomas. 1992. "Spanish Justice and the Indian Cacique: Disjunctive Political Systems in Sixteenth-Century Tehuantepec." *Ethnohistory* 39 (3): 285-315.

# Index

communal lands: and Agrarian Reform
Law, 40, 77, 83, 84-85, 160, 197; in
Oaxaca, 178-79, 182, 185, 186, 187,
189, 190-92
Congreso Nacional de Mujeres
Indígenas (National Congress of
Indigenous Women), 163
Congreso Nacional Indígena (National
Indigenous Congress), 164, 173
conservation: as co-opted by neoliberalism, 68, 71-76, 81-82, 85-86, 114-20,
158-60, 177-78, 201-7, 209-12; of
forest lands, 74, 75, 83, 85, 178-79,
189-91, 202, 206-7, 209-10, 211,
215-16; "green capitalism" and, 114-
20, 158-60, 201-7; Indigenous knowledge and, 26-27, 79, 82, 122, 210,
215-16; Inuit resource/hunting rights
and, 89, 97, 99, 114-19, 210-11;
Nisga'a and, 140-48, 211, 214; and
"noble savage" concept, 27, 72, 154-
55, 158-61, 213; in Oaxaca, 177-78,
188, 189-91, 201-7, 211, 216; peasants
seen as obstacle to, 85, 154-55, 157,
158-59, 160, 211, 215-16; resource
extraction and, 68, 74, 82, 144-46;
and value of pristine/"untouched"
nature, 3, 72, 82, 89, 114; Zapatistas
and, 158-60, 211
Conservation International (CI), 158-59
Constitution Act (1867), 33
Constitution Act (1982), 99, 134
Convención Estatal de Mujeres
Chiapanecas (Chiapas Women's
Convention), 165
Corntassel, Jeff, 48, 50
Coulthard, Glen, 48, 49
Creoles, 38, 39, 152, 153
Cultural Survival, 24

definitions of "Indigenous," 4, 17-18, 20-
24; by ILO, 21, 22-23; by Martínez
Cobo, 21-22; problems with, 22-24;
UNDRIP and, 23-24
Deloria, Vine, Jr., 148

devolution/local self-government: Inuit
and, 97-104, 116; Nisga'a and, 142-43,
144
Douglas, James, 124-25
Duncan, William, 127

Echeverría, Luis, 154
Ejército Zapatista de Liberación Nacional
(EZLN), 156, 161-62, 165, 167, 170-
71; and San Andrés Accords, 157-58
*ejidos* (land plots), 40, 41-42; and communal lands, 40, 77, 83, 84-85, 160,
197; distribution/restitution of
(1930s), 185; on forest lands, 40,
83, 85, 160, 189-91; irrigation lands
turned into, 191-92; liberalization
of, 83-85, 157, 189-91, 215; titling/
certification of, 83, 84-85, 160; usufruct rights under, 40, 192; and wind
industry, 201-7; women's ownership/
inheritance of, 41-42, 83-84, 197,
198-99
environmentalism: neoliberalism and,
68, 71-76, 81-82, 85-86, 114-20,
158-60, 177-78, 201-7, 209-12; neoliberalization strategies and, 73-76;
as "terrorist threat," 1, 2. *See also*
conservation
essentialism, 23, 166-67, 211, 213
Esther (Zapatista woman), 168
extractive colonialism, 8, 16, 27-31,
34-42, 66, 67, 76-77, 82-86, 211-13;
Catholicism and, 35, 37-38, 152-53;
in colonial Chiapas, 150-53; in colonial Oaxaca, 179-83; and colonizer/
colonized dichotomy, 30, 35-38; and
concept of tribute, 8, 28, 35-37, 151-
52, 181-82; and control of mineral
resources, 34-35, 40, 77, 82-83; and
Indigenous citizenship, 38-39, 40-41;
as labour-based, 28-30, 34-37, 38,
150-54, 211, 213; under Mexican
state, 38-42, 77, 82-86, 153-58, 183-
87; and miscegenation, 38, 39, 40-
41; vs reciprocity, 36, 153, 181-82

Printed and bound in Canada by Friesens

Set in Segoe and Warnock by Artegraphica Design Co. Ltd.

Copy editor: Robert Lewis

Proofreader: Helen Godolphin

Indexer: Cheryl Lemmens